How to Develop An Employee Handbook

Joseph W.R. Lawson II

DARTNELL is a publisher serving the world of business with books, manuals, newsletters, bulletins, and training materials for executives, managers, supervisors, salespeople, financial officials, human resources professionals, and office employees. In addition, Dartnell produces management and sales training films and audiocassettes, publishes many useful business forms, and offers many of its materials in languages other than English. Established in 1917, Dartnell serves the world's complete business community. For catalogs and product information write: THE DARTNELL CORPORATION, 4660 Ravenswood Avenue, Chicago, Illinois 60640-4595 USA. Phone: 800-621-5463. In Illinois: (312) 561-4000.

This publication is designed to provide accurate and authoritative information in regard to the subject matter covered. It is sold with the understanding that the publisher is not engaged in rendering legal, accounting, or other professional service. If legal advice or other expert assistance is required, the services of a competent professional person should be sought.

From a Declaration of Principles jointly adopted by a Committee of the American Bar Association and a Committee of Publishers.

Published by The Dartnell Corporation
4660 Ravenswood Avenue
Chicago, IL 60640
Chicago/Boston/London/Sydney

© 1991 The Dartnell Corporation
Printed in the U.S.A. by The Dartnell Press
ISBN 0-85013-190-1

Printed in the U.S.A. by The Dartnell Press
10 9 8 7 6 5 4 3 2 1

About the Author

Joseph W. R. Lawson II is Chairman of the Board and Chief Executive Officer of SESCO Management Consultants.

Lawson has served as an author for The Dartnell Corporation since 1964 and has authored the following publications for management: *How to Meet the Challenge of the Union Organizer; How to Reduce Absenteeism—Cure Tardiness—and Build Employee Morale; Management's Complete Guide to Employee Benefits; How to Comply with the Equal Opportunity Act; and How to Develop a Personnel Policy Manual.*

He received his B.A. degree from King College in Bristol, Tennessee, and his M.S. degree in Industrial Relations from the University of North Carolina. Since 1961, Lawson has represented clients in business and industry as an employee and labor relations consultant to management. He specializes in employee and labor relations, human resource management services, and employer-labor negotiations and arbitration. He is a member of the Commercial Panel and American Arbitration Association. Lawson serves as a professional speaker and instructor for human resource management seminars and union-free employee relations workshops for clients and trade associations.

About SESCO Management Consultants

SESCO Management Consultants is a professional consulting firm specializing in human resource management consulting and labor relations. The firm was founded in 1945 by Dr. J. W. Lawson, Sr., following his early career with the U.S. Department of Labor. During the past 45 years, Dr. Lawson has brought together a staff of professional employee relations and labor relations specialists from business and industry.

SESCO Management Consultants provides the following comprehensive consulting services: Pre-employment Testing, Employee/Supervisory Opinion Surveys, Employee Handbooks/Personnel Policy Manuals, Human Resource Computer Software, Zenger-Miller Certified Training, Outplacement Counseling, Family Business Succession Plans, Criteria-Based Job Descriptions, Pay for Performance Wage/Salary Programs and Wage/Salary/Benefit Services.

Their client newsletter, *The SESCO Report,* is published monthly and available to nonretainer clients on a subscription basis.

The SESCO staff represents clients in all 50 states who are engaged in heavy and light manufacturing, retail and wholesale services, coal mining, transportation, banking, savings and loan, electronics, automobile dealerships, the health care industry, and several national associations.

Preface

Introduction and Purpose

As a result of the continued popularity of Dartnell's management publication, *How to Develop a Personnel Policy Manual,* now in its fifth edition, the publishing staff of Dartnell have observed a strong need among human resource management professionals and other business leaders for a companion volume focusing on perhaps the second most important management-employee relations communications tool—the employee handbook or employee manual.

Because the professional staff of SESCO Management Consultants has specialized in drafting, editing, and publishing employee handbooks and employee manuals for clients in business and industry over the past 45 years, we were invited by Dartnell to author this latest management publication.

This first edition has been especially prepared for immediate, practical use by human resource directors, personnel managers, employee relations managers, general managers, and employers in every industry. The purpose of this new Dartnell human resource manual is to provide business management with the most practical and efficient approach to developing, drafting, publishing, and distributing employee handbooks.

In keeping up to date on the dynamic changes and challenges facing those responsible for human resource management and communications with employees at all levels, there have been significant and important new employment regulations affecting every conceivable type of personnel policy and procedure, including employee benefits administration, that are usually covered in an effective employee handbook.

There are few, if any, "basic" personnel policies, procedures, benefits, standards of performance, or work rules that do not have either federal or state regulations that must be considered and complied with by those responsible for drafting, revising, and publishing employee handbooks.

Additionally, there has been a greatly increased judicial review of numerous employee handbooks, with particular attention given to analyzing whether or not an employee handbook is a bona fide "employee contract" and whether or not the employee handbook can be a bane or a blessing for employers in upholding the "employment at will" doctrines of various state laws. Moreover, present and continuing litigation has been focused on the content of employee handbooks and other personnel policies and procedures when employers have been faced with alleged "wrongful discharge" discrimination lawsuits, as well as other discrimination charges filed by terminated employees alleging age, sex, race, religion, or other charges of discrimination.

Because of this present and continuing period of "people sensitive" legal attentiveness, we caution our readers and subscribers to keep abreast of the new and changing employment law cases currently being reviewed in both the state and federal court systems.

In SESCO's years of consulting with business and industry, we find one of the greatest challenges experienced by an employer is that of having to draft and finalize a particular personnel policy or procedure for the organization. The time element and the pressures of other important business matters have caused many firms, large and small, to procrastinate in this important phase of supervisor-employee communications, yet policies are certainly needed for productive and profitable employee relations.

This first edition has been published to meet the continuing need of large and small employers for a simple, how-to-do-it approach to developing an employee handbook. Each section begins with a "Handbook Checklist" to provide the user with a practical and systematic approach to formulating and outlining desired handbook policies covering all important phases of the employer-employee relationship. The person using this manual can simply place a check mark in the blank beside the subject dealing with a particular policy to be covered in the employee handbook. This checklist is the first step in tailoring personnel policies to fit the particular needs of each employer.

More important, the checklist is designed to stimulate thinking about various aspects of policy that should be formulated and covered in any manual. Recommendations of the SESCO staff on various key aspects of personnel policy are included in several sections.

Sample policy statements are also included. These examples enable the policy writer to review sample handbook policies which reflect and possess, in the author's judgment, the following desirable characteristics:

1. Policies should provide an organization with flexibility and a high degree of permanency.

2. Policies should be harmonious with all other personnel policies.

3. Policies should be designed to meet the individual needs and differences of employees and supervisors.

4. Policies should be in compliance with all federal and state regulations.

5. Policies should be clear and concise, yet avoid too much detail.

6. Policies should never be a liability to the interest of anyone involved in the employer-employee relationship, including owners and the public.

7. Policies should provide for effective communication and understanding by all interested parties and users of the policy manual.

8. Policies should reflect careful study and analysis before being formulated and administered.

The numerous examples of handbook statements are of much practical value because they provide ideas on current policy language. They will help in formulating concise terminology as you draft your own handbooks.

A final note: All policies, statements, and examples cited and used in this manual should be considered as guides and ideas to assist you in appropriately addressing your specific needs and requirements. The particulars of your organizational demands will largely dictate the changes needed to "customize" the handbook policies.

The material presented is intended to serve as a guide and will address the majority of your handbook drafting needs.

We are deeply indebted and offer grateful appreciation to the many organizations and clients we have assisted over the years in developing their employee handbooks. We are particularly grateful to the companies that provided us with their employee handbooks and that gave us permission to use their company name or their handbook statements. However, because of the confidential nature of many policies, several companies have requested that their names not be mentioned in this publication. Therefore, no specific footnote or reference is made to many of the contributors of these various handbook statements.

Joseph W. R. Lawson II
Chairman of the Board and Chief Executive Officer
SESCO Management Consultants

Contents

SECTION 1

Developing an Employee Handbook: Objectives and Concerns

CONTENTS

Developing an Employee Handbook: Objectives and Concerns

1.01 Management Objectives

Why should your organization have an employee handbook? If you believe that consistent, clear employer-employee communication is vitally necessary for productive and profitable employee relations, then your business organization, regardless of size, should not attempt to operate without a clearly worded, up-to- date employee handbook.

An employee handbook is a basic written publication that is designed, published, and distributed for the purpose of providing employees and their family members with two major pieces of information:

1. What can employees and their families expect from your company?

2. What does your company expect from your employees?

Within the covers of a well-written and published employee handbook, those two vital questions are answered clearly, persuasively, and honestly.

Although "face-to-face" and "one-on-one" management-employee communication is most important and essential to establishing and maintaining your "management credibility" (earning the trust, confidence, and respect of employees), it is too easy for verbal explanations given by management and supervisors to be forgotten, misunderstood, or misinterpreted. You need to put in writing all the details, facts, and procedures that concern both employees and their supervisors. Such written or printed personnel policies and procedures reinforce the *intent* as well as the practical understanding of personnel and benefit policies, standards of performance, safety and health rules, and the like. By publishing and distributing this information in an employee handbook, you can measurably improve the management-employee communication that is the hallmark of a successful business organization.

An important employee handbook objective is to be management's fundamental, published communications tool for employees and supervisors to understand what your company expects from employees and what employees can expect from your company. One important purpose or objective of employee handbooks is to *promote consistency in the day-to-day administration of personnel and benefit policies.* Second, a major objective of employee handbooks is to *prevent employee misunderstandings, complaints, grievances, and job dissatisfactions* that often occur due to a lack of understanding or a misunderstanding of personnel and benefit policies.

Advantages of an Employee Handbook to the Employer

The following are a few important advantages and benefits to an employer in having an up-to-date, published employee handbook.

1. **An employee handbook promotes understanding of company personnel and benefit policies.** The employee handbook, properly written and kept current, is the basic management communications tool in explaining to employees the advantages and benefits of working for your company. It can clarify all important employment policies, including pay, benefits, performance standards, discipline, customer service, and other employee obligations.

2. **An employee handbook promotes consistency and management credibility.** A published employee handbook, distributed to all employees and supervisors, is your *roadmap* for consistent, fair, and firm personnel administration and human resource management. It is also a roadmap for all of your management team, giving them a practical communications tool to use daily in administering personnel and benefit policies and procedures.

3. **An employee handbook can save valued time and management operating cost.** Employee handbooks save management substantial time and operating cost by avoiding the need for day-to-day, week-to-week spontaneous, lengthy "brainstorming" sessions to discuss and reach decisions about what should be done and how to handle on-the-job problems and questions regarding various employment and benefit policies and procedures.

4. **An employee handbook is an efficient new employee orientation management tool.** An employee handbook is the most practical and useful management communications tool in the induction and orientation of new employees. Providing a copy of the handbook to the new employee creates a favorable impression and provides excellent two-way communication between the human resource manager or supervisor and the new employee.

5. **An employee handbook is an effective management recruiting tool.** An attractive employee handbook can be presented to prospective employees to provide a positive, persuasive image of your organization and to highlight your major personnel and employee benefit policies. Your employee handbook can make the difference between a quality, skilled employee choosing your organization over a competitor in a tight labor market.

6. **An employee handbook is an effective "union avoidance" management communications tool.** Without question, one of the most important objectives and advantages for a *union-free employer* is having the

management right and freedom to establish and maintain a positive, union-free work environment without the restrictions on management's rights to operate the business and the limitations found in most collective bargaining agreements.

The employee handbook replaces the labor contract in a union-free company. A current, well-written employee handbook provides union-free employees and their families with important facts about the company and the advantages of working in an organization that does not have an adversarial relationship with a labor organization and the restrictions and cost of union membership.

The employee handbook in a union-free organization is an absolute must if management is to avoid defending against a persuasive union organizer who convinces employees that they need to have their employee benefits, personnel policies, and performance standards "in writing" in the form of a union contract and who tells them, "Your employer can take away your present benefits and change your personnel policies at any time because they are not in writing or distributed to you."

7. **An employee handbook documents your fair employment practices and compliance with federal/state equal employment opportunity laws.** The employee handbook is written, good faith evidence of your company's providing fair employment practices and equal employment opportunity for present employees and future job applicants. The enactment of Title VII of the Civil Rights Act placed great importance on the human resource tool of communications. Frankly, a handbook should be the basis of good faith efforts to prove nondiscrimination and to provide equal employment opportunity to everyone in all phases of human resource action. In communicating your equal employment opportunity policy, you may find it necessary to simply reaffirm your past policy. On the other hand, many organizations today are faced with the responsibility of establishing fair employment practices that comply with new laws.

8. **An employee handbook will provide the employer with compliance requirements to communicate "in writing" certain personnel and benefit policies required by state law.**

9. **An employee handbook will assist the employer in complying with federal guidelines.** These guidelines require employees to be notified annually of certain employee benefit descriptions and data under ERISA and Section 89, and Executive Order 11246 requires government contractors to comply with sex discrimination regulations pertaining to written policies for maternity disabled leaves, etc.

10. **An employee handbook can be a valuable legal defense for an employer if and when faced with an employee lawsuit alleging that a**

former employee was entitled to a certain length of employment or "permanent" status. A properly worded, up-to-date employee handbook will contain a "disclaimer statement" that documents the fact that neither the handbook nor any personnel policies or benefit statements within the covers of the employee handbook are for the purpose of establishing an employment agreement or employee contract with anyone. Properly worded disclaimers are continuing to provide the employer with a persuasive defense to employee claims that their handbook is a "contract," provided that the *wording* as well as the *intent* of the disclaimer statement is clear.

In a number of recent court cases, if the employer had not had a current, clearly worded employee handbook with properly worded disclaimer statements, the employer would have been vulnerable to a successful employee lawsuit based upon "oral" or "verbal" promises made to former employees during their employment relative to job security, permanency of employment, job tenure, or based upon verbal statements made to former employees during the hiring process, performance appraisal reviews, or disciplinary interviews regarding additional compensation.

Employers cannot avoid all potential lawsuits by including a properly worded disclaimer statement in a revised employee handbook, but it is recommended that when employers begin revising their employee handbooks, they include not only a properly worded disclaimer statement but also a "reservation of rights" clause. The intent of a "reservation of rights" clause is to inform employees that management has the right to modify or change personnel policies, working conditions, and employee benefits at its discretion. (See Section 4.15 for sample "reservation of rights" clauses and disclaimer statements.)

Advantages of an Employee Handbook to Supervision

Employee handbooks have provided important advantages and benefits to all levels of supervision. The following are several of the most important advantages of having an up-to-date, clearly stated employee handbook:

1. **An employee handbook is the supervisor's reference manual and human resource "guidebook."** It provides the supervisor with written company personnel policies and benefit practices that apply to his or her subordinates on a day-to-day basis. A handbook gives the supervisor a quick reference guide to basic personnel policies and procedures, performance standards for employees, guidelines for progressive discipline, and eligibility for various employee benefits. Although some levels of supervision may have access to a company personnel policy and procedures manual (consisting of substantially more detail and usually in a large three-ring binder format), the employee handbook provides a more con-

venient and practical "summary" in a condensed format of all significant and most widely used employee benefit policies, standards of performance, work rules, and statements of what employees can expect of the company.

2. **An employee handbook is a positive reminder to supervisors of the important need for consistency in their day-to-day "people" management responsibility.** The employee handbook will reinforce the supervisor's day-to-day responsibility for supervising their employees fairly, firmly, and consistently and administering company performance standards and personnel and employee benefit policies.

3. **An employee handbook provides the "newly promoted" supervisor, foreman, or lead person with confidence.** Newly promoted supervisory personnel need to have orientation and training on their new people management responsibility and the communications skills required to work effectively with their subordinates in their new supervisor-employee relationship. The employee handbook can be a most useful and practical communications tool for the newly promoted supervisor in understanding what the supervisor should expect of employees in their day-to-day work environment.

4. **An employee handbook provides the supervisor and employees with common ground for mutual understanding of the employees' responsibilities in the workplace.** When supervisors find it necessary to provide corrective discipline to employees for failure to perform to standards in terms of attendance, punctuality, productivity, safety, etc., they can persuasively communicate with employees one-on-one by referring to the employee's handbook for documentation of the performance standards and expectations of the company toward all employees. The employee handbook thus reinforces the supervisors' authority and responsibility to properly supervise employees with backup reinforcement of published company work performance standards and expectations.

5. **An employee handbook saves much time for supervisors.** Without written personnel policies and procedures, standards of performance, guidelines for progressive discipline, and eligibility requirements for various employee benefit programs, supervisors have to spend much costly time in getting answers to the questions raised by employees on a day-to-day basis. Thus, the supervisor, plant manager, superintendent, or human resource manager will be involved in countless, costly time-consuming meetings brainstorming about which policy or personnel practices and procedures should be applied to various employee questions and about what the company policy and practice should be regarding various daily on-the-job problems.

Advantages of an Employee Handbook to Employees

Since employee handbooks have been developed, published, and distributed to employees, one would naturally expect that the primary benefits and advantages of an employee handbook should focus on the employees and their families. The following are the major advantages and benefits to employees of having a current, clearly stated, attractive employee handbook:

1. **An employee handbook provides *new* employees with their first employee education and orientation of what is expected of them in their new job in terms of on-the-job performance.** It also provides employees with their first education, orientation, and understanding of what the new employees can expect from their new employer. This is the basic, employer-employee communications guidebook to help the new employee get off to a good start in a positive, favorable working relationship with the company.

2. **An employee handbook provides the *new* employee's family with the basic understanding of all employee benefits available to the employee and dependents and of the eligibility and waiting period necessary before certain benefits become effective.** In communicating the employee benefit program and the eligibility and dollar value of employee benefits, the company and the employee's family begin developing a positive, favorable working relationship. When an employee's family has seen, reviewed, and/or read the new employee handbook, they can come away with a favorable first impression of the company. Unless the company provides on-site family functions such as periodic open houses, company picnics, or other employee-family gatherings, the family can benefit from and appreciate the company more when the members have access to an up-to-date, comprehensive employee handbook.

   Throughout the employer-employee employment history, the employee handbook will be used as a reference manual by the employee's family when questions arise regarding eligibility for certain insurance coverages, personal leaves of absence, additional paid time off, etc., since employee handbooks usually end up on a table or on a bookshelf at the employee's home.

3. **An employee handbook can be a very important, useful company publication in attracting desirable new employees in the employee recruiting process.** In tight labor markets or in cities and communities where highly skilled employees are difficult to locate and attract, prospective employees can be given a copy of the employee handbook during the pre-employment interview. Thus, the employee handbook can be the company's "winning edge" in projecting a favorable, positive image of the company and what the prospective employee may expect from the com-

pany in terms of working conditions, employee benefits, performance standards, and opportunity for advancement.

4. **An employee handbook can be an effective substitute for a union contract or labor agreement.** When an employer is committed to establishing and maintaining a union-free work environment, it is absolutely necessary to provide employees with an employee handbook. One of the most common union promises made to nonunion employees during unionization attempts is to obtain statements of policies in writing. A company is at a disadvantage when the union organizer learns that the union-free company does not have any personnel policies, employee benefits, or performance standards shared with employees in a published, printed format. In trying to effectively "tell and sell" certain advantages or benefits of unionization, the organizer will point out this communication void on the part of the employer and promise employees that if they sign a union authorization card and vote for the union in a secret ballot election, the subsequent labor negotiations will result in a *written contract*. The labor agreement will provide employees and their families with detailed employee benefit policies, which the "company cannot take away from you" in the future.

   Although this typical union promise can be effectively debated by management, the nonunion employer should not be put on this defensive path with employees during a unionization attempt. This situation can be effectively avoided with the publication and distribution of an employee handbook long before the union organizer targets the union-free company and begins meeting with employees for the purpose of getting them to sign union authorization cards requesting the union to be their bargaining agent for collective bargaining on wages, benefits, and working conditions.

5. **An employee handbook provides employees with a sense of self-esteem and job security.** An employee handbook can help provide a "motivating" workplace environment because it can be tangible proof to employees that management does care enough about them that it wants them to clearly understand what they can expect of the company. Properly worded in a positive tone, the contents of an employee handbook can provide *effective employee recognition and appreciation* through the writing style, content, and format. Although the employee handbook should not serve or be intended as an "employee contract" or employment agreement, the handbook can be effectively drafted and published in a format that clearly tells employees that they are essential and important to the company's continued growth and operating success.

   The handbook can also create the favorable impression in the individual and collective thought of all employees that the company *values* their suggestions and constructive criticism on how the company can be a more productive, profitable organization, as well as how the company can

Developing an Employee Handbook: Objectives and Concerns

make improvements to create greater job satisfaction and provide a sense of job security for employees and their families.

Advantages of an Employee Handbook to Union-Represented Employees

It is recommended that a separate employee handbook or handbook supplement be provided all employees in an appropriate bargaining unit represented by a labor organization. This will tend to prevent employees in the union from claiming they should have the same benefits outlined in the employee handbook for nonunion employees if benefits are different from those contained in the labor agreement. Furthermore, the employer cannot make unilateral changes in the compensation, employee benefits, working conditions, etc. of employees represented by the union without discussing or negotiating such proposed changes with the union representative before implementation.

One of the more important reasons to provide a separate employee handbook to employees in a union bargaining unit is to reinforce the fact that they, too, are valued employees of the company and are not treated simply as "union members." An attractive employee handbook, correlated with the contents of the labor agreement clauses and contract language, can be a *positive, pro-employee relations management communications tool* with union-represented employees and their families.

Furthermore, if and when a majority of those union-represented employees choose to exercise their federal right to decertify the union as their exclusive bargaining agent, the existence of a valid employee handbook that summarizes and highlights their major employee benefits, seniority rights, and "fair treatment" language can be a reassuring company document that may deter false fears that they will have no employee rights, privileges, or benefits if they vote out the union at the end of the contract term.

1.02 Management Concerns

Employee Handbooks versus Personnel Policy and Procedures Manuals

What is the difference between an employee handbook and a corporate personnel policy and procedures manual? This question is often raised by employers when contemplating the initial development of an employee handbook. The company or corporate personnel policy and procedures manual and the company's employee handbook are two entirely different company publications. Both are distinctive company documents having different "audiences" and different objectives and purposes.

Ideally, the company personnel policy manual should be the *first* management publication drafted, published, and distributed *before* the drafting, publication, and distribution of an employee handbook. The purpose of a personnel policy manual is described in Dartnell's management publication, *How to Develop a Personnel Policy Manual, as follows:*

9

© 1991 The Dartnell Corporation

The purpose of a personnel policy manual is to provide employers, human resource directors, industrial relations directors, and supervisors with a systematic approach to administering personnel policies and practices. The policy manual should be designed as a fundamental communications tool for these members of management to help clarify policies and practices and thus prevent morale problems, complaints, and grievances before they arise.

The typical company personnel policy manual is distributed only to the aforementioned management representatives, including department heads and, usually, middle management personnel.

The personnel policy and procedures manual is a "living management document" that is never "finally published." It is a detailed manual, usually bound in an $8\frac{1}{2}'' \times 11''$ three-ring notebook format. It consists largely of comprehensive, detailed company policies and procedures covering all phases of human resource management, including the following major areas:

- Employment, Induction, and Orientation
- Attendance and Absenteeism
- Wage and Salary Administration
- Management Development and Training
- Employee Benefits Administration
- Seniority, Promotions, Transfers, and Layoffs
- Conduct, Discipline, and Termination
- Complaint and Grievance Procedures
- Employment Expenses and Reimbursement
- Federal Regulations Affecting Personnel Policies and Procedures

The personnel policy and procedures manual typically provides the management team with the detailed policy statement, the purpose of the policy statement, and how the policy is to be administered (procedure).

The employee handbook or manual is primarily developed and published for a different audience—the employees and their families. The employee handbook content is written in a more informal, positive style and format. The content is developed in a substantially briefer format with more of a summary description of the employer's major employee benefits, personnel policies, and performance standards. Whereas the corporate personnel policy and procedures manual has a restrictive, limited distribution to management and supervisory personnel, a copy of the employee handbook is usually provided to everyone within the organization, including managers and supervisors.

Developing Both an Employee Handbook and a Personnel Policy and Procedures Manual

Since the employee handbook and the personnel policy and procedures manual of a company have different audiences and different purposes and objectives, they are never intended to be a substitute for each other. The employee handbook does not and should not contain the substantial details, procedures, explanations, and reasoning behind each personnel policy and procedure of the company. The corporate personnel policy and procedures manual is a detailed roadmap for the management team to follow in their day-to-day management of human resources, explaining, "why," "when," and "where" of all company personnel policy and procedures.

Consistency is a must for both personnel policy manuals and employee handbooks. Although many smaller employers (with fewer than 100 employees) normally do not have the company personnel policy manual published or implemented, most do have the employee handbook published and distributed to everyone. Where there exist both a corporate personnel policy manual and an employee handbook, it is essential that the policies and procedures outlined in both documents reflect the following standards:

1. All personnel and benefit policies should be harmonious in content, intent, and eligibility in both publications.

2. Personnel policy and benefit programs must be in compliance with all federal and state regulations as they apply to the particular company.

3. All personnel and benefit policies should be clear, concise, and up to date.

4. Personnel and benefit policies in both the employee handbook and personnel policy and procedures manual must be administered consistently in order for both management publications to retain their credibility among management and employees.

5. The recipients, or audience, should be identified in the introductory section of the personnel policy manual and the employee handbook. Spell out in the introductory portion of the employee handbook which groups of employees or classifications are subject to the personnel policies, benefits, and work rules outlined in the handbook.

When to Revise or Update an Employee Handbook

Along with the advantages and benefits to employers of publishing and distributing employee handbooks, it is *management's responsibility* to maintain compliance with the recurring changes in both federal and state employment regulations that impact directly on numerous personnel policies and employee benefit programs. There is no "average life expectancy" of an employee handbook. Although numerous employers have published and distributed employee handbooks without revising them over a period of three to five years, that past practice can

© 1991 The Dartnell Corporation

have a haunting, costly impact in today's rapidly changing regulatory enforcement of company personnel policies and benefit programs by both federal and state agencies.

It is one thing to establish and maintain a current employee handbook that clearly and accurately describes your employment policies, benefit programs, and standards of performance. It is equally important that all such personnel policies, benefit programs, and employment standards be in compliance with the latest enforcement policies of federal and state agencies, such as the EEOC, OFCC, NLRB, and various state "human rights" commissions.

Management's Right to Revise and Update Policies and Procedures

When the employer's "audience" of employees consists of people in job classifications and departments that are not represented by a labor organization, the employer has the right to revise and update personnel policies, benefit programs, compensation programs, and working conditions unilaterally.

Caution on Revising Handbooks for Union Employees

However, where there is a union agent representing employees in a bargaining unit and where such employees are provided with an employee handbook in addition to their labor agreement, it is important that management carefully review any collective bargaining obligation it may have to discuss with the union representative any proposed changes or revisions in the employee handbook that would involve the subject or content of "wages, benefits, and working conditions." In such cases, the union representative should be notified and informed of the revision or changes before they are republished and distributed to employees in the bargaining unit.

Company Conditions Necessitating Revision of Employee Handbooks

If and when the following conditions and circumstances develop within the organization, it is recommended that the personnel policies, employee benefits, working conditions, and standards of performance stated in employee handbooks be carefully reviewed and rewritten, republished, and redistributed:

1. Revise and update the employee handbook when company employee benefits, eligibility for benefits, or significant changes have occurred in former personnel policies and procedures, standards of performance, or work rules.

2. Revise and update employee handbook when there is a change in ownership of the company or a merger with a new business organization. Newly negotiated and executed buy-sell agreements between organizations should be reviewed by legal counsel before the new "successor" employer makes any unilateral changes in wages, employee benefits, or working conditions affecting existing employees.

3. Revise and update the employee handbook if and when a group of the company's employees become unionized in an appropriate bargaining unit after the union is certified as the bargaining agent of the National Labor Relations Board (NLRB). Newly unionized employers will be regulated by the NLRB and will be required to "bargain in good faith" over all employment conditions, employee benefits, personnel policies, working conditions, etc. with the certified union bargaining representative.

   Section 8(a)(5) of the National Labor Relations Act requires an employer to "bargain in good faith" with the union representative over the subject areas after the union is certified by the NLRB. This section of the act makes it an unfair labor practice if the employer refuses or fails to bargain in good faith with the union representative over any proposed changes in wages, benefits, or working conditions that may have been published and distributed in the previous or current handbook. If the subject matter of the employee handbook is considered a "mandatory subject of bargaining" by the NLRB, the newly unionized employer will have an obligation to discuss the proposed changes with the union before making them effective or before implementation and communication with employees.

4. Revise and update the employee handbook if the current employee handbook has not been carefully screened for terminology, employer statements, and wording that might cause the handbook to be considered a "binding contract" between the company and employees. There are practical guidelines employers should follow to lessen exposure to employee lawsuits alleging wrongful discharge or other so-called "contract" claims. Some employee handbooks are not properly worded and contain language and phrases that directly or indirectly imply "guarantees" or mandatory requirements before employees can be terminated. Following are several subject areas that should be audited by the employer and the human resource manager on a regular, recurring basis:

   - Avoid employee handbook language that states employees will be terminated only "for just cause." This can destroy or limit the employer's right to terminate an employee "at the will" of the employer under various state laws (see Section 5.02).

   - Avoid using the term *probationary period* in describing the initial try-out or introductory period of employees.

   - Avoid language such as "employees may be terminated with or without cause" during the "probationary period" which may lead one to believe they must be terminated "for cause" after the completion of the probationary period.

   - Avoid describing in detail a "progressive discipline" procedure in the handbook unless you are prepared to consistently follow the procedure before terminating an employee. The following is an example of a progressive discipline procedure:

First Offense—Verbal Correction
Second Offense—Written Correction
Third Offense—Suspension
Fourth Offense—Discharge

- Avoid handbook language referring to "job security," "steady work," or "permanent" employees.

Revising an Employee Handbook May Not Solve Language Problems

The mere issuance of an "amended" employee handbook will not necessarily solve problems created by an earlier version. This was the case in *Thompson v. Kings Entertainment Company*, 674 F.Supp. 1194 (E.D. VA 1986). Thompson was employed as a sign painter at Kings Dominion. In 1980 an employee handbook was issued (the 1980 Handbook) that defined "dismissal" as "a separation initiated by Kings Dominion for cause." In 1984, the theme park was sold, and in July of 1985, the new owner issued a new employee handbook (the 1985 Handbook). Thompson signed a statement acknowledging receipt of the new handbook, which provided that either the employer or the employee "may terminate [the] employment at any time with or without cause and with or without notice." Shortly after the issuance of the 1985 Handbook, Thompson was discharged. He subsequently sued his employer alleging that he had been fired "without cause" and in violation of the 1980 Handbook.

In deciding upon a motion for summary judgment filed by the employer, the court ruled that the 1980 Handbook constituted an offer of employment terms which Thompson had accepted. From the statements contained in the handbook, "a reasonable jury could find that an employee having accepted the [handbook's] offer could only be discharged for cause." Although the court acknowledged that the issuance of the 1985 Handbook could have resulted in alteration or amendment of those employment provisions incorporated from the 1980 Handbook, the court did not believe such amendments became effective automatically upon the issuance of the new handbook. The court construed the 1985 Handbook to be an offer of employment which Thompson could have rejected or accepted.

Following the court's analysis, it was assumed that the employer had bargained away its right to terminate the employee without just cause by issuing the 1980 Handbook. "To permit that employer to unilaterally convert the employee's status to terminable-at-will merely by issuing a second handbook to that effect would do violence to the [earlier] policy." In order to find that the new contract terms had been "accepted" by Thompson, the court felt that the employer "must demonstrate that Thompson was aware of the handbook, that he understood that its terms governed his employment, and that he worked according to those terms." Finally, the court concluded that the employer had not demonstrated that Thompson worked with the understanding that the 1985 Handbook governed his employment. Accordingly, the court found in favor of the employee, declaring that the mere fact that the employee continued to work did not constitute acceptance of the new terms where the employee previously had been granted the right to work until discharged for cause.

Employers must consistently follow the revised personnel and disciplinary policies of revised, amended handbook. In a case decided February 11, 1988, the Circuit Court for the City of Richmond permitted three lawsuits to go forward against Virginia Electric and Power Company (VEPCO). In three separate cases (*Byer v. VEPCO; Kincaid v. VEPCO;* and *Powell v. VEPCO*), former employees charged that VEPCO violated provisions of the VEPCO employee handbook.

Each plaintiff was hired by VEPCO in October of 1981 as a physical security officer at VEPCO's North Anna Power Station. In 1986, each plaintiff was questioned about his possible use of marijuana at a private party in Louisa, Virginia, in October of 1981. Each plaintiff admitted using marijuana at the party. None of the plaintiffs were cited for misconduct for this incident, and there was no evidence that VEPCO knew about the incident before 1986. At all times before 1986, each plaintiff had been an exemplary and exceptional employee and had consistently received good evaluations. After their discharge, VEPCO issued the following memorandum:

> The Company's policy is that *illegal use of drugs, on or off duty, by security personnel* or supervisors impairs their ability to enforce Company policies. Therefore any illegal involvement by these employees will result in termination. [Emphasis supplied.]

At the time the plaintiffs used marijuana in 1981, the employee handbook had no language similar to that contained in the memorandum. The handbook then in effect contained the following statement:

> Every employee should clearly understand that a co-worker under the influence of intoxicants, self-administered drugs, or narcotics poses a threat to their personal safety which may result in serious injury or death. The use of intoxicants while on the job is prohibited and can result in suspension or termination. The illegal use, possession of or sale of narcotics, hallucinogens, depressants, stimulants or marijuana on Company business or Company property can result in suspension or termination. The use of narcotics, hallucinogens, depressants, stimulants or marijuana *off Company premises which affects an employee's ability to perform his/her job,* or which generates publicity or circumstances which adversely affect the Company or its employees can result in discipline, including possible suspension or termination. [Emphasis supplied.]

The employee handbook was not amended to include the memorandum language until well after the plaintiffs used marijuana at the party in 1981.

After finding that the plaintiffs had contracts of employment with VEPCO, the Court permitted the plaintiffs to prove at trial that VEPCO wrongfully terminated them under the handbook in effect when the marijuana use took place. The Court said:

> Thus, if plaintiffs' employment contracts were contracts under which they could only be terminated for just cause and *if just cause in 1981 in connection with marijuana use was defined only by defendant's drug policy as set out in the Employee Pol-*

icy Manual, it cannot be said that plaintiffs' admissions of marijuana use off Company premises in October, 1981, based solely on the allegations of the motions for judgment, constitute just cause for their terminations. [Emphasis supplied.]

It cannot be emphasized too strongly that an employer must comply with the provisions of an employee handbook or policy manual. Progressive discipline procedures must be followed to the letter, and thorough indoctrination of all supervisory personnel in carrying out such procedures must be a continuous process. Furthermore, an employer must ensure that the punishment fits the crime in all cases, that is, that one supervisor is no more lenient than another in determining when to issue reprimands.

Do You Need More Than One Employee Handbook?

In the development of an employee handbook for the first time, it is important that the company focus on the "audience" or intended readers and users of the employee handbook. This is obviously important in determining the handbook's content and subject matter. Many smaller companies usually have only one employee handbook that is drafted, published, and distributed to all employees in the organization, including supervisors, office and administrative personnel, sales, production and maintenance employees, etc.

It is also common to find two employee handbooks in companies where there is a fairly significant number of employees in salaried exempt or salaried nonexempt classifications, as well as a significant number of hourly paid "production and maintenance" employee classifications. The exception would be when both groups of employees can become eligible for the same employee benefits and are employed and supervised under the same type of personnel policies and performance standards.

For employers that have office or plant facilities in different states or municipalities, the content of the employee handbook must be carefully monitored to be certain that all personnel policies, employee benefits, and company regulations, such as the new "no-smoking" policy, comply with local and state regulations.

However, in medium-size and large corporations, it's not unusual to find more than one employee handbook to address the need for different subject matter and content caused by different job classifications, different geographical locations of the facilities, and different employee benefits, working conditions, and personnel policies. Moreover, employers that have employees in collective bargaining units represented by a labor organization usually have a separate employee handbook supplement that is provided to employees who are either members of the union or who work in the bargaining unit represented by the labor organization. The employee handbook or handbook supplements provided to employees represented by a labor union must not differ from the worded intent of their current labor agreement regarding compensation, benefits, standards of performance, work rules, employee rights, seniority rights, or other employee benefits.

SECTION 2

Developing an Employee Handbook: Responsibilities for Drafting, Editing, and Publishing

CONTENTS

SECTION 2

Developing an Employee Handbook: Responsibilities for Drafting, Editing, and Publishing

2.01 Assigning Responsibilities for the Initial Draft or Revision

After you have considered the numerous practical benefits and employee relations advantages of developing and publishing your first employee handbook or of revising and updating your current employee handbook, your first step is to assign this important project to someone within your organization.

Ideally, the initial employee handbook, as well as all revisions, should be authorized and approved by top management. Usually the responsibility of developing the initial employee handbook or revising current handbooks is assigned to the human resources or personnel department of the organization. Thus, the director of human resources or the personnel manager has the primary responsibility for seeing that the employee handbook is properly drafted, edited, published, and distributed. Since the initial and subsequent decisions regarding the contents of a new employee handbook or the necessary changes or additions to a current handbook involve responsible and technical tasks, it is recommended that the management person assigned the responsibility for this project serve as the editor as well as the chairperson of the Employee Handbook Committee.

Establish an Employee Handbook Committee

The editor should have the authority to set up a small committee to assist in gathering the data necessary for producing a complete and comprehensive handbook. The committee should, in effect, do some of the legwork required in bringing information to the committee chairperson.

Because the organizational structure of companies and organizations varies greatly, the choice of a project leader requires some consideration. Although the human resources department is an obvious choice, many small organizations don't have a full-time human resource person or an individual with sufficient skill to handle the job.

However, in every organization there are several people who know current policy and perhaps formulate it on a day-to-day basis. One of these people should have enough background to take charge of the project. This person can be aided by a committee of individuals who have working knowledge of the various departments.

19

Someone from human resources has background on employee relations, someone from accounting has access to wage and salary administration, and an industrial relations person knows much about the union contract.

The handbook committee should be small enough to be functional. It serves to reduce the time and effort that the chairperson/editor must put forth to produce a comprehensive manual. The committee's initial task is to gather data from specified departments. Individual members can make recommendations and should carefully review the area of policy within their realm. It is wise to establish specific policies and timetables for efficient development and publishing of the handbook.

2.02 Primary Responsibilities of the Employee Handbook Committee

The Employee Handbook Committee, appointed by the director of human resources or the general manager, has the following primary responsibilities in preparing the initial or revised draft of the employee handbook for final publishing and distribution to employees:

- Determine what should be covered in the employee handbook and what should be excluded from the new or revised employee handbook.

- Review an available "Employee Handbook Development Checklist" to assist in determining the subject matter to be included or excluded in the initial or revised employee handbook.

- Audit, reread, and evaluate current employee handbook contents for sections or topics that need to be updated and revised to comply with new federal or state employment laws (i.e., employment-at-will cases, wrongful discharge cases, etc.).

- Assist in the drafting of assigned topics or sections of the employee handbook as assigned by the employee handbook editor/chairperson.

- Assist in collecting up-to-date, accurate data on personnel policies and procedures, employee benefits, wage and salary administration, etc. before preparing the initial draft of the employee handbook or the revision of the current employee handbook.

- Involve other department heads, managers, and supervisors in collecting current data for drafting employee handbook policy statements.

- Request that managers, department heads, and supervisors carefully read all drafts of the new or revised employee handbook manuscript before preparing a final draft for printing. It is important to be certain the wording is accurate and the *intent* is clear and consistent.

- Assist the handbook editor/chairperson in determining the format of the employee handbook, cover design, binding, size, and quantity, and in reviewing bids from graphic arts printing firms.

- Assist the handbook editor/chairperson in selecting final artwork, illustrations, cartoons, or photographs to be included in various sections of the employee handbook.

- Assist the editor/chairperson with effective promotion and distribution of the employee handbook after printing.

2.03 Supervisory Involvement in Developing an Effective Employee Handbook

The handbook committee should utilize the ideas and observations of supervisors and department managers to the fullest extent possible. The supervisors and managers are on the firing line daily and are primarily responsible for administering company policies and practices. They know how former unwritten personnel policies or former written policies have affected employee morale and productivity.

Supervisors should be interviewed for the purpose of learning what is going on now. They will be a great help in finding out where present policies, written or unwritten, are working and where they are not working. For example, the supervisors may be able to point out certain policies that have proven unworkable or that are unnecessary and should be revised or abolished. They may also be able to recommend new policies for attaining greater efficiency and more job satisfaction for the employees. The supervisors will be the best informed source on where present policy and practices are being administered inconsistently or unequally among their subordinates. Thus, supervisors will prove of great benefit to the Employee Handbook Committee by helping them determine what the policy and practice should be concerning various subjects.

An important benefit of using supervisors as a source of information for the proposed employee handbook revision is that it gives them the opportunity to participate and be involved in its development or revision. The supervisors are helping to "create" the new or revised handbook. In consulting with them, you will find that there will be greater effort on their part to support handbook policies and practices, because they have helped create them.

For the supervisors to be effective in helping the Employee Handbook Committee, the committee itself must be reasonable in approaching supervisors. Committee members should ask every supervisor to tell them what he or she thinks personnel policies are on a given subject. If a given policy is unknown or ambiguous, the supervisors should be asked to express themselves on how they actually handle a problem that arises in that particular area. The supervisors should also be asked about changes that need to be made in existing policies and practices.

For organizations developing an employee handbook for the first time, the following questionnaire can be extremely helpful to members of the Employee Handbook Committee in working with supervisors. The following set of questions can be applied to any given subject dealing with personnel policies.

**Supervisor Questionnaire for Employee Handbook
Development and/or Revision**

1. Are you familiar with our personnel policy or benefit on _____?

2. Do you think this policy is working in the best interests of both our management team and our employees?

3. Do you feel this personnel or benefit policy meets our present needs?

4. Do you know and understand this personnel or benefit policy well enough to interpret and administer it correctly? Are you aware of any improper understanding or administration of this policy by employees?

5. Do you think we need a new or revised policy on the subject of _____?

6. What do you think the new/revised policy should be?

7. What other suggestions do you have on what should and should not be included in the new or revised employee handbook?

8. What do you think would be a good title for our employee handbook?

Using the questionnaire for interviewing supervisors has practical value. It can help clarify both past and potential personnel problem areas that have resulted in complaints, inconsistencies, grievances, and misunderstandings. It can also assist in developing new policies to prevent problems from arising in the future.

A questionnaire can be of great value as an aid in periodically reviewing overall personnel policies and procedures. We recommend that questionnaires be distributed at least once every year. Furthermore, the interviewing and questioning of supervisors can result in many good ideas on where present training programs need to be revised or improved for the benefit of new supervisors, new managers, and staff personnel.

2.04 Distributing an Employee Handbook Development Checklist to the Management-Supervisory Team

Selecting all of the topics and policy statements to be included in the new or revised employee handbook is an important part of the development process. Distributing an Employee Handbook Development Checklist to the Employee Handbook Committee as well as to all department heads, managers, and supervisors can be a much appreciated and practical first step.

You may wish to customize your own checklist of topics for your first employee handbook or any revision. There is a variety of "checklists" that can be helpful in covering all of the major, important topics of personnel policies and procedures, employee benefits, and other employer-employee relations programs to be considered for coverage in the new or revised employee handbook. Advantages in beginning with an Employee Handbook Development Checklist are as follows:

- A checklist gives the Employee Handbook Committee and management team the same "frame of reference" for all possible handbook policy statements to be included or excluded.

- A checklist saves time in determining the subject matter and content of employee handbooks.

- A checklist assists the Employee Handbook Committee and its chair in getting a consensus regarding the subject matter to be included in or excluded from the new or revised employee handbook.

- A checklist provides the committee with an effective roadmap for monitoring and evaluating current employment policies, work rules, and employee benefits existing in the workplace.

- A checklist can be adapted so that individual members of the handbook committee will know which persons are responsible for gathering the data, drafting the handbook policy statements, and developing the timetable for its completion and submission for review and approval.

Section 4 of this management manual contains separate, customized employee handbook development checklists for special topics covering all of the major phases and events of employer-employee relations in the workplace. For example, there is a detailed employee handbook development checklist for Employment, Induction, and Orientation policies and procedures.

2.05 Using Employee Suggestions in the New or Revised Employee Handbook

Since the employee handbook is really for the purpose of providing *all employees* with clear communications on what they can expect from the company and what the company can expect from them, it's recommended that the Employee Handbook Committee develop and distribute a special "Employee Handbook Questionnaire" to all employees as well as to supervisors prior to the initial drafting of the new or revised employee handbook.

Involving employees in the handbook development process has many advantages both to the organization and to the Employee Handbook Committee. Requesting employees' ideas, suggestions, and input—for example, in a "name the handbook" contest—can create good will, improve employee morale, and foster enthusiastic acceptance of the finished product as employees share it with their families.

The Employee Handbook Committee can prepare a customized "Employee Handbook Development Questionnaire" and distribute it to employees, with an appropriate bulletin board notice or cover letter. It can be presented to them in small group meetings, department head meetings, or one-on-one by their immediate supervisor. Providing employees with a request for their input when developing the first employee handbook or revising a handbook will provide the committee with a tremendous resource of ideas and subject matter as well as an identification of past or current personnel and benefit policies that have become confusing or misunderstood by employees.

Asking employees to give you their opinion regarding what should or should not be included in the employee handbook is a very "proactive management" style of communications and employee involvement. It can provide improved employee morale, self-esteem, and recognition. When the final new or revised employee handbook is printed and distributed to employees and their families, it will be well received and will be more utilized in their future employment relationship with supervisors, department heads, and the organization.

In the appendix to this section is a representative sample questionnaire that can be used by an employee handbook committee in seeking out employee suggestions and ideas about the employee handbook subject matter, content, and format in developing an initial handbook or in revising an "old" employee handbook.

2.06 Sources of Important Personnel Policy/ Employee Benefit/Employment Data

In addition to utilizing the valued input, constructive criticism, ideas, and suggestions from the management team when developing or revising an employee handbook for your organization, there are other important sources of information that need to be tapped, studied, reviewed, and checked out carefully before completing the final draft of the handbook manuscript. These additional important sources of employee handbook information and data include the following:

- Current employee handbook, if one has been previously published and distributed

- Employee handbooks from other operating divisions, subsidiaries, or competitors in the industry and geographical area

- Your corporate or company personnel policy and procedures manual (ideally to be drafted and published the first before developing and publishing the employee handbook)

- Company "SOPs," usually distributed to the management team and found in an SOP manual

- Copies of previously published and posted bulletin board notices concerning employee benefits, personnel policies, standards of performance, employee conduct, etc.

- Employee suggestion systems—namely, written employee suggestions considered to have merit or suggestions that have been approved and implemented during the past two to three years

- Individual or group questions, concerns, or ideas for improving employee communications elicited from the employees themselves in previously conducted monthly "round table" management talks or periodic "department" employee meetings with supervisors

- Analysis of past verbal or written complaints—that is, grievances coming from various steps of the employee complaint/grievance procedures during the past two to three years

- Professional consultants that specialize in developing, writing, and editing employee handbooks or lawyers that specialize in employment law, especially in current federal and/or state cases pertaining to the content of employee handbooks and the changes needed to comply with current state employment law

- Recently conducted employee opinion survey results that highlight areas of misunderstanding, lack of information, or misinformation concerning employee benefits and personnel policies. (Ideally, an employee attitude or personnel opinion survey should be planned and conducted with employees prior to the initial publishing or revision of an employee handbook. It provides management with a highly reliable, valuable source of employment data on what needs to be recommunicated to employees concerning employment personnel policies and procedures, employee benefits administration, conduct on the job, performance standards, etc.)

  For example, one important question on our SESCO personnel opinion survey questionnaire asks: "Is there any personnel, employee benefit policy, work rule or company policies you would like to know more about?" This open-ended question can provide management with important current areas of concern from employees that need to be studied and implemented when revising or developing employee handbooks.

It is highly recommended and absolutely essential that all future revisions of employee handbooks by employers as well as all new handbooks developed for new organizations have their entire contents carefully read and reviewed by a professional consulting firm that specializes in employee handbook development or by an attorney that specializes in employment law.

As described in Section 1 of this manual, there have been numerous employment law cases involving the publication and distribution of certain personnel policies and benefit statements in employee handbooks that have come under close scrutiny by both federal and state agencies such as the NLRB, EEOC, state human rights commissions, labor organizations, and state courts.

The common law "employment-at-will" doctrine is being challenged in numerous states by former employees who allege they were "wrongfully discharged." The employee handbook is often used as major evidence by either the former employee or the company in proving or disproving that the employee handbook is not a "contract" or that the employee handbook contents and disclaimer statements do not provide contractual employment or benefits to present or future employees. (See the Section 5.03 commentary and analysis of state laws restricting an employer's right to "terminate employees at will.")

Once the employee handbook manuscript draft has been prepared and edited by the Employee Handbook Committee of your organization, prior to publishing, printing, and distribution of the new or revised handbook, it must be carefully reviewed by your professional human resource consultant retained for this purpose and/or by your employment law attorney.

2.07 What Should and Should Not Be Covered in an Employee Handbook

A well-written, clearly stated, attractive, and useful employee handbook can be customized to include many or few personnel policies, employee benefits, working conditions, pay systems, progressive discipline procedures, work rules, and other important employer-employee relations programs. The challenge is to decide which personnel and benefit policies, working conditions, etc. should be included in the employee handbook. Following are practical considerations and guidelines to be considered in deciding what should or should not be included in the first draft of your new or revised employee handbook.

The development, writing, and editing of employee handbooks for SESCO's clients over the past 45 years has given our professional staff valuable experience in the general format and content of hundreds of employee handbooks in most all industries. These employee handbooks have covered employees in both exempt and nonexempt salaried positions, hourly paid employees, as well as employees represented by labor organizations.

Although there is no fixed "content" or list of subjects that are covered in all employee handbooks, there is a "general" listing of personnel policies, employee benefits, and employment conditions that have some commonality in most employee handbooks. Obviously, the final content of employee handbooks will vary from industry to industry and within an organization, based upon the company culture, industry, size of the organization, type of employees, and whether the organization has employees represented by a labor organization or is operating union-free.

The appendix to this section contains a representative "Table of Contents" from a well-designed employee handbook along with a sample index, which is located in the last pages of most handbooks.

What Should Be Excluded from Employee Handbooks?

It is customary to exclude from most employee handbooks the following topics or materials:

- Personnel policies and procedures that appear in the corporate personnel policy and procedures manual and pertain only to managerial personnel

- Special "employee benefits" that pertain only to the management team or other classifications of employees that are not included in the "audience" of your particular employee handbook

- Facts, data, or information that is subject to change in the short term or on a regular recurring basis. For example, omit salary or wage rates, salary ranges, company/employee insurance premiums, etc.

- Any language that conflicts with the company's current labor agreement, should the employee handbook be distributed to employees in the bargaining unit represented by a labor organization. Clearly, the labor agreement is a bona fide contract of employment, providing numerous restrictions on management's right to "terminate at will" and usually specifying rather strict guidelines on when employees can be disciplined or discharged only for "just cause." Such wording should not be used in the employee handbook if the handbook is to be distributed to employees who are not covered by the labor agreement.

Remember Your "Audience" When Drafting the Handbook

Employee handbooks should not read like a labor agreement or union contract. They should be written in a friendly, positive tone, even following an "informal" rather than a "formal" standard. Numerous employee handbooks have been written with such an inflated style of writing that only highly educated, college-level people could properly understand the wording or the intent of the contents. The "intent" of employee handbook topics and policy statements must clearly correlate with the actual "language" of the policy statement if it is to have validity, reliability, and consistency in the workplace.

Specialists and professionals in composition and writing for the print media, television advertising, and other mass communications efforts have for a long time prepared their content to the educational level of sixth to eighth graders. One of the most important objectives of the final product of the employee handbook is that it can be read and understood by almost all employees who have the ability to read the English language.

Employee handbooks can be written simply and still accomplish the objective of reflecting a positive, quality image of the organization when the handbook is seen, reviewed, or read by employees, their families, or other "friends" of your organization.

The following are several practical suggestions for the Employee Handbook Committee and the editor/chairperson in drafting the contents of the new or revised employee handbook:

- Provide sufficient "white space" in the margins, and "double space" the typesetting on each page.

- Keep paragraphs and sentences short. Attempt to convey one major subject or idea in each paragraph. Limit sentences to 25 words or less.

- Use "simple" words with no more than three syllables if possible.

- Provide separate "title" pages to provide appropriate identification of new sections or different sections of the employee handbook. Organize the contents of the employee handbook to fit the major topic. For example, all employee benefits, including insurance, paid time off, etc., should be placed in one major section, such as "What Employees Can Expect From the Company—Your Employee Benefits."

- Break up the printed words or language of employee handbooks with appropriate, related artwork, illustrations, or cartoons to identify the major topic or subject of that particular handbook section. Graphic devices will add interest and grab the reader's attention.

- Some handbooks utilize photographs of the facilities, work areas, and certain managerial staff. Photographs can be appropriate as long as they do not become outdated quickly by changes in staffing.

- Try to use personal pronouns in your writing style, such as we, you, or our, to promote an informal, personal style.

- It is ok to use the pronoun *he* rather than *he/she*, provided you explain in the introductory portion of your handbook that masculine pronouns are used for consistency, but the intent is to refer to both male and female employees. The following is an example:

An Introductory Comment to Our Valued Employees

In drafting your employee handbook, we have not used specific gender pronouns for our male and female employees. However, please know that in using the masculine pronoun, our intent is that this should be considered to refer to both male and female employees of our organization.

If you do not find this solution satisfactory, you can avoid the problem by using *you*, as well as plural nouns and pronouns whenever possible (e.g. "*employees may take their* vacations...") and by alternating male and female examples of specific behavior.

- Avoid unneeded words. Nothing weakens writing so much as extra words. Be critical of your own writing and make every word carry its weight.

- Put action into your verbs. The heaviness of much business writing results from overworking the passive voice. Prose can usually be kept impersonal and remain in the active voice.

- Tie in with your reader's experience. The readers will not understand your new idea unless you link it to some old idea they already understand.

- Write the way you talk. As much as you can, use words and phrases that you would normally use in expressing the same thought orally.

- Write to express, not to impress. Present your ideas simply and directly. The writer who makes the best impression is the one who can express complex ideas simply.

This final point reiterates an essential rule of writing employee handbooks—*the policy statements must be absolutely clear.* An employee handbook is no place to display rhetorical ability. Here are some other suggestions to keep in mind:

- Keep your first draft flexible and open to additions and changes. Make your point as clearly as possible and find out if others agree that it is clear.

- Tables and charts are always good when explaining a difficult subject. Even breaking up a section into a tablelike grouping can get the message across as in the following example:

Complete Shift Cycle

12:00 (midnight) to 8:00 a.m.
 8:00 a.m.   to 4:00 p.m.
 4:00 p.m.   to 12:00 midnight

Incomplete Shift Cycle

      7:00 a.m. to 3:00 p.m.
or   8:00 a.m. to 4:00 p.m.
and 3:00 p.m. to 11:00 p.m.
or   4:00 p.m. to 12:00 midnight

- Be your own critic first. Don't be hesitant about rewriting something two or three times. Try to have the first draft as complete as it can be. This may eliminate extensive corrections during review and cut down the number of times the manual will be subjected to review.

- Make enough copies of your first draft to be sure that all who need to review it will be able to do so. Keep track of these copies to avoid missing key corrections suggested by some member of the management team.

2.08 The Organization and Format of Your Employee Handbook

The choice of format and organization is usually decided by the Employee Handbook Committee; nevertheless, it is obvious that some type of outline should be developed and followed throughout.

A checklist for each major section of the employee handbook has been developed for your convenience (Section 4). This checklist is comprehensive, but you may still have to add items that are unique to your organization.

An immediate suggestion is to make additional copies of each checklist for committee members and key executives. These lists can be combined for an overall look at the requisites for a written policy.

Early discussion can center around differences discovered in the outlining of policy areas. When a master copy is completed, the editor/chairperson has a completely developed picture of what is needed. This picture, however, does not provide the order of the material or the substance of the material.

After it is determined which areas of personnel policy will be included in the handbook, it is the job of the editor and the committee to come up with the material (handbooks, previous policies, etc.) that will be the basis of the policy.

Once the research is completed and the information is at hand, it is necessary to establish the organization or arrangement of the manual. The primary requirement here is that the material be organized in a logical manner.

2.09 Writing Drafts of the Employee Handbook

If you have reviewed the recommended steps on how to prepare and/or revise your employee handbook, you should now be ready to begin writing the first draft. A good idea is to review the checklist of policy statements at the beginning of each section. If you have checked off a policy area, you should have a policy statement prepared. The checklists in this manual are followed by a variety of sample policy statements that have been used by other employers.

Each section contains one or more policy statements that are in actual use or that have been adapted from other employee handbooks. If one particular statement meets your needs, it can be used or adapted by you for your employee handbook.

Use the margin of the pages in this guide to note the statement you wish to use, adding or deleting data or information which will help tailor the policy to your requirements. Keep a record of the policy statements (page numbers) that you are planning to use so that you can refer to each one quickly.

There are several policy items on the checklist that do not appear in sample policy statements in the section. That is because this particular policy should be entirely composed by the individual organization. Also keep in mind that these are actual policies, unchanged in wording, and are written to fit a company's current situation.

In drafting the first copy of your handbook, you can use $8\frac{1}{2}'' \times 11''$ sheets that will fit into this three-ring binder, or you can use an index card system ($3'' \times 5''$ cards) that can be kept in a file. If you wish to put the actual policy statements on cards, it is suggested that you use a larger size.

This management guide can be adapted quickly to fit your basic need for a good first draft. By keeping the section guides, the checklists, and the policy statements you wish to use, you can develop your own manual. Add your special, customized policy statements within each major section. When all the the topics have been covered, the manual can be alphabetized to fit your needs.

Get the First Draft Proofed and Reviewed

This is the point at which the manual should be put into order with the organization format you have chosen. It is a good idea to retain the master copy and produce sufficient copies for distribution to key personnel who must help in the review.

Each of the copies should have the name of the individual who receives it written on the cover or first page. This will keep your records clear when it comes to checking any revisions. Besides making changes or suggestions, some of the committee will read the copy closely enough to catch possible typographical errors. These should be caught in proofreading, but experience shows that first handbook drafts usually contain some errors.

After all the handbook review copies have been returned, it will probably fall on the shoulders of the editor to check each revision. A meeting of the committee (probably the final meeting) can resolve the possible differences or conflicts that might arise. This is the final chance to make revisions within the existing body of policy, and since the subject is a current one, some management ideas (changes for the future) might be included now.

Each committee member should approve his or her particular area of administration. As an example, it is important that personnel administration puts the final OK on the employment practices statement. It is also necessary to have legal counsel review handbook statements. Likewise, it's important that financial officers okay the pension plan statement, again with legal concurrence.

Involve your supervisors in the review process. Since it is primarily the supervisor who will work with the employee handbook, it is a good practice to have certain key people read over the entire presentation. After they have studied the policies and policy statements, they might join with the committee for a brief question and answer session. Do they understand the policy? Do they know how to explain the policy to an employee? Do they feel the policy, as it is written, will be understood by the employees?

If there is serious doubt in the mind of a supervisor, or if he or she is unable to interpret a policy statement, this is the time to change it. This doesn't mean the supervisors have the final say, but policy is going to be hard to enforce if this group doesn't comprehend the meaning. It will further result in a widespread problem of control if supervisors in one department are interpreting the policy one way and supervisors in another department are interpreting it another way. Besides avoiding confusion, this meeting will help to eventually cut time and money from the program.

2.10 Publishing the Employee Handbook

With all corrections incorporated into a master final draft, the next step is to have the handbook printed. Cost should be a factor here. It is up to management to set some ground rules. The size of the organization and number of employees will probably determine the number of copies needed. This also has an effect on the actual page count of the manual. It pretty much follows that the larger the company or organization, the larger the manual, but this is not a hard and fast rule.

If you have been following the step-by-step procedures in this guide, you have already determined who will receive a copy of the handbook. The next step is to decide how many extra copies you will need (for replacement, etc.) and how long this particular manual will be in use. If you are producing a loose-leaf manual, you can make additions and changes periodically without too much difficulty. This means the initial run can be a little larger than normal.

Your next decision involves the actual production of the employee handbook. The choice here is wide. Remember, if you decide on a printed and bound edition, there is really no opportunity to make a simple change in the future without running the entire job through again.

The pages can be printed on a mimeograph or duplicator or, for that matter, they can be photocopied, punched, and bound in a loose-leaf binder, which allows for updating and changing pages with a minimum of difficulty. A new employee benefit can be quickly added by distributing new pages to employees.

For a large manual (in pages) the three-ring binder is probably the best bet, but for smaller manuals, the Duo-tang binder (two-holes) is adequate. Both allow for flexibility. Both can have printed covers, or they can have simple labels on the covers. Both plastic and paper covers are available from many sources of supply (including the local stationery store), and the choice should be made on the basis of use and cost.

If the aim is to keep the manual for at least five years, a saddle-stitch binding and printed cover is best provided by a professional printer/graphic arts vendor.

2.11 Keeping Your Employee Handbook Up to Date

It is recommended that your Employee Handbook Committee and management team keep your employee handbook up to date at all times. In Section 1 we discussed the circumstances in which an employee handbook should be completely revised, reprinted, and redistributed to employees. Normally, employee handbooks should be revised, reprinted, and redistributed once every two years, unless changes in the company organization or the content of employee benefits or compliance with new or revised federal and state laws requires immediate revision.

Companies have found it expensive and impractical to revise a manual every time a single policy change is necessary. Instead, they keep management and supervisors informed of policy changes by issuing "Policy Bulletins" or other types of memoranda to the recipients of the handbook. Such bulletins can be retained in the front or rear of the handbook, or if it is a loose-leaf publication, they can be inserted in place of the former statement.

Getting Ready for Your Next Handbook Revision

The time will come when your employee handbook needs revision. Most of the steps outlined in this section will have to be followed again, but the time required for revision can be cut dramatically.

A policy file should be maintained by the current editor of the handbook. If someone else is given the assignment, this file will be valuable to the new editor. If the chairperson/editor is the same, most of the information will be at hand. Each item of policy must be rechecked if this is a true revision. Each item must be approved again. At this point, suggestions can be sought for improvement of the manual in terms of format, organization, presentation, etc.

This is also an excellent time for a critical evaluation of policy itself. Is the current policy up to date? Does the organization operate the same way it did two or five years ago? Have employees accepted the current policy, or has there been dissension?

The same type of evaluation should be conducted for the format of the handbook. Has it been easy to use? Has it been criticized by members of the management team or by employees? Is it a positive, practical management communications tool?

Making the Revision

Having undergone the experience of producing one handbook, the editor can proceed with confidence on the revision. Probably less time will be allocated, but it is wise to remind management that the job still must be thorough. A mistake in a revision is just as bad as a mistake in the original publication.

By retracing the steps in this section, the handbook can be developed and produced with a minimum of effort. Copies of the current policy statements can be made for the individuals concerned and directed to their attention. They can be asked to OK the current policy statement or recommend a revision.

As a final word, when the new handbook is released, try to collect old copies and destroy them—except for record copies. This is the best way to prevent a serious problem, especially when both new and old handbooks look pretty much the same.

Properly document the effective date of your new employee handbook or the new, revised date of any subsequent handbook revision to avoid misunderstanding regarding eligibility for certain employee benefits, or changes in personnel policies, benefits and working conditions. The following sample statement may be appropriate:

> This edition of your employee handbook supersedes all previous employee handbooks that have been distributed to employees of our company.

2.12 Preparing for Final Production of the Employee Handbook

Carefully proofread your first proof! The graphic arts vendor you have chosen to assist your company in printing the final draft of your first employee handbook or any subsequent revisions will provide you with a "final proof" copy, often referred to as a "blue line" proof. Upon receipt of the final proof of your employee handbook, the editor/chairperson and your employee handbook committee will assume one of their final responsibilities—to "proofread" every page and every word of the new or revised employee handbook carefully.

Although typesetting firms often have employees responsible for proofreading their customers' artwork and copy, you must not delegate that important responsibility to the vendor's employees. They will usually do a pretty good job in helping you proofread the final draft. However, assuring that there are no typographical errors, missing pages, or unclear statements in the final proof is the responsibility of the employee handbook editor and the Employee Handbook Committee.

Armed with red pencils, they should carefully *study* the entire proof of the employee handbook, marking those pages, paragraphs, or sentences where there are obvious discrepancies, omissions, typographical errors, or any other inaccuracies.

Calling a meeting of the Employee Handbook Committee with their individual, final review of the proof will enable you to have a more accurate, attractive employee handbook that is free from errors and omissions that could be not only embarrassing but also costly to correct after the handbook has been distributed to employees.

Some employers see fit to make photocopies of the proof of the final handbook draft and submit it to all department heads and supervisors within the organization that are responsible for supervising the employees who will eventually receive the final employee handbook. This can be one of the most important, yet time-consuming responsibilities of your supervisory team. It's the "point of no return" or "last chance" to correct any misunderstandings regarding the intent of the language in the handbook and to keep their "involvement" in this last step prior to the final printing and distribution of the new or revised employee handbook.

2.13 Receiving the New or Revised Employee Handbook from the Printer

Your employee handbook editor will have regular telephone contact with the production house or printer you have selected, after having obtained competitive bids on the printing of your employee handbook. It is then the responsibility of the editor to firm up the delivery date of the new employee handbooks.

2.14 Appendix

- Sample Letter to Employees with Handbook Questionnaire
- Employee Handbook Questionnaire
- Sample Table of Contents
- Sample Index

(Sample Letter to Employees with Handbook Questionnaire)

TO: All Employees

FROM: ABC Company Employee Handbook Committee

SUBJECT: Need to Revise Our Employee Handbook

It has been a long while since your present employee handbook was revised and updated by our company. In addition, we're almost out of stock of our current employee handbook and before reprinting, we believe it would be an ideal time to make a careful review of the present content of our employee handbook to see where we need to make changes to improve the content and update it to better meet the needs of all employees and their families.

We like to believe that an employee handbook is an important management- employee communications tool for all of us. Although you probably have not read the present employee handbook from cover to cover in a long time, we would like for you to assist our Employee Handbook Committee in giving us any suggestions you can think of to help make our handbook more useful and helpful to you and your family.

Please look over the following questions and give us your ideas and suggestions. We will really appreciate your time and help because we believe we can continue to improve the content and subject matter of our employee handbook to help all of us better understand what you can expect from our company and what our company expects from you as we continue to work together and serve our valued customers.

Sincerely,

Editor/Chairperson
ABC Company Employee Handbook Committee

Employee Handbook Questionnaire _____

1. Did you receive a copy of the current employee handbook after
   you were hired?   _____ Yes _____ No

2. Do you still have a copy of our employee handbook?   _____ Yes _____ No

3. Have you ever read your employee handbook from "cover to
   cover"?   _____ Yes _____ No

4. Do you believe the employee handbook is an important
   communications tool for you and your family?   _____ Yes _____ No

5. Do you believe the present employee handbook language is
   clear and up to date?   _____ Yes _____ No

6. Has any of your family members ever used your employee
   handbook to find out information about employee benefits or
   personnel policies of our company?   _____ Yes _____ No

7. Do you believe our company should continue providing all
   employees with an employee handbook?   _____ Yes _____ No

8. List any changes you would like to see made in the current employee handbook on the following topics that would make the subject clearer to understand?

   Pay Policy: _____

   Employee Benefits: _____

   Employee Performance, Conduct, and Work Rules: _____

   Substance Abuse in the Workplace: _____

   Attendance and Absenteeism: _____

   Employee Discipline: _____

   Complaint/Grievance Procedures: _____

   Employer-Employee Communications: _____

Thank you for your time and helpful assistance in completing this important questionnaire for
all of us. Please return it to a member of our Employee Handbook Committee by (date).

(Sample Table of Contents) _____

CONTENTS

(Sample Index)

Index

SECTION 3

Distributing the Employee Handbook

CONTENTS

SECTION 3

Distributing the Employee Handbook

3.01 Schedule a Management Meeting Prior to Distribution

Upon receipt of the handbooks, each member of the Employee Handbook Committee should receive a copy of the newly printed handbook and review the format and content, page by page, against the last, corrected proof. This should be done immediately prior to any scheduled distribution of the new employee handbook with the supervisors and department heads. This is the final review of the employee handbook, following printing, prior to distribution of the handbook with supervisors and employees.

We recommend you meet with all levels of supervision to discuss the new handbook and its objectives prior to distributing copies to your employees. Give every supervisor and manager a copy of the handbook and have all of them sign and date the receipt forms in the last section of the handbook.

Point out what is new, different, or special about the new handbook so that they will be prepared for employees' questions. *They should read the handbook from cover to cover prior to distributing copies to all personnel.*

3.02 Schedule Employee Group Meetings for Distribution

Now is the time you've been waiting for—to put a copy of your new or revised employee handbook in the hands of all employees. For present employees working in the office, plant, or job site, it is recommended that meetings be scheduled during work time on the premises for the sole purpose of announcing and distributing your new or revised employee handbook. Effective distribution can take place either in group meetings with employees or on a one-to-one basis by the department head, supervisor, or director of human resources. Obviously, the most efficient way is the small-group meeting method of distribution.

It is recommended that the director of human resources and the Employee Handbook Committee be involved in the group meetings with employees when the new handbooks are distributed. Such group meetings should be highlighted by a very positive, enthusiastic attitude reflected in the Employee Handbook Committee and/or the department head or supervisors in charge of the distribution of the handbooks.

If your company has followed some of the recommendations for both supervisory and employee involvement in the initial development of the content and format of your new or revised employee handbook, there should be a feeling of positive, favorable anticipation by those attending the employee meetings.

Obviously each company will have a different method of distributing the new employee handbooks in the workplace. However, the following are a few suggestions that have been beneficial and helpful to other organizations at this important, final phase of the employee handbook development process:

1. Have copies of employee handbooks displayed, stacked, or arranged neatly on tables in the room. Prior to physical distribution of the new employee handbook, the president, CEO, or general manager should make appropriate, brief opening remarks covering the following points:

   • Purpose of the new or revised employee handbook

   • Effective date of the new handbook and whether or not it is a revision of a prior handbook

   • The "introductory" or "welcome" portion of the new handbook which describes the practical purpose and objectives of the employee handbook

   • Appreciation for the Employee Handbook Committee and its chairperson/editor for their many hours of time and effort in preparing the new and/or revised employee handbook

2. Following these opening remarks by the CEO or general manager, it is recommended that the director of human resources or the editor of the Employee Handbook Committee ask the department head, department manager, or the supervisors of employees in the group meeting to assist in distributing the handbooks to everyone in the "audience."

3. After the handbooks have been passed out or distributed, employees should be asked to turn to the introductory section of the handbook where they can review the table of contents while the director of human resources or chairman reads aloud the major sections, content, and format of the new or revised employee handbook.

   If the handbook is a revision, the speaker should comment briefly on the major changes or revisions in the "new," revised employee handbook and direct their attention to those particular sections where revisions occurred.

Following the orientation to the new or revised handbook, it is recommended that each employee be asked to turn to the last page of the employee handbook, often perforated and entitled "Acknowledgment and Receipt of Employee Handbook." Employees should be asked to read and acknowledge receipt of the employee handbook by signing, dating, and removing the page. The acknowledgment/receipt pages should then be collected by the department head or supervisor.

It is recommended that all employees be requested to sign their name acknowledging receipt of the employee handbook to enable the company to have a record that everyone has properly received the new or revised employee handbook. A copy of the receipt form should be placed in the employee's personnel file for future reference.

What do you do if an employee refuses to acknowledge receipt of the new or revised employee handbook? If any employee in the room refuses to sign the employee handbook receipt page, *do not* take it lightly. Do all in your power to explain persuasively that the company needs to have documentation that all employees have received the new or revised employee handbook. Thus the company can be certain that all employees and their families have the advantage and benefit of the printed personnel policies, employee benefits, and working conditions outlined in the handbook. Since the employee handbook is to be the company's "basic" communications manual and since the company wants all employees and their families to know "what they can expect from the company in the future," it's only fair and proper that all present and newly hired employees acknowledge that they have received a copy of the employee handbook.

No employee should be disciplined or discharged for refusing to sign the acknowledgment/receipt page or slip in the employee handbook.

The appendix to this section contains representative, sample acknowledgment/receipt statements that have been used by other employers when distributing employee handbooks to present employees or to new employees during their initial induction and orientation process.

3.03 Distribution of the New Employee Handbook to Newly Hired Employees

For newly hired employees, the company's employee handbook is one of the most important management-employee communications tools to help that employee get off to a proper, positive start with the company. Most human resource directors, personnel managers, or supervisors use the employee handbook as an important employee orientation tool.

Some employers request that employees read and study the employee handbook *before* they sign and date the receipt form. Other employers will begin their employee orientation of employee benefits, personnel policies and procedures, working conditions, and performance standards by referring to the various sections of the employee handbook that describe these important phases of a successful employer-employee relationship.

3.04 Sending a Follow-up Letter to Employees

Following the on-site distribution of your new or revised employee handbook to present and new employees, it's recommended that you further *reinforce* the purpose and objectives of your employee handbook by preparing a personalized letter on company letterhead and mailing it to the homes of all present and new employees.

The purpose of this employee communication from management is to convey to employees and their families the reasons why the employee handbook is provided to them and how it can benefit them in the future when questions arise concerning employee benefits, working conditions, time off, eligibility for certain benefit plans, etc.

The appendix to this section contains sample representative letters that have been mailed to employees' homes or handed to employees in the workplace following distribution and receipt of their new or revised employee handbook.

3.05 Appendix

- Sample Disclaimer and Acknowledgment Page
- Acknowledgment of Employee Handbook
- Employee Handbook Receipt and Acknowledgment
- Acknowledgment and Receipt of Employee Handbook
- Letter to Employee after Receipt of Employee Handbook

(Sample Disclaimer and Acknowledgment Page) _____

We have prepared this handbook as a guide to the policies, benefits, and general information which should assist you during your employment. However, neither this handbook nor any other company communication or practice constitutes an employment contract. The company reserves the right to make changes in the content or application of its policies as it deems appropriate, and these changes may be implemented even if they have not been communicated, reprinted, or substituted in this handbook. It is also understood that nothing in this handbook or any other policy or communication changes the fact that employment is at-will for an indefinite period unless terminated at any time by you or the company.

I understand that no employee or representative of the company, other than the president, has any authority to enter into an employment contract or to change the at-will employment relationship, or to make any agreement contrary to the foregoing. I acknowledge receipt of the employee handbook and understand that my continued employment constitutes acceptance of any changes that may be made in content or application of the handbook.

Employee's Signature: _____

Date: _____

Supervisor's Signature: _____

Date: _____

(Acknowledgment of Employee Handbook) _____

Dear Fellow Employee:

We are providing you with your personal copy of our new employee handbook. Please sign and date this form and return it to our personnel office within seven (7) days of receipt of your new handbook. This will assist us in being sure that all of our valued employees have received our new employee handbook.

I understand and agree that this revised version of the company employee handbook super-sedes all prior versions that have been issued by the company and that it will be effective on _____ .

    (date)

Thank you.

Employee's Signature: _____

Date: _____

(Employee Handbook Receipt and Acknowledgment) _____

I have received a copy of the employee handbook. The employee handbook contains personnel policies and work rules which will apply to me. I agree to read the employee handbook and follow it during my employment. I further understand the company may amend the handbook at any time and in such case, any new changes in personnel policy or employee benefits and working conditions will be communicated to me by the company.

I understand and agree that this revised version of the company employee handbook supersedes all prior versions that have been issued by the company and that it will be effective on _____ .

   (date)

Employee's Signature: _____

Date: _____

Employee's Name (Printed): _____

(Acknowledgment and Receipt of Employee Handbook) _____

(The following acknowledgment form also contains a disclaimer statement.)

I understand that the information contained in this employee handbook represents guidelines only and that the company reserves the right to modify or amend this employee handbook at any time or to terminate any personnel policies, procedures, or employee benefit programs at any time, or to require and/or increase contributions toward any employee benefit program.

I understand this employee handbook is not a contract of employment between me and the company and I should not consider it as such.

I further understand that no representative of the company, other than the president, has any authority to enter into any agreement guaranteeing employment for me for any specific period of time. I further understand that any such agreement, if made by any manager or supervisor, shall not be enforceable unless it is in writing and signed by both me and the company president.

Printed Name of Employee: _____

Employee Signature: _____

Date: _____

Management Witness: _____

Signature Management Witness: _____

Date: _____

(Letter to Employee after Receipt of Employee Handbook)

SUBJECT: Your Employee Handbook—"Working Together at ABC Company"

Dear _____ :

By now you should have received your new (or revised) employee handbook. This handbook is very special because it summarizes what you can expect from us and what we expect from you. It will help you get to know your company better, and we hope you'll read it all the way through and keep it to refer to often in the future.

Our goal here at (name of company) is to make our company the best place to work, and we believe that this new handbook will help us continue to achieve that goal.

Your employee handbook is yours to keep. We want you to share it with your family. It contains important information about vacations, holidays, group insurance, and other employee benefits, work rules, employment policies, and procedures.

Finally, I want to take this opportunity to thank you for your good work effort and your loyalty over the years. Our employees are our most important asset, and we realize the strong contribution you have made to the success of our organization.

If you have any questions about anything contained in your new handbook, please ask your supervisor or our director of human resources who will be glad to answer any questions you may have.

Sincerely,

President/CEO
ABC COMPANY

SECTION 4

Drafting and Editing Employee Handbook Policies

CONTENTS

SECTION 4

Drafting and Editing
Employee Handbook Policies

4.01 The Employee Handbook Development Checklist

Observations and Recommendations
Using the Employee Handbook Development Checklist

In this section you are provided with SESCO's "Employee Handbook Development Checklist." This checklist was prepared by our professional staff of handbook consulting specialists to assist clients in drafting, editing, and publishing new employee handbooks.

We have found this Employee Handbook Development Checklist to be a most helpful and practical tool for the person who is responsible for heading up an Employee Handbook Committee or for beginning the initial development and decision making on which subjects will or will not be included in the first draft of the new or revised employee handbook.

For the Employee Handbook Committee or the management team of any organization, putting a copy of this Employee Handbook Development Checklist in their hands can be the most practical, beneficial instrument for obtaining their valued input and understanding on what needs to be included in the employee handbook draft or on which statements should be revised and updated in your present employee handbook.

Some employers may also wish to consider providing a copy of the complete or a condensed version of the Employee Handbook Development Checklist to employees in order to get their involvement and valued input and suggestions when it is time to draft or revise your employee handbook. It was recommended in Section 2 that you involve your supervisory employees in the initial development of employee handbook subject matter regarding subjects to be included, excluded, or revised and updated. A sample supervisory questionnaire was also provided in Section 2 for this purpose (see Sections 2.03–2.04). In addition, we recommended that you seek out employee suggestions for handbook subject matter in your new or revised employee handbook (see Section 2.05).

In this section, you will find separate Employee Handbook Development Checklists for the major subject areas relating to the employer-employee relationship of most organizations. Each of the major subject areas contains a special commentary of observations and recommendations from our professional staff related to specific employee relations subject matter. Following this commentary are sample or "model" employee handbook policy statements. The Employee Handbook Committee editor can review and use the sample or model policy statements as a help in drafting personalized, or customized, employee handbook policy statements covering each of the major employer-employee relations areas.

As previously observed and recommended in Section 2.06, the final draft of any new or revised employee handbook should be carefully read and reviewed by a professional consultant that specializes in employee handbook development or by an employment law attorney. The primary reason for this recommendation was also described in Section 1 of this manual.

There have been numerous employment law cases involving the publication and distribution of certain personnel policies and benefit statements in employee handbooks that have come under close scrutiny by both federal and state agencies such as the NLRB, EEOC, state human rights commissions, labor organizations, and state courts.

The common law "employment-at-will" doctrine is being challenged in numerous states by former employees who allege they were "wrongfully discharged." In many cases, the employee handbook is used as major evidence by either the former employee or the company in proving or disproving that the employee handbook was not a "contract" or that the employee handbook contents and disclaimer statements did not provide contractual employment or benefits to present or future employees.

Once your employee handbook manuscript draft has been prepared and edited by the Employee Handbook Committee of your organization—prior to publishing, printing and distribution of the new or revised handbook—it must be carefully reviewed by your professional human resource consultant retained for this purpose and/or by your employment law attorney.

4.02 Employee Handbook Development Checklist

Introductory Material for the Employee Handbook

The following checklist can be used to help determine the various subjects to include in your handbook. Sample handbook statements covering many of the items in this checklist appear in this section. They can be used to help draft your personalized employee handbook statements.

Our Employee Handbook Should Include:

1. Introductory and welcome statements   Yes ___ No ___ Maybe ___

2. Welcome letter by chief executive officer ___,
   human resources manager ___, administrator ___   Yes ___ No ___ Maybe ___

3. Who is the "company"?   Yes ___ No ___ Maybe ___

4. The history of our company   Yes ___ No ___ Maybe ___

5. Organization chart for our company   Yes ___ No ___ Maybe ___

6. Company products and services   Yes ___ No ___ Maybe ___

7. Purpose of employee handbook   Yes ___ No ___ Maybe ___

8. New or revised edition of handbook   Yes ___ No ___ Maybe ___

9. Introductory disclaimer statement on
   employment-at-will   Yes ___ No ___ Maybe ___

Sample Policies: Introductory Statements ⎯⎯⎯⎯⎯⎯⎯

Sample Policy 1
This handbook has been prepared so that you may be better informed about policies, procedures, benefits, and other issues concerning your employment here. We appreciate the service of those of you who have been with us for some time, and we welcome our new employees.

To a very large extent, we have operated on the principles in this handbook for a long time. Our working conditions and some things about our jobs have changed over the years as our company has grown and as things have changed in our industry. These facts have necessitated changes in company policies and practices from time to time. This manual contains information which will insure the smooth operation of our plant and your well-being as an employee here. (The company reserves the right to delete, amend, or modify these policies and practices as the need may dictate.)

All employees are expected to be familiar with and abide by the policies in this manual; and all those with authority to do so have a duty to administer these policies fairly and consistently and to enforce them when necessary. If you have questions about anything presented here, please see your supervisor for clarification and/or explanation.

Sample Policy 2
This handbook is offered to give our employees a general description of work rules, benefits and personnel policies of (name of company). The handbook should not be construed as an employment contract or an agreement for employment for any specified period of time. The corporation reserves the right to make changes to this handbook as conditions require. When changes are necessary, you will be provided with supplements or a new handbook.

Sample Policy 3
With the publication of this booklet, your management endeavors to take another step forward in our continuing effort to maintain a close informative relationship among those who work together at (name of company).

For our new employees, this booklet will introduce our organization to you and give information about our various benefits and policies which apply to you as an employee. For those who have been with us, this booklet contains the current status of our benefits and policies. These benefits and policies have been developed over the years as a result of our effort to constantly improve the conditions of employment of all our employees.

Since the costs of the benefits provided to our employees must be paid for out of the revenue derived from the sale of our products, the performance of each and every employee is important to the continuation of these benefits, as well as to the success of our operations. For these reasons, we believe it is important that you should know about the benefits, policies, and opportunities available to you, as well as the duties and responsibilities of your job.

From time to time, some of the policies included in this booklet may be changed. When such changes have been properly determined, they will be brought to your attention through written communications or bulletin-board announcements. Our bulletin board is also used to communicate other matters of importance for your attention.

If you have any questions with regard to these or any other matters affecting your job or your employment with the company, please discuss the matter with your supervisor or the management.

It is our hope that you will enjoy working here and that you will be able to advance steadily as you make yourself more valuable to the company for our mutual benefit.

This book is not to be construed or intended as a contractual agreement.

Sample Policy 4

The intent of the Hospital Employee Guide is to give focus and direction to important aspects of your involvement with the hospital. It is not intended in any way to be a contract, but instead this guide should be viewed as providing general information about policies, practices, responsibilities, and benefits affecting you while employed at the hospital. The hospital also reserves the right to change or revise personnel policies from time to time. If you have questions about policies, procedures, or benefits that appear in this guide or any questions that relate to your employment situation, either your supervisor or the Personnel Department will be available for clarification.

Sample Policy 5

Our mission . . . incorporates five elements:

- To be a *growing company.* Growth comes from selling more to existing customers, attracting and keeping new ones, and expanding operations.

- To be a *profitable company.* Profitability fuels growth and reflects how well we meet our customers' needs.

- To be a *worldwide company.* Beyond the obvious benefits of increased sales and earnings from foreign operations, a multinational presence minimizes the impact of economic downturns in any one country.

- To be a *retailer of groceries.* Food is the primary reason shoppers go to supermarkets; groceries are our basic strength. We will reinforce it with improved presentation, greater selection and more aggressive merchandising.

- To be a retailer of *related consumer goods and services.* Consumers like the convenience of one-stop shopping, so we will actively promote related goods and services that contribute to growth and profitability.

To fulfill this mission, we have adopted six major objectives, broad in scope but specific in purpose. As tangible statements of principle, they represent what we stand for and the higher ideal we seek.

The objectives focus on people: satisfied customers, dedicated employees, discerning stockholders. Our objectives are also results-oriented, aimed at achieving excellence and sustaining a competitive advance. They are:

To attract and retain customers by meeting their needs with quality, service, and value. Using creative market research to identify consumer preferences—and following up quickly with a competitively superior combination of quality and service—will bring shoppers in today and keep them coming back tomorrow.

To operate at the lowest cost consistent with providing quality and value. Only by trimming every unnecessary expense can we give customers the merchandise and services they want at prices they like.

To be innovative, aggressive, and productive in the operation of our business. We are exploring new ideas and emerging technology to support growth, enhance productivity and cement its innovative leadership position in the industry.

To attract, develop, and reward quality people to operate our company. Bright, friendly, and effective employees, well-trained and highly motivated, hold the key to our success.

To return value to stockholders through real earnings growth and strong financial position. Our owners have the right to expect good results. We in turn are obliged to protect their investment and enhance its value.

To forge a partnership among all employees to sustain the growth and vitality of our company. Pride, unity, and cooperation—the shared values of 156,000 employees—will shape the company's destiny.

Sample Policies: Welcome Statements _____

Sample Policy 1

Welcome to (name of company). As a new employee, you are joining the family that has made this Company the leading (type of company) company in the world.

As a newcomer, you will want to know more about your job, your work rules, your benefit plans, and many other things. The Personnel Department orientation and the first-day instruction by your supervisor should answer many of your questions. The following pages will help you become more familiar with our more important rules and procedures.

If there are any questions still unanswered in the Employee Booklet, feel free to consult your supervisor. Your supervisor will welcome the opportunity to discuss any aspect of your job with you. Or you may come to the Personnel Office.

I wish you every success in your new job, and I trust that your association with (name of company) will be rewarding and satisfying.

Sample Policy 2

It is a pleasure to welcome you to (name of company) and to wish you success in your new job. We hope that you will quickly feel at home.

Starting a new job is an important event and means as much to us as it does you. Whatever position you hold on our team is important. We have built our company to be a leader in its field through teamwork, cooperation, and service. Your commitment to these ideals is absolutely necessary for us to continue our mutual success.

The following pages will provide newcomers and those of you who have been with us for some time a better understanding of the privileges and responsibilities that go with employment at (name of company). Please note, company policies as stated in this handbook will act as guidelines for our activities.

This booklet was prepared to help make you aware of what you can expect from the company and what the company will expect of you. It is not meant to cover everything. If you have questions, please ask. Your supervisor or someone in the Personnel Department will be glad to talk with you about your job or the company.

We are proud to have you as a part of our team. We hope you will share with us in our sense of pride in our company and grow through your experience with us. Please share your employee handbook with your family at home. They, too, will learn important information about your new job, our company, and benefits of working with us.

Sample Policy 3

An interesting and challenging experience awaits you as an employee of ABC Company. To answer some of the questions you may have concerning the company and its policies, we have written this handbook. Please read it thoroughly and retain it for future reference. The policies stated in this handbook are subject to change at the sole discretion of the company. From time to time, you may receive updated information concerning changes in policy. Should you have any questions regarding any policies, please ask your supervisor or a member of our human resources department for assistance.

This handbook is not a contract guaranteeing employment for any specific duration. Although we hope that your employment relationship with us will be long-term, either you or the company may terminate this relationship at any time, for any reason, with or without cause or notice. Please understand that no supervisor, manager, or representative of ABC Company other than the President, the General Counsel, or the Vice-President of Human Resources has the authority to enter into any agreement with you for employment for any specified period or to make any promises or commitments contrary to the foregoing. Further, any employment agreement entered into by the President, the General Counsel, or the Vice-President of Human Resources shall not be enforceable unless it is in writing.

We wish you continued success in your position and hope that your employment relationship with us will be a rewarding experience.

Sample Policy 4

We are happy to present you with a copy of our employee handbook. This booklet has been designed to help you know your company better. Whether you have been with us for a short time, or for many years, we want you to know how much we appreciate the contribution you are making to the continued successful operation of our company.

In return for your loyalty and cooperation, we believe it to be our responsibility to keep you accurately informed of our company's policies and procedures. This booklet is a summary of the principles for which we stand, the benefits to which you are entitled, and the obligations you assume as an employee.

We do not intend that any "rule" or "policy" cause an undue hardship for any employee. We set them forth in this booklet simply to let you know what to expect from us and what will be expected of you. These policies are not unchangeable, but will remain in effect unless changes are considered necessary because of general economic conditions or because of conditions pertaining to our particular industry.

Please read your handbook carefully and keep it for future reference. If you should have any questions concerning the policies or benefits outlined in this booklet, please ask your supervisor about them. Your supervisor will be glad to help you.

Sample Policies: Who Is the Company? ————————————

Sample Policy 1

We cannot provide good service and fine products to our customers without employees who are interested in doing good work. That is one of the reasons why you are so important.

It is you, the employee, with all other employees who make up our company. We are a team and we must work together toward the common goal of providing a quality product and efficient service to our customers. You are an important aspect of our company—*you, the employee.*

And in all successful companies, there are two more important groups of people. These are (1) customers and (2) stockholders.

Our customers are people. They are as necessary to our business as the plant we work in. We do our best to satisfy the needs and desires of all our customers because we know that our business depends upon them; they are another important aspect of our company—*our customers.*

Our stockholders are also part of our company. Someone has to provide us with money and financial support to buy merchandise, trucks, and equipment. That makes them partners with us. These individuals who have invested money in our stock are another important aspect of our company—*our stockholders.*

As you can see, our company consists of three very important groups of people—employees, customers, and stockholders.

Sample Policy 2

How many times have you heard someone talk about the "company" as if it were one person or a small group of persons?

How many times have you heard that the "company" did this or did that—or sent something to someone—or told somebody to do something?

Is it buildings and machinery? These items are certainly necessary and someone has to provide them or there would be no jobs. But buildings and machinery are useless without people to manage and operate them.

Is it your supervisor? You'll admit supervisors are important persons. They must see that assigned work gets done on time and that there is a high level of performance by people without unnecessary cost. But they are not "the company."

Is it the company president? Every company must have one top manager, just as every shift has one top foreman or supervisor. The manager has the responsibility to make sure that there is proper planning and organization to meet the objectives of the company; to see that there is coordination between people in departments and between departments so that work gets done as scheduled. But the president is only part of "the company."

62

Is it you? To be sure, you're mighty important, too. But you'd find it very difficult to do your job without the investment and equipment furnished by the owners, or without your foreman, the president, or other company officers.

Who, then, is "the company"? It's you, and all of the others. It's the combined, cooperative efforts of everyone directed toward a goal of productivity and excellence of service. Another major factor is the company's "image" or the reputation it enjoys with our customers and in our community where we're located. Perhaps this one word, *reputation*, comes closer than anything else to describing "the company" because it represents the end result of our efforts and is an important part of our future.

SAMPLE POLICY: ORGANIZATION CHART

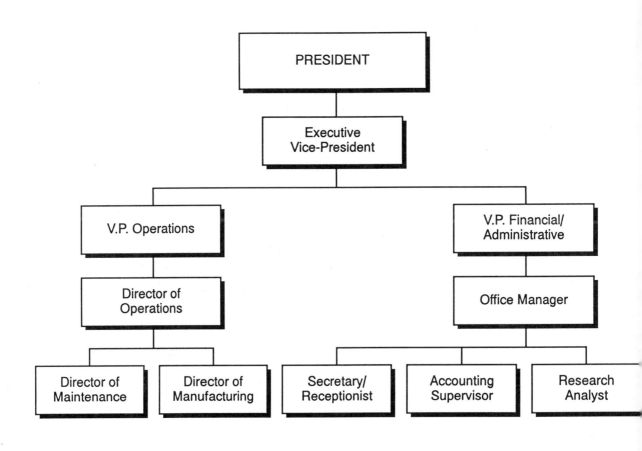

4.03 Employee Orientation and Training

SESCO Observations and Recommendations
Current Trends in Training and Management Development

The Training Scene Today—Training and developing employees and managers is becoming the number one priority in today's workplace. Today's employer no longer has the option to train or not to train, but the question simply is, how much and when? Training is being brought to the forefront by the changing nature of the work force. There will be fewer and fewer people available to us in the labor pool, so we must keep training those we have at the present, so they will stay with us. As we move farther into the Information Age, there will be the need for training and retraining for jobs which did not exist a few years before. Every business, no matter what it is, will encounter this problem. Also, as the world becomes more technical, more training will be demanded.

The training field is on the move. It is becoming increasingly sophisticated and professional. To meet this challenge, there are better equipped trainers and more various types of training materials than ever before in history. This is good for employers because it allows them more resources from which to choose when selecting and delivering training, and provides more tools to meet training needs.

The time in which we live is the era of the lifelong learner. We will have to continue to learn all of our lives or we will become obsolete. This lifelong learning has to be deliberate, planned, and continuous, and we have to be committed to growing and developing.

Who Needs Training?—There are basically three areas of training that need to be focused on in the years ahead: one is the *employee*, the second is *management*, and the third is *customer service providers*.

First, let us look at the employees. Recently the American Society of Training and Development and the United States Department of Labor conducted a study of what employees want to learn in the workplace. Today's employees want and need training in the following basic skill areas:

1. Learning to learn—the ability to learn new skills

2. Listening—the ability to really hear what others are saying

3. Oral Communication—the ability to orally communicate effectively

4. Problem Solving—the ability to solve problems on one's own

5. Creative Thinking—the ability to come up with new ideas and innovative methods

6. Self-Esteem—the ability to feel good about one's self

7. Personal and Career Goals—the ability to set clear goals

8. Interpersonal Skills—the ability to relate effectively to others

9. Team Work—the ability to work on a team

10. Negotiation—the ability to build consensus

11. Organizational Effectiveness—the ability to understand the direction in which the organization is heading and to be able to make a contribution to the achievement of those goals

12. Responsibility—the ability to assume responsibility

These are the needs of employees in the twenty-first century. We need to begin providing this training for them as the employees begin to take more and more responsibility for what happens in our organizations.

The second area on which we need to focus in the 1990s and in the year 2000 is *management training*. Patricia Aburdene, who (along with John Naisbitt) wrote the book, *Reinventing the Corporation*, has projected ten trends for the 1990s. One of those ten trends says, "managing in the 1990s requires a new breed of leadership." Aburdene contends that the manager in the 1990s will not give orders—he or she will basically be a person who encourages and develops people. The five traditional roles of managers—organizer, director, planner, coordinator, and controller—are beginning to fade into the background. We are now seeing roles such as leader, communicator, team member, teacher, learner, career consultant, and coordinator come to the forefront. These are not roles that the traditional manager in today's organization has been trained to fulfill. Likewise, the manager of tomorrow will have to be an innovator and a creative leader. This will require training our managers in new ways of managing.

The traditional role of the supervisor is also changing and will require training. The supervisor will be more of a team leader and a team coordinator, rather than one who directs. Tomorrow's supervisors will supervise people who know more than they do. Supervisors will coordinate employees' efforts. The changing role of the supervisor will require new skills that our present supervisory people do not possess.

The third area that will become a focus of training in the 1990s and in the year 2000 will be *customer service*. Today we are being required to provide better customer service more than ever before. To remain competitive, we have to satisfy the needs of today's customer, which are different from the needs of yesterday's customer. Today's customer is more intelligent, wants better value for the money, is willing to pay a higher price for better service, and will complain if we do not provide the service. Thus, we need to train all people in an organization to be customer service providers, and we need to establish a well-designed, ongoing customer service training program in an organization—no matter how large or small.

What Kind of Training?—Training today is shifting from random instruction to training designed to meet particular needs—from training which is nonspecific to that which is specific. For example, we are no longer including role plays in training which are not related to the situation. Now we are asking for real situations that happen on the job and are walking through them in a training experience. The other demand is that training be highly transferable to the workplace. We are training people specifically to do certain things. The employers who are spending training dollars want a return on their investment.

   Priority of Training—The training dollar is staying within the budget of American businesses; it is no longer disappearing. At one time when there needed to be a budget cut, the first thing that went was the training dollars. Today, we are investing in human capital and leaving training dollars in the budget.

4.03 Employee Handbook Development Checklist

Employee Orientation and Training

The following checklist can be used to determine the various subjects to include in your handbook. Sample handbook statements covering many of the items in this checklist appear in this section. They can be used to help draft your personalized employee handbook statements.

Our Employee Handbook Should Include:

1. Equal employment opportunity   Yes ___ No ___ Maybe ___

2. Affirmative action program   Yes ___ No ___ Maybe ___

3. Sexual harassment guidelines   Yes ___ No ___ Maybe ___

4. Introductory period/employment-at-will   Yes ___ No ___ Maybe ___

5. Definition of employee status—full-time, part-time, temporary, nonexempt, exempt   Yes ___ No ___ Maybe ___

6. Hiring former employees, friends, relatives and the handicapped   Yes ___ No ___ Maybe ___

7. Employee recruitment and selection   Yes ___ No ___ Maybe ___

8. Employment of former employees   Yes ___ No ___ Maybe ___

9. Employment of relatives   Yes ___ No ___ Maybe ___

10. Employee referrals   Yes ___ No ___ Maybe ___

11. Reception and evaluation of applicants (procedure)   Yes ___ No ___ Maybe ___

12. Selection of employee (procedure)   Yes ___ No ___ Maybe ___

13. Pre-employment physical examination   Yes ___ No ___ Maybe ___

14. Employment application retention requirements   Yes ___ No ___ Maybe ___

15. Fee payment of employment procurement   Yes ___ No ___ Maybe ___

16. Induction and orientation procedure   Yes ___ No ___ Maybe ___

17. Substance abuse testing   Yes ___ No ___ Maybe ___

18. AIDS policy statement   Yes ___ No ___ Maybe ___

19. Immigration Reform and Control Act   Yes ___ No ___ Maybe ___

    A. Completion of I-9 form   Yes ___ No ___ Maybe ___

    B. Identification of proper documents for
       verification   Yes ___ No ___ Maybe ___

    C. Retention requirements   Yes ___ No ___ Maybe ___

    D. Procedures upon investigation of
       Department of Labor   Yes ___ No ___ Maybe ___

20. Parking

21. Statement of commitment to training   Yes ___ No ___ Maybe ___

22. Tuition reimbursement policy   Yes ___ No ___ Maybe ___

23. Statement on cross-training   Yes ___ No ___ Maybe ___

24. Statement on supervisory/management training   Yes ___ No ___ Maybe ___

25. Statement on employee training   Yes ___ No ___ Maybe ___

26. Explain on-the-job training program   Yes ___ No ___ Maybe ___

27. Pay while in training   Yes ___ No ___ Maybe ___

28. Explain special educational seminars and
    workshops provided by company   Yes ___ No ___ Maybe ___

29. New employee training   Yes ___ No ___ Maybe ___

Sample Policies: Equal Employment Opportunity _____

Sample Policy 1

(Name of company) is an equal opportunity employer. In accordance with federal, state, and local laws, we recruit, hire, promote, and evaluate all personnel without regard to race, religion, color, sex, marital status, age, national origin, veteran status, and handicap, except where such characteristic is an appropriate bona fide occupational qualification. Job applicants and present employees are evaluated solely on ability, experience, and the requirements of the job.

Sample Policy 2

Equal Employment Opportunity is an integral part of (name of company) way of life. Since our beginning, we have adhered to a policy of equal opportunity for available positions.

Title VII of the Civil Rights Act prohibits discrimination because of race, color, religion, sex, age, handicap, marital status, or national origin in all employment practices, including conditions of employment. It is our policy and intent to comply with all applicable state and federal laws prohibiting employment discrimination.

Not only are all qualified persons given employment consideration, but also those already employed continue to be assured of opportunities for advancement according to their abilities. (Name of company) policy and practices is based on the premise that a person's value is determined by character, loyalty, education, experience, and performance.

Sample Policy 3

Your company is bound to a policy of nondiscrimination and equal employment opportunity because of our strong belief that adherence to the principle involved is the only acceptable way of life.

We are further committed to a policy of equal employment opportunity by our strict adherence to federal, state, and city laws on fair employment practices.

This policy of equal employment opportunity extends to all policies, procedures, and programs of your company.

Action relating to employees or applicants for employment is now, and will continue to be, fair and equitable for all. This policy includes but is not limited to the following: hiring, promotion, demotion, or transfer, recruitment or recruitment advertising, layoff or termination, rates of pay or other forms of compensation, training and selection for training.

All employees are expected to support company endeavors in this regard to make this EEO policy 100 percent successful.

Sample Policy 4

We believe in people. We need people. It is our objective to employ well-trained and capable people to operate and manage the company productively, safely, and profitably.

It is our intent to provide employees an avenue for utilizing their skills to the fullest and an opportunity for advancement to the highest available position earned through their skills and efforts, and then to compensate them fairly in both their wages and protection for them and their families.

It is our pledge to respect the dignity of both employees and prospective employees and to carry out our relationships with them without discrimination because of race, color, religion, sex, age, national origin, veteran status, or handicap.

Sample Policy 5

Our company provides equal employment opportunities (EEO) to all employees and applicants for employment without regard to race, color, religion, sex, national origin, age, handicap, or status as a Vietnam-era or special disabled veteran in accordance with applicable federal laws. In addition, we comply with applicable state and local laws governing nondiscrimination in employment in every location in which the company has facilities. This policy applies to all terms and conditions of employment, including but not limited to hiring, placement, promotion, termination, layoff, recall, transfer, leaves of absence, compensation, and training.

To further the principle of equal employment opportunity for all, our company has developed affirmative action plans for minorities and women, the handicapped, and Vietnam-era and special disabled veterans. These plans, or relevant portions of them, are available for your inspection upon request. Please ask your supervisor or a member of the Human Resources Department for information regarding these plans.

We expressly prohibit any form of unlawful employee harassment based on race, color, religion, sex, national origin, age, handicap, or status as a Vietnam-era or special disabled veteran. Improper interference with the ability of our employees to perform their expected job duties is not tolerated.

Sample Policies: Affirmative Action _____

Sample Policy 1

The company is an equal opportunity employer and, through its Uniform Employee Selection Procedure and other policies, attempts to ensure that no job applicant or employee is discriminated against because of race, color, religion, sex, age, national origin, Vietnam era veteran status, or handicap. Written Affirmative Action Programs specify the company's policy for females, minorities, handicapped, disabled veterans, and veterans of the Vietnam era.

For more information concerning these Affirmative Action Programs, you should contact your Human Resources Department.

Sample Policy 2

Job applicants and employees who are disabled veterans, veterans of the Vietnam era, or handicapped who wish to take advantage of the company's affirmative action program should contact the Manager, Equal Employment Opportunity. Our company is committed to taking positive, affirmative steps to promote equal employment opportunity for all employees of our company.

All managers, supervisors, and employees are individually and collectively responsible for understanding the intent of the company's affirmative action program. Our company is committed to equal employment opportunity through affirmative action, and we expect our supervisors, managers, and employees to take the positive steps outlined in our written affirmative action program to correct any problem that comes to their attention concerning equal employment opportunity and affirmative action.

We expect all employees to be responsible for complying with the intent of our policy. Should any employee act contrary to our company's affirmative action program and equal employment opportunity policy, they will be subject to disciplinary action up to and including termination.

Sample Policy 3

This statement will reaffirm our policy on equal employment opportunity for all females, minorities, handicapped, disabled veterans, and veterans of the Vietnam era.

This company will take affirmative action to recruit, employ, and advance in employment, females, minorities, handicapped, disabled veterans, and veterans of the Vietnam era for all positions in which they are qualified to perform. We will impose only valid requirements for employment and promotional opportunities.

Our policy will be extended to all personnel policies and procedures to include hiring, upgrading, demotion or transfer, recruitment or recruitment advertising, layoff or termination, rates of pay or other forms of compensation, and selection for training.

Our Equal Employment Opportunity Officer will administer all policies and procedures to en-sure success of our Affirmative Action Program for all females, minorities, handicapped, dis-abled veterans, and veterans of the Vietnam era.

Sample Policies: Sexual Harassment _____

Sample Policy 1

It is the policy of this company to maintain a working environment free from all forms of sexual harassment or intimidation. Unwelcome sexual advances, requests for sexual favors, and other verbal or physical conduct of a sexual nature are serious violations of our policy and will not be condoned or permitted. Not only is sexual harassment a violation of our policy, but it may also violate Title VII of the Civil Rights Act. Any employee who is subjected to sexual harassment or intimidation by a fellow employee, manager or supervisor, should contact (name of person). All complaints of sexual harassment will be promptly and confidentially investigated. Any employee, manager, or supervisor who violates this policy will be subject to appropriate disciplinary action up to and including discharge.

Sample Policy 2

As a part of the company's continuing affirmative action efforts and pursuant to the guidelines on sex discrimination issued by the Equal Opportunity Commission, the company endorses the following policy:

1. It is illegal and against the policies of this company for any employee, male or female, to sexually harass another employee by (a) making unwelcomed sexual advances or requests for sexual favors or other verbal or physical conduct of a sexual nature, a condition of an employee's continued employment, or (b) making submission to or rejections of such conduct the basis for employment decisions affecting the employee, or (c) creating an intimidating, hostile or offensive working environment by such conduct.

2. Any employee who believes he or she has been the subject of sexual harassment should report the alleged act immediately to the Director of Human Resources. An investigation of all complaints will be undertaken immediately. Any supervisor, agent, or other employee who has been found by the company after appropriate investigation to have sexually harassed another employee will be subject to appropriate sanctions depending on the circumstances, from a warning in his or her file up to and including termination.

The company recognizes that the question of whether a particular action or incident is a purely personal, social relationship without a discriminatory employment effect requires a factual determination based on all facts of this matter. Given the nature of this type of discrimination, the company recognizes also that false accusations of sexual harassment can have serious effects on innocent women and men. We trust that all employees of the company will continue to act responsibly to establish a pleasant working environment free of discrimination. The company encourages any employee to raise questions he or she may have regarding discrimination with the company (e.g., Personnel Officer).

Sample Policy 3

It is the policy of (name of company) to strictly prohibit any conduct which constitutes sexual harassment and to discipline any employee guilty of committing such conduct. This policy is based on Title VII of the 1964 Civil Rights Act and court decisions.

Sexual harassment is defined as sexual advances, requests for sexual favors, and any other conduct of a sexual nature (including sexually explicit language, jokes, etc.) when:

1. The employee must submit to the offensive conduct as an explicit or implicit condition of employment.

2. The employee rejects advances and risks losing a job, promotion, privileges, or benefits; whereas the employee who submits gains favors and advantages.

3. The employee's job performance is interfered with as a result of the offensive behavior, or the work atmosphere becomes hostile and intimidating.

Any employee who believes that he or she has been subjected to sexual harassment shall immediately report the conduct to the Personnel Director who will investigate the incident thoroughly. The Personnel Director will present the investigated incident to the Management Committee who will decide the appropriate discipline which the situation warrants. This could include termination. It is the responsibility of each member of management, from the President to the first-line supervisor, to create an atmosphere free of sexual harassment. In addition, it is the responsibility of each employee to respect the rights of fellow employees.

Sample Policy 4

Through reasonable management, (name of company) will endeavor to prevent any form of job harassment from occurring in our workplace. Submission to unwelcome sexual advances, requests for sexual favors, and any other unbecoming verbal or physical conduct is not a condition of employment. Neither submission to nor rejection of such conduct will be used as a basis for employment decisions.

Likewise, any annoyances of a racial or ethnic nature will not be tolerated. Such conduct is not only socially unacceptable, but also unreasonably interferes with work performance and creates an intimidating, hostile, and offensive working environment.

Should you ever experience any job harassment problem, please exercise the steps in our company complaint procedure. Or, at your option, you may directly contact any member of management in confidence, including the President. You may expect prompt and concerned reaction to your problem.

Sample Policies: New Employee Status
(Orientation, Tryout, Review Period)

Sample Policy 1

Your first 90 work days are a trial period during which your company will give you every consideration and assistance to help you succeed. This is a trial period for you and for (name of company). If things just "aren't working out" for our mutual benefit, you may decide to terminate this relationship without prejudice. (Name of company) reserves the same right.

At least once a month, your supervisor will evaluate your work, personal traits, willingness, and general fitness for the job. If your progress is unsatisfactory, your supervisor may recommend that you be given another trial period at the same or another job, or you may be terminated.

Sample Policy 2

As a new employee, you are regarded as being in an orientation period until you have completed sixty (60) calendar days of continuous service. The primary purpose of the orientation period is to provide you with a learning period and give the company an opportunity to evaluate your performance.

All new employees are hired on this sixty (60) day trial basis, during which time you are evaluated by your supervisor on your performance on the job, your cooperativeness, and your dependability, among other performance factors.

Regular employees enjoy certain privileges which are not available to employees in orientation, such as job bidding and shift selection privileges. Employees in orientation do not participate in the company benefit program. (Employees are eligible for paid holidays during orientation.)

Like regular employees, employees in the orientation period can be terminated at any time at the discretion of the company. When an employee completes the orientation period, length of service will be retroactive to date of employment.

After completing the orientation period, an employee's continued employment will be subject to the company's policies regarding rules of conduct and performance standards. You will then be given a seniority status, which is your length of service with the company, which is used for making such decisions as vacation and shift selection, and layoff in the event of a reduction of staff due to economic conditions.

Sample Policy 3

The first 60 days that you work for us are considered your orientation period. During this period, you will work closely with your supervisor to learn how to do your job and you will learn about our policies, procedures, benefits, and work rules. This period will also allow you the opportunity to find out whether or not you are going to like it here. It also gives us a chance to determine if your work, your performance, and your attendance measure up to our standards of a good employee. After you complete the orientation period, you become a "regular" employee entitled to participate in the benefits offered by the company as you meet the required eligibility dates.

After 45 days of your orientation period, a review of your progress will take place and you will be given guidance to the areas of your work performance which require improvement. Your supervisor will work closely with you to help you improve your performance. Of course, during this period or at any time during employment, you may be released or you may resign, as employment may be terminated at the will of either the employer or the employee.

Sample Policy 4

In thinking about how "permanent" your job is, it is proper to consider how sure we can be of our company's ability to furnish jobs to qualified persons.

We cannot say you will have a job forever; but we can state that our management team's goal is to do its best to guide our company successfully toward a future of solid, competitive growth.

By doing our job productively with a goal of excellence, each of us can help our company continue to grow and prosper.

All employees must understand that their employment is for no definite period of time and that just as you may terminate your employment at any time without notice or cause, so too may the company terminate or modify the relationship at anytime without notice or cause.

In consideration of your employment, you agree to conform to the company's rules and regulations, and you understand that no representative or agent of the company, with the exception of the President, has any authority to enter into any agreement for employment for any specified period of time or to make any agreement contrary to this policy. In no fashion does this guideline handbook or anything else presented to you in written or verbal form serve as a guarantee (promised or implied) of future employment.

Sample Policies: Definition of Employee Status ———————

Sample Policy 1

A regular "full-time employee" is an employee who works a normal workweek, in accordance with an established schedule of at least 40 hours per week on an annual basis, with overtime hours as required.

A regular "part-time employee" is an employee who works under 40 hours per week.

A "temporary employee" is an employee who is hired for specified or limited periods during the year and who may work less than 40 hours per week.

Part-time and temporary employees will receive some benefits, such as Worker's Compensation Insurance and Social Security Protection. Hospitalization insurance, life insurance, vacation, holiday, paid sick/personal days, and profit-sharing benefits are not available for part-time and temporary employees.

Sample Policy 2

For purposes of wage and salary administration and eligibility for overtime payments and employee benefits, our employees are classified as follows:

- *Full-time Regular Employees*—Employees hired to work the company's normal, full-time, thirty-five hour workweek on a regular basis. Such employees may be "exempt" or "nonexempt" as defined below.

- *Part-time Regular Employees*—Employees hired to work fewer than thirty-five hours per week on a regular basis. Such employees may be "exempt" or "nonexempt" as defined below.

- *Temporary Employees*-—Employees engaged to work full-time or part-time on the company's payroll with the understanding that their employment will be terminated no later than upon completion of a specific assignment. (Note that a temporary employee may be offered and may accept a new temporary assignment with the company and thus still retain temporary status.) Such employees may be "exempt" or "nonexempt" as defined below. (Note that employees hired from temporary employment agencies for specific assignments are employees of the respective agency and not of the company.)

- *Nonexempt Employees*—Employees who are required to be paid overtime at the rate of time and one half (i.e., one and one-half times) their regular rate of pay for all hours worked beyond forty hours in a workweek, in accordance with applicable federal wage and hour laws.

- *Exempt Employees*—Employees who are not required to be paid overtime, in accordance with applicable federal wage and hour laws, for work performed beyond forty hours in a workweek. Executives, professional employees, outside sales representatives, and certain employees in administrative positions are typically exempt.

You will be informed of your initial employment classification and of your status an an exempt or nonexempt employee during your orientation session. If you change positions during your employment as a result of a promotion, transfer, or otherwise, you will be informed by the Human Resources Department of any change in your exemption status.

Please direct any questions regarding your employment classification or exemption status to the Human Resources Department.

Sample Policies: Employment of Former Employees _____

Sample Policy 1

Former employees who have left (name of company) in good standing will be considered for job openings along with other applicants at the time openings become available.

Sample Policy 2

If an employee terminates for any reason and later desires to be reemployed, his/her previous service record will be carefully reviewed. If there should be any question regarding his/her re-employment, the matter will be referred to the (department) for decision.

Sample Policy 3

It is the policy of (name of company) not to rehire an employee more than once. Employees who voluntarily quit will be eligible for rehire status, and the above policy will be in effect for employee benefit determination. If, after rehire, an employee again voluntarily quits, he or she will be ineligible for rehire.

Sample Policy 4

It is the policy of our company to hire the best qualified employees available for all jobs. However, it is necessary that judgment be used in the hiring or placement of employees who have terminated their employment under favorable circumstances.

Each application will be considered on its own merits after review of the applicant's record, the type of job available, and other relevant factors. Management will make these decisions on an individual basis, giving primary consideration to the best interests of our company. In no event will discharged employees be considered for reemployment. Likewise, no spouse of any employee will be hired.

Sample Policies: Employment of Relatives ——————

Sample Policy 1

The company recognizes that there are certain disadvantages inherent in the employment of relatives. These disadvantages can be harmful to the best interest of the company, and they can also be of equal or greater harm to the employees. While the potential for harm exists at all levels and in all areas of operation, it becomes greater as job content increases in breadth and complexity, such as technical, professional, and managerial positions and when the duties include the handling of confidential material.

In recognition of the above, the company has established this Employment of Relatives Policy to place certain restrictions on the hiring of new employees and the assignment of present employees. This policy should be carried out as follows:

1. The restrictions shall apply only when all present or prospective employees involved:
   a. are or would become regular employees; and
   b. are working or would work for the same subsidiary company.

2. The restrictions shall apply only to close relatives of an employee or prospective employee.

3. For the purpose of the policy, an employee's close relatives are defined as: Spouse, Brother, Sister, Parent, Child, Grandparent, Grandchild, Uncle, Aunt, Nephew, Niece, Son-in-law, Daughter-in-law, Brother-in-law, Sister-in-law, Spouse's Brother-in-law, Spouse's Sister-in-law, Mother-in-law, Father-in-law.
   In addition, recognizing that there may be relationships other than the above which are actually close relationships, other relatives or relationships may be included, depending upon the circumstances of individual cases.

4. Under no circumstances shall any of the following situations be permitted, whether such situation would arise because of employment, transfer, promotion, marriage, or for any other reason:
   a. One close relative would directly or indirectly supervise another.
   b. One close relative has access or would have access to confidential information or records. Positions in the Human Resources or Payroll Departments and confidential secretarial positions are examples of positions to which close relatives cannot be assigned.

5. Even when there would be no conflict with the above two restrictions, close relatives of a present employee may not be hired without the full knowledge and written approval of the President of the company.

6. When an employee marries, or a close relationship among employees is otherwise created, and the resulting relationship conflicts with the restrictions in policy 4 above, efforts shall be made to resolve the conflict through reassignment. If reassignment is not feasible, one of the employees must resign within three months of the creation of the relationship. If neither employee voluntarily resigns, the com-

pany will terminate one of them at the end of the three-month period. Except in unusual circumstances, the employee with the shortest period of continuous service shall be selected for termination.

Sample Policy 2

Our company permits the employment of qualified relatives of employees as long as such employment does not, in the opinion of the company, create actual or perceived conflicts of interest. For purposes of this policy, "relative" is defined as a spouse, child, parent, sibling, grandparent, grandchild, aunt, uncle, first cousin, or corresponding in-law or "step" relation. The company will exercise sound business judgment in the placement of related employees in accordance with the following guidelines:

- Individuals who are related by blood or marriage are permitted to work in the same company facility, provided no direct reporting or supervisory/ management relationship exists. That is, no employee is permitted to work within the "chain of command" of a relative so that one relative's work responsibilities, salary, or career progress could be influenced by the other relative.

- No relatives are permitted to work in the same department or in any other positions in which the company believes an inherent conflict of interest may exist.

- Employees who marry while employed are treated in accordance with these guidelines. That is, if in the opinion of the company, a conflict or an apparent conflict arises as a result of the marriage, one of the employees will be transferred at the earliest practicable time.

This policy applies to all categories of employment, including regular, temporary, and part-time classifications.

Sample Policies: Employee Referrals— Recruitment Bonuses

Sample Policy 1

Over many years, employees working for our company have been the best source of new employee referrals as we continue to grow to a larger organization. You may wish to recommend some of your friends to apply for a vacancy in our company. Our human resources department will be happy to interview anyone you recommend. Naturally, all applicants for employment will be hired only if they meet the requirements of the vacant position. When you refer any friend to our human resources department, be sure to tell them to mention your name.

We should be glad to consider your friends for employment if a suitable position is open and their references are satisfactory.

Sample Policy 2

If you know someone who is interested in finding a good job, please refer him or her to our personnel office. For each applicant you refer that is hired for a full-time job with our company, you will receive a recruitment bonus of $25 awarded at the end of the new employee's first 30 work days and another $25 at the completion of the employee's first 90 work days of employment with our company.

Sample Policies: Orientation ⎯⎯⎯⎯⎯⎯⎯⎯⎯⎯⎯⎯⎯⎯

Sample Policy 1

During your first few days of employment, you will participate in an orientation program conducted by Human Resources and various members of your department, including your supervisor. During this program, you will receive important information regarding the performance requirements of your position, basic company policies, affirmative action plans, your compensation, and benefit programs, plus other information necessary to acquaint you with your job and the company. You will also be asked to complete all necessary paperwork at this time, such as medical benefit plan enrollment forms, beneficiary designation forms, and appropriate federal, state, and local tax forms. At this time, you will be required to present the company with information establishing your identity and your eligibility to work in the United States in accordance with applicable federal law.

Please use this orientation program to familiarize yourself with the company and our policies and benefits. We encourage you to ask any questions you may have during this program so that you will understand all the guidelines that affect and govern your employment relationship with us.

Sample Policy 2

Your immediate supervisor is one of many who wants you to succeed in your job. Only by working together as a team with our supervisors and other employees can we continue to be successful and at the same time satisfy our customers and stockholders.

Your supervisor is an experienced employee who will give you full opportunity to learn the best ways of doing your work. If you have any problem or difficulty in performing your work properly, or if you have a question about any job duties, please talk over your problem with your immediate supervisor. He or she is always willing to help you and is the best source of information.

Sample Policies: Immigration Reform and Control Act

Sample Policy 1

In compliance with the Immigration Reform and Control Act of 1986, we require all newly hired employees to present documented proof of identity and eligibility to work in the U.S. Employees will be required to furnish this information within three working days of hire date.

Sample Policy 2

The Immigration Reform and Control Act of 1986 requires that all employees hired by (name of company) provide documentation proving that they have a legal right to work in the United States.

In compliance with this act, all job offers extended to successful applicants are made contingent upon the receipt of the required documentation and completion of INS Form I-9. Only those successful applicants who provide the required documentation and complete Form I-9 will be permitted to begin work.

Sample Policies: Parking ─────────────────────────

Sample Policy 1
Large, surfaced parking areas are provided for your convenience.

The following suggestions are offered for your convenience and safety while driving on (name of company) property. Your compliance is essential to the orderly and safe operation of vehicles at our plant.

> Observe the posted speed limits and direction signs.
> Use only one parking space.
> Do not block other cars.
> Do not park in areas reserved for visitors, salesmen, and customers or in restricted "no parking" or "handicapped" areas.
> Designated tow areas will be enforced.

Special parking areas are available for employees who are temporarily or permanently handicapped. If you have a need for this service, see the on-duty Security Officer.

Sample Policy 2
We have provided a well-lighted, paved parking area for employee use only. Additionally, a designated area is provided for motorcycle parking only and automobiles are strictly prohibited from parking in this area. Speeding and/or reckless driving in the parking and drive area are against company policy, and violations should be reported to your supervisor for the safety and well-being of all employees. Employees are not to park in unauthorized areas, such as in the shipping dock turnaround area.

Should you suspect vandalism of your vehicle, please report this to your supervisor immediately upon discovery. Likewise, report any harassment or unusual happenings.

Sample Policy 3
Adequate parking is provided for all employees in the parking lot. Employees may park in any parking zone in the area that is striped for parking, excluding the areas designated for company vehicles.

We must ensure at all times that sufficient space is available in the parking lot to permit immediate access for fire equipment, if necessary. Therefore, all cars or trucks that are parked in unauthorized areas may be towed away at the employee's expense. Office or plant personnel should park in the employee parking lot and not on the street to the side or front of the building.

All personnel must have a parking sticker to park on company property. The company cannot be held responsible for any vandalism, theft, or damage that may occur to any vehicle while parked on company property.

Sample Policy 4

Parking lots are provided for use by all employees. Spaces not reserved are available on a first-come basis.

You will be expected to observe the parking regulations. A copy of these regulations is supplied to each employee when initially hired. Please note the areas where parking is not permitted, and regulations regarding how to park, exiting from the driveways, and picking up passengers at the entrances.

The Personnel Office issues a numbered employee sticker to place on the lower left corner of the rear window of your car. If you change cars, please request a new sticker from the Personnel Office. All employee cars on the parking lots must carry this sticker.

Please exercise courtesy in the use of the lots.

Sample Policy 5

Our company provides you with parking facilities. However, we cannot be liable for fire, theft, damage, or personal injury involving employees' automobiles. Protect your property by locking your car doors. Courtesy and common sense in parking and driving will avoid accidents, personal injuries, and damage to your car and to those of others.

Sample Policy 6

The company has, in most cases, provided an area for employees to park their personal vehicles while they are working. All employees are advised that they park at their own risk in using these facilities. The company shall not be responsible for any loss or damage occurring to vehicles of employees or visitors while parked at company lots. This includes, but is not limited to, alleged damage from possible generating plant emissions.

Sample Policies: Tuition Reimbursement ───────────

Sample Policy 1

Our company realizes that our future success and long-term growth depend in part on the development of our employees. Education benefits our employees and our company. This process of employee education is supported through our Tuition Reimbursement Program. This program strives to balance both personal development and ongoing business needs by reimbursing tuition and certain fees for courses or degree requirements directly related to an employee's current job, next logical position, or long-term career development. Company approval of tuition reimbursement does not imply that an employee will be transferred or promoted as a result of these studies.

Under the Tuition Reimbursement Program, the company will reimburse to full-time regular employees 100% of tuition, registration, graduation, and laboratory fees for the satisfactory completion of approved courses. Part-time regular employees are reimbursed on a prorated basis.

In order to participate in this program, an employee must:

- Have been employed at our company as a full-time regular or part-time regular employee for at least six months.

- Be at an acceptable or better level of job performance at the time of application and not on warning for any reason.

- Complete a "Request for Tuition Reimbursement" form, *each semester,* and have it approved by his or her supervisor.

- Submit the completed form to the Program Administrator at least two weeks prior to the course registration date. (Note: Pass-Fail or Audited courses must have the employee's department manager's authorization prior to submission to the Program Administrator.) The approved form will be returned to the employee indicating authorization to enroll in the course.
  - Incorrect or incomplete forms will be returned and, therefore, may cause delays in the ability to register for the intended course.

- Attend programs accredited by organizations such as the American Council on Education/Council on Postsecondary Accreditation or the American Association of Community and Junior Colleges.

In order to receive reimbursement, the employee must:

- Maintain regular employment until course completion.

- Obtain a "C" or better grade.

- Submit all copies of the preapproved "Request for Tuition Reimbursement" form along with the following information to the Program Administrator within 60 days of course completion:
  - Evidence of satisfactory completion of the course(s), such as a grade report or a letter from the professor on school stationery.

— An invoice or bill from the institution showing a breakdown of charges.

Tuition Reimbursement Program refunds will be made by the Payroll Department. All relevant tax laws will be followed when preparing payments.

While this program provides competitive and liberal coverage, there are some limitations:

- Expenses for books, travel, application, activity, and health fees, parking, late enrollments, deferred payment fees, or miscellaneous fees are not covered.

- Below "C" grades, dropped courses, or incomplete courses are not covered.

- Entry tests and preparatory tests are not covered. Job-related tests, training programs, or programs by nonaccredited vendors are also not covered under this policy.

- Loans, direct payments, prepayments to schools, or advances cannot be made.

- The company does not refund any expenses covered through grants, scholarships, veterans' benefits, student financial aid programs, etc.

- Requests for Educational Leaves of Absence and Executive MBA Degrees must be approved by the Vice-President of Human Resources and the General Manager.

Sample Policy 2

Our company has established an educational assistance program to help eligible employees develop their skills and upgrade their performance. All full-time regular employees who have completed a minimum of one year of service are eligible to participate in the program.

Under our program, educational assistance is provided for courses offered by approved institutions of learning such as accredited colleges, universities, and secretarial and trade schools. Courses must be, in the company's opinion, directly or reasonably related to your present job or part of a degree program or in line with a position that the company believes you can reasonably achieve. Courses must not interfere with your job responsibilities and must be taken on your time.

Reimbursement covers actual costs of tuition and registration fees only and is limited to a maximum of six credits per semester for approved courses, based on the following schedule:

Grade Received	Amount of Reimbursement
A	100%
B	75
P (pass/fail courses)	75
C	50
Lower than C	0

Employees eligible for reimbursement from any other source (e.g., a government-sponsored program or a scholarship) may seek assistance under our educational assistance program but are reimbursed only for the difference between the amount received from the other funding source and the actual course cost up to the maximum reimbursement allowable under this policy based on the grade received.

To be eligible for reimbursement, you must submit a tuition reimbursement form to your supervisor prior to the scheduled commencement of your course(s), receive written approval from your supervisor and the Human Resources Department in advance, be actively employed at the time of course completion, and receive a qualifying grade.

Sample Policy 3

The company wishes to encourage and assist employees who continue to add educational qualifications in their career fields which will improve their personal development and job performance. In this line, with prior approval, the company will reimburse an employee up to $1,000 of tuition per school year should he/she desire to continue education in job-related courses of study or courses toward the attainment of a degree. Employees must secure proper written approvals prior to starting course work. Required forms are available from the Human Resources Department. In addition, the employee must be in active employment status at the completion of the course to receive reimbursement.

Sample Policies: Training

Sample Policy 1

From time to time, our employees will be required to attend various training programs and workshops conducted or offered by our company. These training programs are designed to provide knowledge and skills to ensure better job performance. Our company will pay for the required training.

In addition to required training, our company will offer educational and development programs to be attended on a voluntary basis. These voluntary training programs are designed to help interested employees qualify for jobs within our company involving more responsibility and pay.

Sample Policy 2

Our company sponsors inhouse training and orientation programs that are available to employees interested in developing their administrative, managerial, and secretarial skills. A complete list of training and development courses can be obtained from the director of human resources. You may request, with your supervisor's approval, to participate in these courses provided you meet the eligibility requirements and complete the training request form. It is recommended that you and your supervisors discuss your desire to participate in our inhouse training programs and the value of the particular course before you complete the training request.

4.04 Compensation, Wage and Salary Administration

SESCO Observations and Recommendations
How to Pay Your Employees Fairly

One of the most important policy statements in an employee handbook should be that of wage and salary administration or "how you compensate your employees." The employees' salary or pay plan is of major importance to all employees. Although many handbooks do not devote much space or wording on this important subject, we recommend that new employee handbooks being developed or employee handbook revisions devote more space and wording on your company's policy and procedure involving your wage and salary administration program.

A review of numerous employee handbooks would indicate that most companies do provide a very general policy statement about their wage and salary program. There are important reasons why this subject should be covered in some detail in your new or revised employee handbook.

Employer Advantages of Communicating the Basics of
Wage and Salary Program in Employee Handbooks

1. Employers need to assure employees that their wages or salaries are paid on a competitive basis relative to the labor market and the industry in which they work.

2. You want to assure your employees that your pay policy provides for wage and salary equities within each job classification compared to other jobs in the company or facility.

3. Each job classification is paid fairly compared to other organizations in your industry and in your area.

4. You want to communicate and reassure your employees that your wage and salary program provides for compensation to all employees that is competitive with other employers having similar job classifications, in the same industry, and in the same geographical area.

5. Employers need to communicate through the employee handbook the fact that their wages or salaries are subject to semiannual or annual reviews based upon performance or cost of living or some other criteria so that employees will know how often their wage rate or salary will be reviewed and possibly increased by management.

6. The most important advantage of communicating your wage and salary program through your employee handbook is that it properly documents your "nondiscriminatory" compensation and benefit programs that will possibly come under the review and scrutiny of one or more federal or state regulatory agencies, such as the Federal Wage-Hour and Public Contracts Divisions, the Equal Employment Opportunity Commission

(EEOC), or the Office of Federal Contract Compliance (OFCC), and National Labor Relations Board (NLRB).

There have been numerous cases where proper and current policy statements in employee handbooks have provided employers with substantial "good faith documentation" that their wage and salary programs do not discriminate against any minority employees or other protected employees in various job classifications.

In developing, publishing, and communicating your wage and salary administration program, you eliminate much secrecy and insecurity among employees as to how they're compensated and remove concerns of wage inequities and other distorted beliefs of wage classification inequities.

7. Now, if you have not developed a formal wage and salary administration program at your organization, then the odds are very good that you have pay rates which are "out of line" right now. The longer you wait to develop such a program, the more difficult it will become to bring these rates back in line and implement your new program.

Further, you simply will not be able to attract and retain good, qualified employees without fair and competitive rates of pay; and the only way that you will know for sure that your rates of pay are proper is through the development of a formal wage and salary administration program. Otherwise, it's simply a "hit-or-miss" affair.

8. Publishing your wage and salary policy statement in the employee handbook will help establish management credibility (trust, confidence, and respect) of your wage and salary program. Properly communicating the purpose of your wage and salary program—how it functions, how it is administered, why it is competitive—will cause your employees to feel that they are being compensated fairly and competitively.

What to Cover in Your Employee Handbook Policy Statements on Wage or Salary Administration

We recommend the following major points be clearly communicated in your employee handbook policy statements dealing with wage and salary administration:

- Jobs within your establishment differ in responsibility, working conditions, complexity, and other important factors. Rates of pay which employees receive for performing their jobs reflect differences in skill levels. In other words, the job of bookkeeper should be paid fairly, compared to the job of machine operator, compared to the job of computer programmer, compared to the job of supervisor, and compared to every other job in the organization.

- The overall pay structure at your organization should compare favorably with other organizations in your area and in your industry. As an exam-

© 1991 The Dartnell Corporation

ple, a secretary at your organization should be paid fairly compared to a secretary at XYZ Company just down the road. If you operate a hospital, your X-ray technicians should receive competitive pay rates, compared to other X-ray technicians in other hospitals in your area.

- Your rates of pay are fair both internally and externally. You know that your pay rates are proper and you can defend them to both your board of directors and your employees. Your board of directors approve an appropriate amount of money on employee compensation. You can explain to your employees that their rates of pay are fair and competitive compared to other organizations in the area and compared to other employees in your establishment.

- You conduct annual wage and salary surveys—they provide you with the knowledge that the rates of pay you provide your employees are fair and competitive.

- Your wage and salary policy statement should also remind employees that their "total" compensation includes not only their take-home pay from their regular wages and salaries but also their costly employee benefits.

Communicate Your Employees' "Hidden Paycheck"—the Dollar Value of Your Employee Benefits in Your Employee Handbook

National statistics from the U.S. Chamber of Commerce indicate that average employer benefit contributions approach 37 percent of payroll expense. Employee benefit costs usually average in excess of $6,000 per year, per employee. Unless benefit costs are communicated to each employee, the primary advantages for providing benefits are lost.

A benefit policy statement in your employee handbook can be one of the most effective ways to communicate employee benefit plans, including the company's cost for providing the benefits. The use of this policy statement can serve to enhance employee productivity, morale, and loyalty.

What to Exclude from Employee Handbooks Concerning Your Wage and Salary Program

It is recommended that your policy statements on wage and salary administration in new or revised employee handbooks exclude the following:

1. Job evaluation factors, points, and descriptive evaluation factors

2. Actual salary ranges or wage ranges within a pay grade or labor grade

3. Actual hourly rates or salaries according to a given job classification or salary position

    These wage and salary details should be properly covered in your company's personnel policy and procedures manual—not in your employee handbook. Such information should be conveyed to the employee in a one-on-one performance evaluation and review when appropriate. There are also situations where such wage and salary data can be posted on company bulletin boards or individually provided the employee during employee orientation or annual performance reviews.

4. Avoid a policy statement dealing with the confidentiality of wages or salaries that stipulates they are not to be discussed with other employees, with the exception of supervisors or the personnel office. Such statements or comments can have serious repercussions in terms of negative morale among employees who often refer to it as a "wage and salary gag order."

   More importantly, there have been unfair labor practice charges filed by the NLRB against employers that have attempted to publish and enforce such "no discussion" wage and salary policies alleging confidentiality of a wage and salary program. Such policies have been held to be in violation of the National Labor Relations Act. For example, a recent NLRB decision held that an employer violated the NLRA when it established and communicated a wage and salary policy that prohibited employees from discussing their wages with other employees. The prohibition also reminded employees that they would be subject to termination if they were found communicating their wage and salaries with other employees.

   One employee was discharged for discussing wages and a pay increase with other employees. He filed an unfair labor practice charge against his employer dealing with Section 8(a)(1) and Section 8(a)(3) of the National Labor Relations Act. These unfair labor practice charges make it an unfair labor practice for an employer to interfere with, threaten, or coerce employees in the exercise of their rights to engage in concerted activities for their mutual aid and protection guaranteed under Section 7 of the National Labor Relations Act. Section 8(a)(3) prohibits employers from discharging an employee in the exercise of such rights to engage in union activity, collective bargaining, or other concerted activities for their mutual aid and protection. We recommend that no such restrictions pertaining to discussing or talking about wages or salaries be included in any employee handbook statements (*Brookshire Grocery Company,* 294 NLRB No. 34, May 31, 1989).

Communicate Your Employee Performance Review Policy

Your employee handbook should also contain a policy statement on the purpose and procedure of employee performance evaluations and reviews. All supervisors and employees should receive semiannual or annual performance evaluations and reviews. This important feedback on employee performance should be provided based upon an *objective-based* evaluation of the employee's performance on the basis of job-related criteria rather than subjective evaluations.

To avoid potential discrimination charges from the EEOC on claims of "adverse impact," employers must comply with the EEOC guidelines requiring employers to validate any selection procedure or criteria used as a basis for making employment decisions if they have an adverse impact on a protected group. The EEOC has defined this regulation to include not only hiring but also promotion, demotion, referral, and retention. If you establish and maintain a performance appraisal and review policy as part of your wage and salary program, which is most common in industry, use customized performance appraisal forms and train supervisors to conduct their performance reviews on an objective basis that is directly related to job performance.

Equally important is that once you commit to conducting performance appraisals and reviews, management must be consistent and schedule such performance appraisals and reviews with all employees when due. It is anticipated that some state laws that look upon employee handbook statements as "implied contracts of employment" could look upon an employer's failure to conduct a performance appraisal review at established intervals as a breach of implied promise to conduct such performance appraisal reviews.

Managers and supervisors responsible for conducting these performance appraisals and reviews should be properly trained in the definitions and job criteria evaluated, and to communicate both the negative and positive performance appraisals with all employees.

4.04 Employee Handbook Development Checklist

Compensation, Wage and Salary Administration

The following checklist can be used to determine the various subjects to include in your handbook. Sample handbook statements covering many of the items in this checklist appear in this section. They can be used to help draft your personalized employee handbook statements.

Our Employee Handbook Should Include:

1. Wage and salary policies—compensation philosophy   Yes ___ No ___ Maybe ___

2. How wages and salaries are determined   Yes ___ No ___ Maybe ___

    A. Job evaluation plan—criteria for job descriptions   Yes ___ No ___ Maybe ___
    B. Merit or performance appraisals   Yes ___ No ___ Maybe ___
    C. Salary ranges by classifications   Yes ___ No ___ Maybe ___
    D. Progression raises   Yes ___ No ___ Maybe ___
    E. Incentive wage policies   Yes ___ No ___ Maybe ___
    F. Pay for performance   Yes ___ No ___ Maybe ___

3. Wage and salary differentials   Yes ___ No ___ Maybe ___

    A. Shift differentials   Yes ___ No ___ Maybe ___
    B. Differentials for learners and apprentices   Yes ___ No ___ Maybe ___
    C. Call-in pay—call-back pay   Yes ___ No ___ Maybe ___
    D. Report-in pay   Yes ___ No ___ Maybe ___

4. Overtime pay policies   Yes ___ No ___ Maybe ___

    A. Employees subject to overtime premium pay   Yes ___ No ___ Maybe ___
    B. Employees exempt from overtime premium pay   Yes ___ No ___ Maybe ___

5. Promotions   Yes ___ No ___ Maybe ___

    A. Criteria for promotions   Yes ___ No ___ Maybe ___
    B. Raises for promotions   Yes ___ No ___ Maybe ___

6. Payroll deductions   Yes ___ No ___ Maybe ___
    A. Legal   Yes ___ No ___ Maybe ___
    B. Company   Yes ___ No ___ Maybe ___

7. Bonus plans   Yes ___ No ___ Maybe ___

8. Hours of work   Yes ___ No ___ Maybe ___

    A. Flextime work schedule   Yes ___ No ___ Maybe ___
    B. Shift schedules and workweek   Yes ___ No ___ Maybe ___
    C. Recording compensable hours of work   Yes ___ No ___ Maybe ___

Sample Policies: Wage and Salary _____

Sample Policy 1

To attract and retain above-average employees, our company endeavors to pay salaries competitive with those paid by other employers in our industry and in the applicable labor markets in which we maintain facilities. In line with this objective, we monitor our wage scales to ensure that they are kept in line with local as well as national economic conditions.

Each position at our company has been studied and assigned a salary grade. Each grade has been assigned a corresponding salary range. Periodically, we may revise job descriptions, evaluate individual jobs to ensure that they are rated and paid appropriately, and review job specifications to ensure that they are directly job related.

Your salary will be reviewed on an annual basis, and if you are granted a salary increase, it will normally be effective on your anniversary date.

Your total compensation consists not only of the salary you are paid but also of the various benefits you are offered, such as group health and life insurance and your retirement plan, as described in a later section of this handbook.

Questions regarding our salary administration program or your individual salary should be directed to your supervisor or the Human Resources Department.

Sample Policy 2

Under the free enterprise system, different jobs receive different rates of pay. Jobs that are more complex and that fewer people have the skills to perform receive greater rates of pay.

Within the company, your job has been evaluated according to the duties and skills required. The jobs that are evaluated as having similar requirements of skill and complexity are in the same pay range. The jobs in pay range 1 are (insert your job titles here). These have the fewest skill requirements. Pay range 2 jobs are (insert titles here). These have the next highest skill and complexity requirements. Pay range 3 jobs are (insert job titles). These have the highest requirements. In short, how much pay you receive depends primarily on how your job is evaluated.

Progress through your own pay range will depend upon meeting performance standards. If you increase skills and learn the job, you will move up in your job's pay range. If you do not demonstrate to your supervisor's satisfaction that you are increasing skills and performance, your pay rate will not be stepped up in the pay range. You should discuss performance expectations with your supervisor and assure that you are receiving the proper skills training and experience so you will not miss an opportunity to receive a pay increase. Remember: You are personally responsible for assuring that you qualify for a pay step increase. For improved performance, you will continue to receive step increases until you reach the maximum for your pay range.

To make sure we are competitive, our company conducts wage and benefit surveys once a year. Appropriate pay adjustments are based on the following factors:

- Pay levels of other companies in our industry located in our area

- Inflation

- Overall performance and progress of company operations.

Sample Policies: Merit and Performance Appraisals _____

Sample Policy 1

All employees of (name of company) are expected to work as a team. You were employed to work for the company, not just to do a specific job. At times you will be asked to assist in areas other than your regularly assigned duties. Cheerful cooperation in our team effort is expected from all employees.

Each employee's job performance will be reviewed with the Vice-President at least once a year. This process will provide each employee with an opportunity to note major accomplishments and progress as well as performance problems.

The performance appraisal process will inform employees of their standing in the organization and communicate expected standards of performance. It is also used to discuss work standards, areas where improvement is needed, and possible merit increases.

Sample Policy 2

To ensure that you perform your job to the best of your abilities, it is important that you be recognized for good performance and that you receive appropriate suggestions for improvement when necessary. Consistent with this goal, your performance will be evaluated by your supervisor on an ongoing basis. You will also receive periodic written evaluations of your performance. If you are a nonexempt employee, such evaluations will normally occur after you have been employed for six months, on your first anniversary date, and annually thereafter. In addition, if you are promoted or transferred to a new position, your performance will normally be evaluated in writing after you have been in your new job for six months. We endeavor to conduct written performance reviews of each employee's performance annually.

All written performance reviews will be based on your overall performance in relation to your job responsibilities and will also take into account your conduct, demeanor, and record of attendance and tardiness.

In addition to the regular performance evaluations described above, special written performance evaluations may be conducted by your supervisor at any time to advise you of the existence of performance or disciplinary problems.

Sample Policy 3

All of us like to know how we're doing on the job. Day-by-day comments from supervisors help, but now and then there is a need to review all phases of your work performance.

In our company we have a method which we call "Performance Review." It's a procedure which requires each supervisor to evaluate the performance of every employee under his or her supervision. Your supervisor will discuss your performance with you at the time of each performance review, point out how well you are carrying out your job, and suggest where and how improvements can be made.

Your review will be based on such factors as the quality and quantity of your work that has been performed during the past year, knowledge of your job, initiative, attendance, personal conduct record, and your attitude toward your job and other employees.

Our performance review gives you an opportunity to have a face-to-face discussion of your performance with your immediate supervisor and to learn how you can maintain and/or improve your on-the-job performance.

If you have any questions about how you are doing or what we can do to help you improve your performance, please ask your supervisor to visit with you in private. He or she will always try to help you in every way possible.

Sample Policies: Wage and Salary Differentials _____

Sample Policy 1

When employees are called in for emergency work, the company desires to ensure that these employees are adequately compensated for their special efforts; therefore, they shall be paid a minimum of four (4) hours at their straight time rate of pay or actual hours worked at the prevailing premium rate of pay, whichever is the greater, unless the employee works into his/her regularly scheduled shift.

If prior arrangements have been made with an employee for an early call-in, then this provision would not apply.

Call-in time will apply if an employee is called back to work after he/she has left company property following his/her regular shift.

Sample Policy 2

Emergency call-in work is paid at a minimum of two hours at time and one-half.

Call-in pay is paid to you when you are called to work at a time other than your regular shift and you had not been informed the previous day.

If you are on a five-day workweek and are called to work without prior notice earlier than your regularly scheduled hours, you will be paid time and one-half for those hours worked prior to your regularly scheduled starting time, with a minimum of two hours at time and one-half.

Because employees on the three-day workweek or four-day work period have premium time built into the regular work day, these employees are not eligible for the call-in pay provisions outlined above.

Sample Policy 3

If you should be required to return to work during time other than your normal working hours, and work for three (3) hours or less, you will receive a minimum of three (3) hours of pay.

If the office is unable to operate during regularly scheduled working hours and if notification of the office closing was not broadcast over the radio stations as described in the inclement weather section of this handbook, employees who report for work shall receive a minimum of three (3) hours pay for reporting.

Sample Policy 4

Wage rates for the classifications covered by this handbook are available through the Personnel Office. The current rate of pay for each job classification remains posted on the bulletin board.

When an employee is temporarily assigned to work in another classification, he shall receive his regular rate of pay or the rate for the temporary classification, whichever is higher, provided the temporary assignment is for a period of at least four hours. This provision applies only to temporary assignments.

Sample Policy 5

An employee who reports to work and has not been notified by the company not to do so, shall be given not less than four hours of work and pay or not less than four hours of pay at the regular straight-time pay rate, except where work is not available due to power failure, machine breakdowns, or other conditions beyond the control of the company. Should employees refuse the work assignment or make themselves unavailable for work, they shall not receive reporting pay. Any time an employee is called into work outside his normal schedule, he will be given not less than two hours of work and/or pay.

Any employee returning from vacation, leave of absence, suspension, or any other period of time away from scheduled work, shall call the personnel office no later than 5:00 p.m. Friday prior to the next scheduled workweek to be informed where and when to report to work the following week. The company shall not be liable for reporting pay should the employee fail to call the plant.

Sample Policies: Overtime Pay ————————————

Sample Policy 1

From time to time, as the need arises, you will be asked to work beyond your regular scheduled work period or workweek. For this extra work, all hourly paid employees will be paid overtime for all hours worked in excess of 40 hours during the regular workweek at one and one-half times their straight time rate.

An employee is required to work overtime when asked to do so, unless the employee has a valid reason that is acceptable to the supervisor or plant superintendent.

Sample Policy 2

In order to meet production needs and work demands, it is necessary for certain employees to work overtime on occasion. Working overtime is not an employee option. When a supervisor requests that an employee work overtime the employee is expected to do so.

(Name of company) will pay overtime to all hourly employees at the rate of time and one-half for all hours in excess of 40 hours per week.

Sample Policy 3

As a public utility, our company has an obligation to provide the most reliable service possible to our customers. In order to accomplish what is expected of us, it is frequently necessary for management to request employees to work overtime. Sometimes overtime is scheduled to meet unusual work demands, and on other occasions it is on an emergency basis, to restore service after storms, etc. Every employee when hired accepts the responsibility to work overtime when necessary.

Generally, overtime is any time worked outside an employee's regular schedule. For employees who are paid a premium for overtime (nonexempt employees), the overtime rate is normally one and a half times the employee's regular, straight-time rate.

Sample Policy 4

If you are classified as a nonexempt employee (see the classification of employment policy section), you will receive compensation for approved overtime work as follows:

1. You will be paid at straight time (i.e., your regular hourly rate of pay) for all hours worked between the thirty-fifth and fortieth hours in any given workweek.

2. You will be paid one and one-half times your regular hourly rate of pay for all hours worked beyond the fortieth hour in any given workweek.

3. You will be paid one and one-half times your regular hourly rate of pay for all hours actually worked on Saturdays or Sundays, regardless of the number of hours worked during the regular workweek.

4. You will be paid one and one-half times your regular hourly rate of pay for all hours worked on a company-observed holiday in addition to receiving your regular holiday pay.

Your supervisor will attempt to provide you with reasonable notice when the need for overtime work arises. Please remember, however, that advance notice may not always be possible.

You will normally receive payment for overtime in the pay period following the period in which such overtime is worked, providing that your time record form has been properly prepared, approved by your supervisor, and forwarded to payroll for processing in a timely manner.

Sample Policy 5

When overtime is to be worked, the company will give preference to the most senior qualified employee with the least amount of overtime, who regularly performs the job on which overtime is to be worked. The company will then proceed up the list by the least amount of overtime worked until all employees who regularly perform the jobs have been asked to work.

In the event no one who regularly performs that job wishes to perform the overtime work, the most senior employee in the next lower job in the progression line, with the least amount of overtime, will be asked to work. After reaching the bottom of the line of progression, the company will start with the next higher classification and work up. This procedure will be followed through all steps within the line of progression and then proceed by plant seniority beginning with employees who have accrued the least amount of overtime, until employees are secured to perform the overtime work.

In the event no one who regularly performs that job wishes overtime, should that job be critical, as determined by the company, the junior qualified employee will be required to work. Failure to work agreed overtime without notice and/or reason will be subject to corrective action.

Overtime which is refused by an employee will be recorded in his overtime record. Available overtime worked during unexcused absent periods will be charged to his record. New employees are to be assigned an amount of overtime equal to the high amount charged within the department assigned.

Whenever possible, when overtime work is necessary, the company will notify the employee involved in the job classification where overtime is to be worked, at least three and one-half ($3\frac{1}{2}$) hours before the end of the shift on which the overtime is to occur. When it is necessary to call an employee in for overtime, where possible, the call will be documented.

Whenever a department is scheduled for more than eight (8) hours a day for the week or the balance thereof, the change in scheduled hours will be posted before the end of the day shift of the preceding day.

Overtime premium pay is earned by hourly employees who work more than eight (8) hours a day or more than forty (40) hours per week, whichever is greater. All work performed on the seventh consecutive day of work in any payroll workweek will be paid at double time the regular straight-time rate of pay.

Sample Policy 6

The company makes a concentrated effort to schedule and finish work within a normal work period. However, on occasion, due to an unusual demand, an unexpected equipment breakdown, material flow, or a temporary lack of capacity, it is necessary to schedule work past the regular eight (8) hour day. Should that need arise, the expectation is that every employee will cooperate and cheerfully work the overtime assigned.

The company will distribute overtime work as fairly as possible among employees in a classification where the overtime is required. To be offered overtime work, you must have sufficient skill, ability, and experience to perform the required job. Whenever possible, advance notice will be given when overtime is expected. As a condition of employment, you are expected to work overtime when asked by your supervisor.

Nonexempt employees will be paid time and one-half their regular hourly rate for all work performed over forty (40) hours in any one workweek. Holiday pay will be considered time worked when computing overtime pay for the week in which the holiday occurs.

Sample Policies: Payroll Deductions ⸻

Sample Policy 1

The company is required to deduct Federal and State Withholding Tax (income tax) from your paycheck. This deducted amount is turned over to the U. S. and State Treasuries and you are given credit for it on your income tax at the end of the year. The amount of the tax deduction is determined by your earnings and the number of your dependents. At the close of each year you will receive a slip (W-2) showing your total earnings for the year and the amount of taxes withheld.

Also, deductions for Social Security at the rate established by law are deducted from your paycheck. The company matches your contribution to the Social Security Tax.

Other deductions, for items such as insurance and personal purchases, must be authorized in writing by you before they can be taken from your paycheck.

Sample Policy 2

The law requires that the company deduct from your paycheck your federal income tax, state income tax, and Social Security tax. The amount of your check is your wages less such tax deductions and any other sums the company is authorized to deduct, such as premiums for life insurance, medical insurance, savings plan, garnishments, etc. These deductions are remitted to the proper agencies by the company. You should retain your check stub as a record of your earnings and deductions.

Sample Policies: Bonus Plans ——————————————

Sample Policy 1
We like to be able to share our success with our employees. In years past, we have been able to provide Christmas bonuses to our employees, and while this bonus is not guaranteed, we hope that we will be able to continue to reward your dedication and efforts in the future.

Sample Policy 2
By looking for new ways to work more effectively in order to reach our business goals, we can have a positive influence on business results. When business goals are met, we will be able to share in that success directly through a performance bonus. The annual bonus is based on the achievement of preestablished business sector or site operational goals. The goals will be set by senior management at the beginning of each year. When results are finalized and we know how we did, if the goals are achieved, bonuses will be announced and paid.

In order to receive a performance bonus when payable, you must:

- be a regular employee, not currently participating in any other incentive or bonus plan;

- satisfy plan service and eligibility requirements;

- maintain an acceptable level of performance; and

- not have been issued a formal warning during the plan year.

Sample Policy 3
All employees can earn extra cash for perfect attendance for each full calendar quarter. The purpose of the attendance bonus plan is to encourage you to come to work every scheduled workday because your regular attendance is necessary for the best operation of our company and our customers' satisfaction.

If you have perfect attendance for a full calendar quarter, you will be paid $_____ in cash at the end of the quarter. This can mean an additional $_____ a week, $_____ a quarter, and $_____ a year more money in your pocket. All you have to do is come to work every scheduled workday.

If you are absent for any one of the following reasons, you will still be eligible for our attendance bonus at the end of each calendar quarter:

- Death in your immediate family (children, legally adopted, brother, sister, husband or wife, mother or father, mother-in-law or father-in-law).

- Absence due to paid holidays and paid vacations.

- Absence in any calendar quarter for any other cause will disqualify you for your attendance bonus that quarter.

Sample Policies: Hours of Work

Sample Policy 1
Most jobs in our company normally require 40 hours of work each week—eight hours a day, five days a week, though some employees are on other schedules. Our customers expect around-the-clock service. This makes it necessary for many plant and other operations to run on a continuous basis. For this reason, shift schedules are established for these jobs so that a working force is continuously on duty. Such work is rotated where practicable. Your supervisor will tell you exactly what your daily working hours will be.

Sample Policy 2
The official payroll workweek for all employees of (name of company) begins Thursday, 12:01 a.m. and ends at 12:00 midnight the following Wednesday. Naturally, your particular work schedule will depend on your job. Your supervisor will explain your work schedule to you. Should you have any questions on when you are to be at your work station and ready to work, please ask your supervisor.

Sample Policy 3
Many employees are required to punch a time card each day. If you are, you have a time card with your name and payroll number on it. This card is the official payroll record from which your pay is computed.

You should punch your time card at the beginning and end of your workday and at the beginning and end of your lunch period, also. Do not punch in more than five (5) minutes before or after your scheduled starting or quitting time unless requested by your supervisor. All the time you work must be shown on your time card. In addition, all days not worked that are to be paid, such as vacation days and funeral leave, must be shown on your time card by your supervisor if payment is to be received.

Please be certain to punch your time card you are supposed to. If you forget or make an error, you are expected to notify your supervisor at once. Your supervisor will make the correction, and both you and the supervisor will initial the correction. When clocking out on the last day of the week, review your card carefully to see that all hours of work are recorded properly.

Punching the time card of another employee or having another employee punch your time card is prohibited and will be grounds for disciplinary action.

Sample Policy 4
Flexible Work Hours—Our company provides employees with an opportunity to work a flexible work schedule, referred to as "Flextime." It is available to those employees in certain job classifications whose normal workweek is 40 hours.

Under the flexible work schedule, an employee may start his shift at any time between 7:00 a.m. and 9:00 a.m. and may cease work between 3:00 p.m. and 7:00 p.m. These are flexible work hours in these brackets. However, every employee must work between 9:00 a.m. and 3:00 p.m. These hours are "fixed" hours and make what is called the "core day": a minimum of six (6) hours a day, allowing for a 30-minute lunch period.

With Flextime, all employees are required to work a five-day week. The 30-minute meal period is not flexible. Extra hours worked cannot be accumulated for use during the following week. The flexible work hour preferences of employees are subject to the department's work schedule and must be approved by the immediate supervisor.

Each department may adapt the Flextime schedule to meet its own work requirements and staffing needs. Check with your immediate supervisor to find out how your department has modified its work hours schedule.

Sample Policy 5

Each and every employee fills out his/her own time attendance record. This card is the official payroll record from which pay is computed. Unless an employee is authorized overtime, he/she logs only the normal starting and ending time on his/her card.

Nonexempt employees are not allowed to work before or beyond the normal starting/ending time without specific overtime authorization. Any time away from the premises during the work shift must be recorded (i.e., personal business, medical appointment, lunch periods).

Salaried (exempt) employees are required to record their work hours and time away from the job on the appropriate form each week.

4.05 Attendance, Absenteeism, and Leaves of Absence

SESCO Observations and Recommendations
Importance of an Attendance Improvement Program in the Employee Handbook

Every employee handbook should contain your company's attendance improvement and/or absenteeism control policy. It should provide clearly understood attendance and punctuality standards of your company. If the employee handbook is to clearly communicate to employees and their families what they can expect from their company and what the company expects from them in terms of on-the-job performance, it is highly important that your employees and their families understand your expectations as to punctuality and attendance.

There is no better company document to share with the prospective or new employee than the employee handbook and reference to your company policies on attendance, punctuality, and absenteeism.

Since employee absenteeism is costing American business over *$10 billion a year* with over one-third of our nation's workforce showing tendencies to be chronically absent from work—such statistics reconfirm the need to communicate clearly your absenteeism and attendance policies in your new or revised employee handbook. It is estimated that absenteeism costs in industry are directly related to lost profits and a direct ratio of 1 percent absenteeism costing a loss of 1 percent profits.

It is obvious that excessive absenteeism has many direct and indirect costs to employers: lost production, poor service, poor substitution of untrained employees, increased insurance premium rates, training replacement costs, reduced earnings, and employee benefits to employees—resulting in the higher cost of goods and services to the American consumer.

Some of the "hidden" costs of tardiness and absenteeism include such costly areas as quality fluctuation, overstaffing, idle machinery and equipment, work schedules disrupted, scrap and material waste, excessive overtime, higher inventories, and hundreds of hours lost by supervision and human resource personnel involved in conducting employee discipline and counseling sessions on absenteeism.

The following SESCO observations and recommendations can be beneficial in developing a new or revised attendance improvement or absenteeism control policy.

Four Factors in Improving Attendance

The first step in improving attendance and in maintaining good attendance is to recognize that absences can be controlled. Beyond this, there are four basic factors which should be considered in any program to control absence: example, information, expectation, and administration.

Example: Management personnel should start with themselves and set an example by being on the job every day they are scheduled to work.

Information: The supervisor should see that every employee understands the company's position on attendance: employees are expected to be at work every day they are scheduled to work. Any absence is undesirable. Frequent absence is unacceptable.

Employees are to be told to report any absences to their supervisors. If the supervisor is not available at the time the call is received, the supervisor is to call back and discuss the absence with the employee or the employee's representative. The supervisor should, in a sympathetic but firm manner, get all the details concerning the nature of the illness and estimated duration of the absence. It should be clear that minor indispositions or inconveniences are not valid reasons for absence.

Employees should know that attendance will be considered in rating their performance for pay increases and for promotions. Each employee should understand his or her personal responsibility for good attendance.

The supervisor should explain the sickness benefit plan to every employee: payments are made to eligible employees who are ill and unable to work. It is wrong for any employee who is able to work to accept such payments.

Expectation: Most employees have good attendance. Good attendance is not exceptional; it is expected. This expectation should be communicated to all.

Each employee should recognize that a valid and reasonable explanation is expected in any case of unexcused absence.

Before being hired, each employee should be given a medical examination to assure that he or she will be able to meet the daily requirements of the company.

Employees are expected to take all reasonable precautions against accidents or illness which might result in absence.

Administration: An effective absence control program calls for regular attention to attendance and a critical examination by each supervisor of all cases of absence or tardiness, including those where no payments are involved. Supervisors should be consistent in their attitude toward attendance and in their treatment of absence problems. In dealing with absence, however, as in other parts of the job, they must use good judgment.

What Causes Absence?

In administering an Attendance Improvement Program, the supervisor should recognize that there are causes of absence beyond the usual ones of unexpected illness or accidents. Absences, examined carefully, can signal conditions needing treatment. Among these are the following examples.

Oncoming Illness: Some serious illness such as cancer, tuberculosis, etc., give warnings in their early stages with periods of short absences. When an employee with an excellent record of attendance starts missing days with increasing frequency, he should be counseled by his supervisor, and told of the company's concern for his well-being. The supervisor should then offer to schedule a health examination for him, for example, in the Medical Department. On scheduling the examination, the supervisor fills out Form M-105, Memorandum of Special Information, which informs the Medical Department of the reason the visit is scheduled.

Proneness to Accident or Illness: An employee who has a wide variety of illnesses or accidents is frequently suffering more from an emotional condition than from a physical condition. Simply making the person aware of the frequency of his absence, and of your interest in helping him to improve his attendance may be help in itself.

Evaluation and advice by the company's Medical Department or community agencies are available for help in these and other problem absence cases. In such instances the employee should be informed of why he is being asked to visit the Medical Department or consult an agency.

Morale: A high absence rate within a group may indicate a morale problem. In such circumstances it may be desirable for managers to examine their own behavior and the handling of work situations to see if these might indicate any reason why people would find it unpleasant to come to work. Examine working conditions. For example, experts have found that poor ventilation can cause real or imagined illness.

Poor attitudes can affect attendance. If a person thinks his work is not important, or that other people are not depending upon him, he may feel that "just one day" or "just one more day" of absence won't matter.

Permissiveness: In an atmosphere where no one, especially the supervisor, thinks that occasional absence is a cause for concern, an employee will be more inclined to have an occasional absence. The supervisor should indicate interest and concern at each instance of absence.

Desire for Attention: If a person gets little attention on the job, he may find he can get the attention he wants by occasionally missing a day of work.

Personal Problems: Family problems and certain medical problems can result in absence. An opportunity to discuss reasons for absence may help the employee or indicate other counseling needed.

Immaturity: Some employees may find it hard to face the demands of regular work. They must do so, or leave.

A Program for Attendance Improvement

Absence cannot be controlled on a hit-or-miss basis or through periodic campaigns. Absenteeism is controlled through careful, consistent attention to the attendance of every member of the supervisor's group.

Absence control is a job of managing—and an important indicator of a supervisor's ability to manage. As with other parts of the management job, the control of absence works best with a planned program. The following are some of the basics of any such program:

Appraise Attendance and Performance: Since the objective is to eliminate absence, every absence should receive the prompt and careful attention of the immediate supervisor.

Pattern absence. One indication of an attendance problem is absence which falls into a pattern. This pattern might be one of Friday or Monday absences, or it might relate to work load changes or certain days of the month. In any case, a regular pattern is a signal.

Increasing absence. Any indication of a growing number of absences, either for an individual or for the group as a whole, may signal the start of an absence problem and should alert the supervisor.

Consistent absence. Frequent absence by any member of the group, no matter how valid the reasons for absence, should be examined critically to determine if medical help is needed or if the individual is unsuited for work in that business.

Inform Employees: It is largely within the first year of service that habits and attitudes are developed that determine attendance performance for the rest of the employee's career. Therefore, place emphasis on the importance of regular attendance and punctuality during the induction period and from the first day on.

Some employees are not aware that perfect attendance is a goal. Others have the mistaken belief that they are entitled to a certain number of "sick days" off per year. Clear up misconceptions quickly and easily by informing employees of all the attendance expected of them. This should be done on a regular basis to keep the idea before all employees, and at the first sign of any increase in absence.

Examine Conditions and Work Habits: Watch for unsafe work conditions or work habits. Either can contribute to injury and absence. Deal with such conditions or habits quickly and effectively. Once supervisors are aware of a situation calling for action, they must assume responsibility for any injuries that result from failure to correct the situation. Invite comments on working conditions from employees, and make periodic tours of the work area to see that there are no conditions that could cause illness or injury. See that employees wear safety glasses, seat belts, and other protective equipment when called for and that they perform their duties in a safe manner.

Maintain Attendance Records: Simple records show at a glance when absence of individuals or a group is on the increase and action is needed. In addition, a record of reasons for absence can signal a developing condition and serve as a basis for discussion with employees whose attendance is not satisfactory.

Display Active Interest in Attendance: An active interest in attendance is good management practice. It involves the setting of standards, human relations, and administration.

Discuss attendance in meetings and at other opportunities to make employees aware of its importance. Let your people know the standard of attendance expected of them. If perfect attendance is a goal of the group, as well as a goal of each individual, an employee may hesitate to spoil a good record.

Welcome an employee back to work after an absence. Interest shows concern for the person's well-being, indicates that he was missed, and provides an opportunity for him to tell you of any problem with which you or the company may be able to help.

Personal visits to absent employees are an important part of the overall supervision of absence cases. The visitor or supervisor should recognize that the purpose of the visit is to convey concern regarding the employee's health and to be sure everything possible is being done to permit early return to the job. In this connection, the visitor or supervisor should gather the following information:

On Incidental Absence Cases

1. Whether the employee has seen a doctor.

2. Whether the employee could return to work later in the day.

3. Whether the employee could perform part-time work or do modified work.

On Disability Absence Cases

1. Whether, in certain cases—particularly postoperative cases—the employee could perform part-time work or do modified work.

2. Whether the employee's appearance indicates the possibility of return to duty earlier than anticipated by medical reports.

Where any doubt exists regarding these inquiries, the information should be reviewed with the company's Medical Department through lines of organization or with top management.

First-day visits may be profitably employed in cases of poor attendance, off-duty accidents, and other special situations. Normally, first-day visits should not be made when the employee is hospitalized.

Follow-up visits should be scheduled as appropriate to ensure that the employees are receiving proper care and return to duty as soon as their condition permits.

Attendance performance can slip very quickly. Continuous attention to attendance is a must, from an administrative point of view.

Discuss Absence with Individuals: Advise employees promptly when their attendance is not satisfactory. A warning can often nip a problem in its early stages, before it spoils the attendance average for the group. A conversation may be all that is needed. It can improve performance, provide an opportunity to correct an attitude problem, indicate the need for medical attention, or serve as a basis for disciplinary action if performance does not improve.

Consult the Company's Medical Department: When supervisors feel that a medical evaluation would be helpful and the employee consents, send a form to the Medical Department requesting an evaluation or examination. The evaluation may include a review of the medical history, a comprehensive physical examination, necessary laboratory studies, and consultation with the private physician. Be careful to explain that this represents an effort to improve the employee's health and should not be considered as disciplinary action.

The following medical reports may result in the following:

1. No medical condition is found to account for the employee's poor attendance.

2. A condition exists for which remedial measures can be taken. The employee should be advised to consult his personal physician for any necessary treatment. The responsibility for deciding on the action to be taken, if remedial measures are not followed in a reasonable interval, rests with the employee's department.

3. A chronic condition exists which may result in future intermittent absences. Where feasible, these employees should remain under the observation of the Medical Department and their personal physicians. The employees' department should encourage them to follow the recommended medical advice. If this does not result in satisfactory attendance, the employees' department must decide at what point action is to be taken.

Take Disciplinary Action: Disciplinary action—withholding increases, suspension, demotion, or separation from the company—is taken only after careful consideration and consultation with supervisors. It is used when other efforts to improve attendance have failed. When disciplinary action is called for, delay is unfair to the company, the group, and the individual involved. The goal of disciplinary action must be positive. Its aim is to improve overall performance and morale, not damage either one.

Commend Good Performance: Good attendance warrants as much attention as poor attendance. Commend individuals and the group for periods of perfect attendance. Encourage a sense of pride in attendance performance.

Set short-range goals of perfect attendance for one month or one quarter, so that members of the group can see these goals accomplished.

See that long-term perfect attendance is recognized. Take an interest in outstanding performance in the attendance part of the job and your people will too.

In Case of Poor Attendance

Few aspects of the supervisory job test management skill and judgment more than a case of poor attendance. Many factors are involved, such as past performance, length of service, health, indications of improvement, unusual circumstances, and group morale.

With so many variables, there is no one right answer on what to do in a case of poor attendance. Each case must be handled individually, in a manner fair to the employee and the company. To do this, the supervisor must be flexible, never arbitrary.

There are no simple solutions to cases of poor attendance, but there are some simple steps for arriving at a solution. Among these steps are the following:

Get All the Facts: Records of past attendance performance are among the best source of facts when you have an attendance problem.

Clear, detailed information on each absence will often profile a developing health problem, indicate preventive measures, or serve as a basis for disciplinary action. (Any notes made at the time of an absence should be recorded with the thought in mind that you may have to use them at some time in the future if the employee develops an absence problem.)

Talk with the employee to be sure you know of any new circumstance that might have caused his absence, and to be certain that you have a mutual understanding of the amount of absence and its seriousness.

Analyze the Situation: Using the information you've gathered on past performance, consider the trend in the employee's attendance. Is his performance showing marked improvement or decline? Has the employee been on the edge of an absence problem for some time, or is this a new development? Can you trace the start of his increased absence to some change in circumstances, such as a change in job or group, an accident, a death in the family, or the like? Ask yourself if there is any indication that the employee may be fighting a health problem. Consider the employee's length of service. Is he so close to retirement that an early retirement should be offered? Or is the employee new to the company and showing signs of being unsuited for work in the business?

In considering any case for action, one of the questions which should be kept in mind is, "Are there other, more serious cases of absence in this group which should be treated first?" Most people have a strong sense of justice, and taking action on a less serious case before a more serious one can cause a morale problem.

Consider Courses of Action: Think about the employee and his or her attendance problem. Consider all the courses of action open to you: a conversation, disciplinary action, or even no action at all. Which will accomplish the most for the employee and the company?

Set the Matter Aside: Impulse is a poor companion in solving personnel problems. Your personal feelings toward the employee may color your judgment if you act too quickly, and a course of action, once started, may be difficult to discontinue. A good decision is not damaged by sleeping on it, while a poor one may lose its appeal.

Reexamine the Situation: Take another look at the facts. Do they add up the same as they did before, or has something new come to mind? Do the "facts" say what they seem to say, or do they tell more than one story? Do the absences add up to indifference on the part of the employee, or do they indicate trouble at home?

Get an Outside Opinion if Needed: Good supervisors want to solve their own problems, but there are times when another opinion can be invaluable. If you suspect the case may involve a physical or emotional problem, the company's Medical Department or professionals in community agencies can give you expert advice. If you feel you are too close to the problem to make a good decision, a talk with your own supervisor may be helpful.

Write out Your Recommendation: Often just putting your ideas down in black and white will show up any weakness in logic and help you to organize your thinking. By making a recommendation on paper, you are defining a line of action. The recommendation may end up in your own wastebasket, when it belongs there.

Get Authorization as Needed: Disciplinary action that could involve suspension, loss of pay, demotion, or dismissal is always serious. In such matters you'll want the advice of your supervisor. To get agreement for such action, you will be expected to present clear and accurate information on the employee's record of attendance, the reasons for absence, the conversations held with the employee, and any warnings given.

Take Necessary Action: Once the decision has been made for disciplinary action, follow through. Be certain the employee understands what the action is, why it is being taken, and what will be expected of him in the future.

In cases other than those of separation from the company, make it clear that the disciplinary action is the end of the matter if the employee's performance becomes satisfactory.

Follow up on Improvement: Criticism can be discouraging even when it is given in good faith and for good cause. Be certain to recognize an improvement in attendance and the effort behind this improvement as soon as it becomes apparent.

Leaves of Absence: Job Rights for Reservists and Members of the National Guard

It is recommended that every new or revised employee handbook contain a company policy statement which provides a military leave of absence for employees who are in the active reserves of the armed forces or members of the National Guard. Because of the increasing number of men and women that have joined the volunteer armed forces, there are also a large number of employees that will remain in the active reserves or members of the National Guard. They need to know what their on-the-job rights and responsibilities are to their employer. These rights and responsibilities, as well as the notification request for a leave of absence, need to be spelled out in an employee handbook policy statement.

Requiring employees to provide copies of their military orders to their immediate supervisor as soon as possible is important in order to readjust staffing and work schedules of employees affected. The following guidelines, observations, and recommendations can be helpful in developing your company policy statement pertaining to military leaves of absence for reservists and members of the National Guard.

Congress has recognized that strong, ready National Guard and Reserve forces are essential for national defense under "Total Force Policy" and that the support of civilian employers is necessary if the services are to be able to recruit and retain National Guard and Reserve personnel and to get them to participate in training to maintain and increase their readiness. Therefore, Congress has provided certain protections for reservists and members of the National Guard with respect to their civilian employers.

The Veterans' Reemployment Rights (VRR) law provides that a reservist or member of the National Guard "shall upon request be granted a leave of absence by such person's employer for the period required to perform active duty for training or inactive duty training [drills] in the Armed Forces of the United States." The law further provides that a reservist or member of the National Guard "shall not be denied retention in employment or any promotion or other incident or advantage of employment because of any obligation as a member of a Reserve component of the Armed Forces."

The reservist or National Guard member is required to "request a leave of absence" when military drills or active duty for training will conflict with civilian working hours; however, the "request" is just a notice, because the employer has no right to deny the request or to veto the timing of the military training. The timing, frequency, and duration of the military training are determined by the military authorities.

The reservist or National Guard member is not required to possess written training orders at the time he or she requests a military leave of absence. Because of clerical problems within the military services, reservists and National Guard members sometimes do not receive written orders until shortly before the training is to start or even after it has started. As soon as the National Guard members or reservists are informed of the dates of the military training, they should notify supervisors and request a leave of absence, even if they have not yet received written orders. Reservists or National Guard members can minimize the employers' inconvenience by giving supervisors as much advance notice as possible of any anticipated military training periods.

The right to a military leave of absence applies to "inactive duty training" (drills) as well as active duty for training. Drills are normally, but not always, conducted on weekends. Reservists or National Guard members normally do not receive written orders with respect to regularly scheduled drills. They may receive a written order assigning them to a unit, and the unit establishes its own drill schedule, which may or may not be put in writing.

If a reservist or National Guard member receives a written drill schedule for a significant period of time, such as a fiscal year, he or she can write to an employer, attach a copy of the drill schedule, and request a leave of absence for each scheduled drill. An employer cannot require a reservist or National Guard member to make a separate request each month, so long as the drill schedule remains.

A request for a leave of absence can be either oral or written; however, reservists and National Guard members are encouraged to make written requests to help avoid misunderstandings. There is no limit on the frequency or duration of military leaves of absence under the provisions of law. So long as reservists or National Guard members receive orders for military training, their civilian job rights are protected.

The employer is not required to pay reservists or National Guard members for the hours or days when they do not work because of military training obligations. It is unlawful to require them to use their earned vacation time for their military training.

After completing military training, the reservists or National Guard members must report back to the civilian job at their first regularly scheduled shift after the completion of training and the time required for return from the place of military training to the place of civilian employment, unless their return is delayed by factors beyond their control, such as an automobile accident during the return trip. If reservists or National Guard members are late in returning to the civilian job, without adequate cause, they are subject to the employer's usual sanctions for tardiness or unexcused absence.

Upon reporting back to their civilian jobs, reservists or National Guard members must be put back to work immediately, without loss of seniority, status, or rate of pay because of the military absence. The military absence is not considered to interrupt employees' "continuous service" status regarding pension.

It is unlawful for an employer to discharge reservists or National Guard members because of their military obligations or to discriminate against such a person with regard to promotions or any "incident or advantage of employment." Even if the reservist or National Guard member has been guilty of some misconduct or inefficiency unrelated to military obligations, the employer cannot treat him or her more harshly because of part-time service in the National Guard or Reserve.

When a person first joins the National Guard or Reserve, he or she is usually required to undergo "initial active duty training" (IADT), unless the person has previously served on active duty. During IADT, reservists or National Guard members undergo basic military instruction and perhaps receive some training in a military specialty.

With two important exceptions, IADT is treated exactly like regular active duty with regard to reemployment rights. After completing IADT, a person must apply for reemployment within 31 days, rather than 90 days, as in the case of regular active duty. Furthermore, time spent on IADT does not count toward the four-year limitation on regular active duty.

In addition to performing IADT, active duty for training, and inactive duty training, reservists and National Guard members also sometimes perform regular active duty, when they are called to active duty voluntarily or involuntarily. Reemployment rights for persons performing regular active duty are described in the Department of Labor fact sheet entitled "Reemployment Rights for Returning Veterans." "Temporary active duty" (TEMAC) is considered to be regular active duty with regard to reemployment rights.

4.05 Employee Handbook Development Checklist

Attendance, Absenteeism, and Leaves of Absence

The following checklist can be used to help determine the various subjects to include in your handbook. Sample handbook statements covering many of the items in this checklist appear in this section. They can be used to help draft your personalized employee handbook statements.

Our Employee Handbook Should Include:

ATTENDANCE AND ABSENTEEISM

1. Defining absenteeism   Yes ___ No ___ Maybe ___

   A. Excused   Yes ___ No ___ Maybe ___
   B. Unexcused   Yes ___ No ___ Maybe ___
   C. Progressive discipline for unexcused absence   Yes ___ No ___ Maybe ___

2. Punctuality   Yes ___ No ___ Maybe ___

3. Time away from work   Yes ___ No ___ Maybe ___

4. Policy on excessive absenteeism   Yes ___ No ___ Maybe ___

5. Policy on attendance control   Yes ___ No ___ Maybe ___

6. Excused absences   Yes ___ No ___ Maybe ___

7. Attendance award program   Yes ___ No ___ Maybe ___

8. Policy on return to work after illness/injury   Yes ___ No ___ Maybe ___

9. Inclement weather   Yes ___ No ___ Maybe ___

LEAVES OF ABSENCE

1. Eligibility and procedure for personal leaves of
   absence   Yes ___ No ___ Maybe ___

2. Types of leave granted   Yes ___ No ___ Maybe ___

3. Length of leaves   Yes ___ No ___ Maybe ___

4. Can employee continue insurance coverage?   Yes ___ No ___ Maybe ___
   Who pays premium?   Yes ___ No ___ Maybe ___

5. Does seniority continue?   Yes ___ No ___ Maybe ___

6. Does employee receive pay for holidays occurring

during the leave?   Yes ___ No ___ Maybe ___

7. Reemployment privileges and obligations   Yes ___ No ___ Maybe ___

8. Military leaves of absence   Yes ___ No ___ Maybe ___

9. Jury duty leave   Yes ___ No ___ Maybe ___

10. Military reserve or National Guard leave   Yes ___ No ___ Maybe ___

11. Sick leave   Yes ___ No ___ Maybe ___

12. Funeral leave   Yes ___ No ___ Maybe ___

13. Educational leave   Yes ___ No ___ Maybe ___

14. Paternal care leave   Yes ___ No ___ Maybe ___

15. Elder care leave   Yes ___ No ___ Maybe ___

16. Maternal child care leave   Yes ___ No ___ Maybe ___

Sample Policies: Attendance and Absenteeism _____

Sample Policy 1

We are counting on each employee to be at his work station five minutes before the start of his shift in order to exchange pertinent information, and to remain there until released by his supervisor or replaced by the next shift. No one, while on company time is to leave the building without the permission of his supervisor. Any employee leaving the plant during working hours must log/clock in and out.

In the event of illness or family emergency, notify your supervisor or plant manager immediately—at least one hour before start of shift—indicating the extent of the anticipated absence, so your work may be assigned to others. During prolonged absence, contact your supervisor at least once a week.

Failure to call in will result in a written warning to the employee. After two such written warnings without adequate explanation, an employee is subject to immediate termination.

If you find that you cannot return to work as scheduled following an absence, you must notify your supervisor at that time. All employees are important to the smooth running of (name of company) and we encourage you to return with proper notification any day of the week.

If you are absent for three consecutive scheduled days without notifying your supervisor, we assume that you have voluntarily quit your job.

Repeated tardiness, absence without good reason, and washing-up or changing your clothes early will indicate that you do not value your position with (name of company). These behaviors cannot be tolerated and will be cause for disciplinary action or discharge.

Sample Policy 2

Your regular attendance is essential to the efficient flow of work and is considered a measure of your desire to perform your job. The nature of this business dictates that repeated absenteeism or tardiness cannot be accepted by (name of company). Irregular attendance increases the need for unpredictable overtime by the (name of company) people who are rarely absent or late to serve our customers.

If you cannot report for work due to illness, please contact your supervisor as early as possible before the start of your shift. If your supervisor is unavailable, leave your message with the (name of company) person responsible for taking such messages.

Please ask permission for an excused absence from your supervisor as soon as possible if you need to be away from work for reasons other than illness.

Sample Policy 3

You are expected to be punctual in reporting for work. Tardiness of a few minutes does not require calling your supervisor, but an employee who expects to be delayed more than one-half hour must inform the supervisor. Excessive tardiness is cause for discharge.

Absence from work or tardiness affects your income and hurts production. The ability of the company to operate efficiently and meet its schedules depends upon your regular attendance. Habitual absence and tardiness cannot be tolerated. All employees are expected to call their supervisor within one-half hour of reporting time on any day on which they expect to be absent. If a prolonged absence is anticipated, you should contact the Personnel Department about a leave of absence; otherwise, you should notify your supervisor regarding the expected length of the absence and should also call the supervisor every other day during that period.

Some absence and/or tardiness cannot be controlled and is understandable and excused. Frequent absences or tardiness are not acceptable.

Absences are divided into two categories: (a) Excused or authorized. Examples of excused absences are vacation, jury duty, bereavement, temporary layoff or nonpaid time off at the company's request. (b) Unexcused or unauthorized. Examples of unexcused absences are time off for personal reasons, no-show, or an illness that is either not work related or does not require a disability leave of absence.

The following chart shows the appropriate disciplinary action for excessive absenteeism.

A.   3 incidents in any   6-month period—Verbal warning
B.   6 incidents in any 12-month period—Written warning
C.   8 incidents in any 12-month period—1 day suspension
D.   10 incidents in any 12-month period—3 day suspension
E.   12 incidents in any 12-month period—Discharge

NOTE: An employee with a record of habitual absenteeism may still be subject to discharge even if the employee does not reach twelve absences in a twelve-month period.

Any unexcused absence occurring during a new employee's tryout period is subject to the verbal warning step. More than one unexcused absence during the tryout period will be cause for immediate discharge.

Sample Policy 4

Regular attendance contributes significantly toward better team effort and productivity; each employee is very important to the smooth operation of the City. Good attendance is an essential component of solid employee performance.

Occasionally, however, it may be necessary for you to be absent from work as a result of illness, injury, or other personal reasons. In such cases, you are expected to give your supervisor as much advance notice as possible before the beginning of your scheduled starting time. This advance notification is necessary in order that proper arrangements can be made to handle your work during your absence. If you must leave work, your supervisor should be notified as far in advance as possible.

Absences are classified into two categories—Excused and Unexcused—as follows:

> *Excused Absences*—Excused absences are earned through length of service, or are a result of factors beyond your control, such as holidays, vacation days, sick time, work compensatory time, and leaves of absence.

> *Unexcused Absences*—Unexcused absences occur upon failure to report to work as expected. Any unexcused absence of any duration will be considered an occurrence. Employees receive disciplinary warning for each occurrence. Two or more occurrences of unexcused absence within a 90-day period will result in disciplinary measures up to and including dismissal. Three or more occurrences of unexcused absence within a 12-month period will result in dismissal. Two consecutive days in which an employee fails to report to work as expected will be considered a voluntary quit on the part of the employee.

Sample Policy 5

Absence from your job, as well as tardiness, creates problems in scheduling work and in many cases it means someone else will have to do your work as well as his own assignments. Management recognizes that some absence cannot be avoided, but you as an employee have a responsibility to be on the job.

In the event you must be absent from your job for any reason, your immediate supervisor must be contacted for approval and given an explanation of the circumstances requiring your absence. You should notify your supervisor as soon as you know you will be absent, giving at least two hours' notice.

If your absence is prolonged, keep in touch with your supervisor so that work will be properly scheduled.

It is important that your remember you were hired to do a job that is considered important and necessary, and you should be on the job each day.

Sample Policy 6

To maintain efficient production schedules, the company insists on regular, punctual attendance of all employees. Excessive absenteeism or chronic tardiness will be cause for discharge or other disciplinary action.

To afford employees time off for personal reasons, including illness, the following attendance policy will be in effect:

> a. Each employee will be allotted a maximum of six (6) days off without pay per calendar year. It is company policy that all employees notify their supervisor and/or the Personnel Department at least one-half ($1/2$) hour before their shift or not later than one and one-half ($1 1/2$) hours after the start of their shift if they are to be absent or tardy for any reason.

b. Three (3) days of tardiness constitutes one (1) day of absence for the purpose of records outlined in Section a.

c. Beginning with the seventh day of absence in a calendar year, the disciplinary action, as outlined in this handbook, will be applied.

d. The policy, as outlined herein, will not be applied for extended illness, etc. where a leave of absence is applied for and granted by the company. In cases of medical absences due to serious illness for a period of three or more consecutive workdays, there will only be a charge of one absence.

Any time an employee is absent three (3) consecutive days without notice, the employee will be considered as having voluntarily quit.

When an employee returns from absence, he will report directly to his supervisor.

An employee with an unexcused absence will be subject to corrective action listed below, beginning with the seventh absence in a calendar year or the first unexcused absence.

Corrective Action
Annual Period Covered: January 1–December 31

First Offense: Verbal reprimand
Second Offense: Written reprimand
Third Offense: Three (3) days without pay
Fourth Offense: Five (5) days' suspension, pending investigation
                         and disciplinary action up to discharge

Current attendance policies will be posted at all times on the bulletin boards.

Sample Policy 7

The company relies on all its employees to contribute productively to the company's success and profitability. Therefore, regular attendance and punctuality at scheduled work times are expected of all employees.

Attendance and punctuality are considered when reviewing recommendations for promotions and transfers.

PUNCTUALITY—Employees are expected to report at the scheduled work time. This includes returning from breaks and meal periods, as well as reporting for scheduled overtime. You must notify your supervisor as soon as you are aware that it will not be possible to report to work on time.

ABSENCE—Absence is defined as any lost time (one-half day or full day) from work. While company policy provides a liberal schedule for vacation and personal holidays as well as other allotments of time off for special circumstances, the company recognizes that an occasional absence may be required as a result of a personal illness, an emergency, or other personal matters that must be handled during your regularly scheduled workweek.

Notification: You must notify your supervisor as soon as you know you will be absent. In the case of an accident or sudden illness that requires hospitalization, you should have someone notify your supervisor within 24 hours.

Types and Treatment of Absences

The following types of absences are not counted toward your attendance record:

- Company-paid holidays, paid vacation periods, and paid personal days.

- Occupational illness or injury—if you must miss work due to an on-the-job injury or occupational illness, you will be covered by Worker's Compensation and the company's Short-Term Disability Plan (explained in detail later in this section).

- Legally required absence—includes time missed due to jury duty, military training or duty, and if, through no fault of your own, you are required to appear in court as a witness or for other legal reasons. You must provide a subpoena or other substantiating document to your supervisor. Documented occasions will not be included on an attendance record.

The following types of absence will not be counted toward your attendance record as long as you do not exceed the allotted number of days. In each case you must seek your supervisor's approval as soon as you know that an absence may be necessary. Your supervisor may require verification of the event that necessitates the absence.

- Death in the family—upon the death of your spouse, son, daughter, mother, father, brother, sister, mother-in-law (of your current spouse), father-in-law (of your current spouse), or any relative living with you, you are permitted a paid absence of up to five days. You may take one day off with pay at the death of your brother-in-law, sister-in-law, grandparent, grandparent-in-law, or grandchild. This time is allotted to make any necessary arrangements and to attend the funeral.

- Emergency or major household disaster—up to one day's paid absence is permitted if you must miss work due to an emergency at home, such as a burglary, leaking gas line, or similar situation. Under unusual circumstances, a maximum of three days' absence with pay will be granted in the event of a fire, flood, or other major disaster that destroys an employee's home or its contents. This time period should be used to arrange for reconstruction, relocation, or any other matters that must be resolved.

- Injury or illness in the family and planned absencesDone day's absence, up to a maximum of three days each calendar year, may be used if you must be absent for any of the following reasons:
    - a family member living with you is so ill that you must stay home to provide care or to make arrangements for extended care of the sick family member.
    - household move—if you are changing your principal residence and the moving or delivery of furniture is involved.
    - house settlement on your principal residence.
    - birth or adoption of a child—if you become a father or adoptive parent, you may be absent either the day the mother enters the hospital, the day the child is born,

the day the child comes home, or a day to attend to adoption business (see also Maternity Leave Plan, explained in detail later in this section).

— graduation for you, your spouse, or your child from high school, college, or university.

— if your doctor or dentist can see you only during your regular workday. You should make every attempt to schedule any appointment at the beginning or the end of your workday to keep your absence to a minimum.

The following absences will be counted toward your attendance record:

• Personal illness or injury—if you must miss work due to a personal illness or injury, you will be covered by the company's Short-Term Disability Plan (explained in detail later in this section).

• Any unexcused absence—includes any time off from work taken without your supervisor's approval.

• Any time in excess of the allotted, excused time off for a death, injury or illness in the family, or a planned absence as described above.

REPORTING OF ABSENCES—You must notify your supervisor and indicate on your time record when you have been absent for any reason, including vacation, personal holidays, sick days, etc.

EXCESSIVE ABSENTEEISM—Although the company maintains a liberal policy to provide for employees who are occasionally absent, frequent and extended absences, even for legitimate reasons, can impair an operation, reduce productivity, and diminish the employee's effectiveness and value to the company.

Excessive absenteeism is defined as six occasions of includable absences (as previously explained) in a 12-month period or more than 15 days of absence per year for two consecutive 12-month periods. The 12-month period is a "rolling month," measured from the current date back 12 months; not a calendar year

Progressive Discipline Steps for Excessive Absenteeism

• Verbal discussion—normally takes place after four occasions

• Written correction—normally issued after five occasions

• Final written correction notice—normally issued after six occasions in a 12-month period or more than 15 days' absence per year for two consecutive years.

EXCESSIVE LATENESS—Employees are expected to be at their work station and ready to work at the scheduled time. An employee's chronic lateness places an unfair burden on other employees in the department. Excessive lateness is defined as when an employee is late at a rate greater than an average of once a month.

Progressive Discipline Steps for Excessive Lateness

- Verbal discussion—normally occurs when lateness averages more than once a month over a period of eight consecutive months

- Written correction—normally issued when lateness averages more than once a month over a period of 10 consecutive months.

- Formal written correction notice—normally issued when lateness averages more than once a month over a period of 12 consecutive months.

Sample Policy 8

Being on the job, ready to work and on time, is very important. Each of us was hired for a specific contribution to the overall business. When you are absent or late, you are missed and the department experiences some disruption.

If you are going to be absent or late unexpectedly, you must call your supervisor at or before the assigned starting time. Without this notification to your supervisor, your absence will be counted as unexcused and could have a detrimental effect on your future employment.

Further, you are expected to remain at your work assignment for your full work session except for lunch and break periods. Do not leave the job without your supervisor's permission.

Anyone who is absent for more than one day must stay in regular contact with his/her supervisor (i.e., three-day virus infection—call each day; medical leave for survey—call once each week).

Sample Policy 9

Any absence from work must be excused by your supervisor. Each employee is responsible for notifying his/her supervisor prior to the absence to gain approval. Failure to do this will be considered an unexcused absence. An employee receiving two unexcused absences in any twelve-month period will be discharged.

There are many types of absence. Each has its own set of rules and procedures. The following specifics will apply.

Casual Absence—Absences of short duration: one or two days for personal illness or other incapacity. Each casual absence of two to eight hours in any given workday is considered to be an occasion. Two days of absence equals two occasions. Employees having seven occasions within one year (January 1 through December 31) will receive a verbal correction. An employee with twelve occasions within one year will receive a written correction. A written correction for excessive absence will remain in the personnel file for six months and will negatively affect consideration for upgrades and promotions. Also that employee will not receive any pay raises during that six-month period.

Medical Absence—Absences of longer duration and related to more serious illnesses or infirmities (i.e., surgery, disabling accidents, or physical conditions, etc.). If one of these conditions occurs, first you must contact your supervisor; and second you must contact the company nurse who starts the request for leave documents. *No employee has authorization for leave until the forms have been processed and are approved. Failure to promptly accomplish these two steps will be considered an abandonment of your job.* When returning from a medical leave or if you have been under the care of a doctor or dentist for an acute illness, injury or surgery, you must present to the company nurse a written release for full duty without restrictions. The same conditions apply for a casual absence of three or more days. No one can return to his/her work station without a "Return to Work Authorization" issued by the nurse.

Personal Business—Absence from work to attend to a personal problem or business. Supervisors have the authority to grant a personal business absence. The need to be away from work should occur *very rarely* and each absence of two to eight hours will count as an occasion. Nonexempt employees would not be paid for a personal business absence.

Required Absence—Absences like jury duty, court appearance, military reserve training, bereavement, and company business. All reasons must be communicated to the immediate supervisor.

Unexcused Absence—Absences from work without proper notification to the immediate supervisor. It is the employee's responsibility to speak directly to the supervisor and to continue contact as frequently as the supervisor indicates. Having two incidents (i.e., two different days) of unexcused absence within any twelve-month period will result in a discharge from employment.

An employee who will not or cannot correct a pattern of chronic excessive absences or has a record of numerous medical leaves will be replaced by someone more dependable. Mitigating or aggravating circumstances will be discussed before any such disciplinary action is taken. Overall absence records from year to year are also a consideration when evaluating an employee's dependability.

Sample Policies: Inclement Weather _____

Sample Policy 1

(Name of company) is a service company and, therefore, will always remain open for those employees who can get to work during severe weather. However, in case of a severe snowstorm, flood, etc., as determined by the National Weather Service, the following policy will be in effect:

1. If an employee is unable to get to work, he/she will be allowed to charge such an absence to a vacation day, float time, or sick leave provided he/she has the time remaining. Such time may not be borrowed from the upcoming year.

2. In the event a severe storm should occur the day before or on the day after one of (name of company) stated holidays, holiday pay would be paid to all eligible employees, whether or not they worked the day before or the day after the holiday.

3. The lateness policy will be suspended for the duration of the severe weather.

This policy will hold unless you are called by the company and informed not to report for your shift. Only with major storm damage to the building would this notification be made.

Sample Policy 2

In the event of severe snow or ice storms it may be necessary to adjust normal work schedules. The company will make decisions on closings and openings based upon the best information available and respond to potential hazardous weather conditions that affect all of our employees.

If a severe snowstorm overnight makes it undesirable to open in the morning, the employee is not paid. However, if the employee is able to get to work and be productive in his/her regular job, he/she will be paid for the day at the regular rate. The company may, at its discretion, schedule or permit a makeup day or hours.

If in our management's best judgment we elect to close our offices and plant before the normally scheduled closing time because of threatening weather, employees will be paid for the entire scheduled work day.

If for some reason an employee feels that he/she must leave because of poor weather, even though we are not officially closing, that employee must have the approval of his/her supervisor to take the rest of the day off. In this instance, the employee will not be paid for hours not worked. We will assume and expect that the individual concerns of the employee, as well as the department, will be addressed in a sensitive manner.

Employees will be notified of company closings/openings by radio as follows:

(City)
(Radio Station)

As weather improves in the morning, the company may elect to open for business. Employees should call by telephone if conditions improve and travel is no longer hazardous to see if a later opening is planned.

Sample Policy 3

If during foul weather, (name of company) is open for business by 11:00 a.m., the following policy applies to absences:

1. All individuals who report to work on a day of foul weather, as described above, will be paid at their normal hourly rate for the hours actually worked.

2. Each individual who fails to report to work on a day of foul weather as described above, will be required to make a decision to
   a. Be paid for that day lost, charging the time against "vacation," if that individual has vacation accrued.
   b. Not be paid for that specific date.

Sample Policy 4

Employees unable to report to work because of snow will be given an excused absence if, in the opinion of their supervisor, the weather justified an excused absence.

Employees reporting to work in snowy weather will be allowed to work, but may be assigned to jobs other than their regular jobs.

In the event of severe weather, employees are urged to listen to (radio station) for plant schedule changes. Employees reporting for work after a plant closing has been broadcast will not be paid.

Sample Policies: Leaves of Absence _____

Sample Policy 1

A written leave of absence is required for all absences exceeding five working days and may be requested after completion of 90 days continuous service.

A leave of absence of less than 30 days can be granted by your supervisor. If a leave of absence exceeds 30 days, it must be approved by the manager of your area and the Personnel Director. Approval for a leave is based on the reason for the absence, the length of your employment, your performance record, your attendance and punctuality record, and the work schedule in your area.

The company cannot guarantee to hold a particular job open during any leave or any other absence longer than 30 days. Those returning from longer leaves would be entitled to the first available opening for which they are qualified if their former position has been filled during the leave.

A leave of absence should not be taken lightly since it may work a hardship on the company and your fellow workers who will have to fill in for you.

Your employment is subject to termination if you leave without prior approval or if you fail to return to work on the expiration of the leave of absence. In an emergency situation, you should contact your supervisor as soon as possible to make the necessary arrangements for an extension of leave.

Personal Leave of Absence: A request for a personal leave of absence must be submitted in writing to your supervisor at least five working days prior to the day the leave is to begin, except in case of an emergency. A personal leave of absence may not exceed 60 days and is not subject to extension.

Medical Leave of Absence: If you are sick or disabled and a doctor verifies that you are unable to work for an extended period of at least five working days, you must notify your supervisor and submit a written request for a medical leave. Granting a medical leave of absence is subject to approval of the supervisor and Personnel Director. Any paid sick days or personal paid absence days should be taken before you are placed on medical leave, and those days will not be paid simultaneously with disability pay provided under the Health Plan.

While on medical leave, the company will request a report from your doctor every four weeks on the status of your illness or disability. You will be eligible for up to 90 days with proper doctor's verification. Extension of medical leave beyond 90 days must be in writing and requires approval of the Personnel Director and Vice-President of the area. An authorized "return to work" note will be required before you may resume your normal work responsibilities and should be presented to your supervisor immediately upon your return to work.

Sample Policy 2

A leave of absence for cause may be granted by the company provided that it does not seriously disrupt operations.

A leave of absence will not be granted to any employee having less than one year of continuous service with the company.

A request for a leave of absence must be presented to your supervisor in writing, stating the reason for leave and the length of time requested. An employee failing to return to work at the end of a leave of absence will be dropped from the payroll and lose all seniority.

A leave of absence may not exceed 45 days.

Holiday pay will not be paid for a holiday which occurs during a leave of absence.

A leave of absence will be granted for:

1. Jury duty, with pay for the difference between jury duty pay and straight time earnings while on jury duty.

2. Death in the immediate family, not to exceed ten days.

   A. Payment will be made for only regular work days.
   B. No payment will be made for days after burial.
   C. Immediate family includes the following:
      Father
      Mother
      Husband
      Wife
      Children
      Brother
      Sister

3. Military leave. An employee who returns from service in the Armed Forces will be reemployed in accordance with whatever law or laws are in effect and which apply to his or her case.

   An employee who is a member of a reserve military organization or of the National Guard and who attends regular military training camp, will be given the necessary time off for such training which will not be considered vacation time.

4. Other requests for leaves of absence for other reasons will be considered on an individual basis.

An employee who is out sick for more than three days is required to have a doctor's statement that he or she is able to return to a full workweek.

An employee who is returning from a leave of absence of ten days or less will be returned to his or her former job, if practical, or to a job for which he or she is qualified or can qualify.

134

An employee who is returning from an indefinite leave (maternity, illness) or who is returning before the expiration of a leave is to give at least a one-week notice prior to the date of return.

If, because of an emergency or for any other reason, you are absent from work, you should immediately advise your supervisor, and keep him or her advised until you return to work, so that if you have good cause for absence you will not be dropped from the payroll and your seniority and other employment benefits will be protected. If you are absent from work for three consecutive working days without notifying your supervisor and obtaining approval for your absence, you may be automatically dropped from the payroll.

Sample Policy 3

Generally, a leave of absence will not be granted to any employee having less than one year of continuous service with the company, except when the request for leave of absence is for entering the military service or for maternity.

If it becomes necessary for you to stay away from work for an extended period, you may protect your service record with the company by obtaining a leave of absence. Application for a leave of absence must by made to your supervisor and approved by a member of management prior to being granted. Leaves of absence may be granted for reasons such as the following:

1. Personal illness or accident

2. Illness or accident in your immediate family

3. Personal emergencies

4. Maternity

Military Reserve: If you are a member of the Reserve Corps and are required to take annual training for a period of no more than two weeks each year, you shall make special arrangements for such time off through your supervisor. During such time, you shall be treated as an employee on leave of absence. In such cases, however, your insurance and other benefits will be continued.

Military Reserve and National Guard Leave Pay: All regular full-time employees called to serve not more than ten days' annual training tour per calendar year of duty with the National Guard or Armed Forces Reserve, will be paid the difference between gross wages for such government service and the amount of straight-time (regular gross wages) earnings lost based on the employee's regular scheduled straight-time rate. (Unless the time is taken as vacation or the amount of Armed Forces Reserve or National Guard pay is more than the employee's regular straight-time weekly wages.)

Such payments for up to ten days per calendar year, are to be made following the showing of satisfactory evidence of the amount of pay received for such service.

Insurance Status During Leave: Before taking a leave of absence, an employee should check with the Personnel Department regarding the status of all insurance benefits during the period of absence.

Sample Policy 4

Under certain circumstances you may be eligible for a leave of absence. For those employees who have been with the company three months (except for Military LOA), leaves of absence are granted for the following reasons:

Personal: Should not extend beyond six weeks unless it falls in the category of emergency.

Emergency: Leave should not extend beyond three months. While on Personal or Emergency leave, you will be responsible for full payment of all insurance premiums.

Medical (including maternity): Is granted for one month, but may be extended each month for a period not to exceed six consecutive months.

Layoff: Due to a lack of work, a layoff may be extended for a period not to exceed three months. Insurance premiums regularly paid by the company will continue to be paid by the company for the duration of the three months. This is applicable not more than once during a six-month period. Laid-off employees may continue other insurance coverage at their own expense for the duration of the layoff.

After you are absent from work for seven calendar days, you must be placed on leave of absence or be released.

Length of the leave depends on your reason for requesting it. If it is necessary for you to be gone more than one month, the Personnel Department will make every effort to place you in the same or similar job, on your return. Before returning from a leave, notify Personnel in advance so that arrangements can be made for your return to work.

Failure to return from leave: You will be considered to have voluntarily resigned if you fail to return from leave at the specified time, or if you seek or accept any work with another employer, or if you operate your own business during a leave of absence, or if you fail to return to work at the specified time and have not requested extension of leave, or if your leave (other than Military) exceeds six months.

Procedure for leave of absence: All employees requesting a leave of absence must complete a Leave Request Form in the Personnel Office.

If, for unusual circumstances, the leave of absence should be extended beyond six months, approval must be given by Corporate Personnel for a one-month extension.

Rehire or reinstatement from leave: In the event of reemployment within twelve months of termination because of failure to return from a leave of absence, an employee who has five years of continuous service (including time on leave) will be shown as reinstated and will be entitled to full benefits, vacation, personal days, etc.

An employee with less than five years of service who is terminated because of failure to return from leave will be shown as rehired and will be eligible for benefits as a new employee.

Sample Policy 5

Each request for a leave of absence will be considered on an individual basis. The leave may be approved or not approved after your immediate supervisor and the Division Officer have considered all facts, the reason for the request, etc. The duration of the leave, if approved, may also vary in different cases, but in no case will leave be granted in excess of two leaves per year or granted for more than six months, except under very unusual circumstances.

Donating Blood: The (name of company) feels that giving blood is both an honor and a privilege, and all employees are encouraged to donate as often as possible. You will be paid for time spent at the bloodmobile. In the event of a blood call by the Red Cross, your company has and will continue to pay for the time you spend, during working hours, at the bloodmobile and, for obvious reasons, this time must be paid as straight time.

Sample Policy 6

In unusual cases and for compelling reasons, you may require a leave of absence. The company will consider such leaves of absence without pay, consistent with business requirements.

Requests should be made to your Department Supervisor in writing (approved forms must be obtained from the Department Supervisor) and the recommendation is subject to the approval of the Director of Personnel. You may be granted a personal or medical leave of absence without pay up to eight weeks' duration. (Additional time off may be granted upon/before expiration.) The disability policy set forth in the benefits section also applies.

Where unusual circumstances exist, the company may grant additional leave of absence. Each case will be judged on its own merit.

If one is gainfully employed by another company while on a leave of absence from (name of company), that person shall be terminated and all seniority will be lost.

Funeral Leave: Your company recognizes your desire to be absent in the event of a death in your immediate family (spouse, child, mother, father, brother, sister, mother-in-law, father-in-law, step-parents, grandparents, and grandchildren). You will be allowed a total of three working days off between the date of death and the day following the burial inclusive. Allowed time off, up to eight hours each day shall be paid at your job classification, straight-time hourly rate in the event you were scheduled to work and would have worked such days if there had been no such death. Time lost for scheduled hours of work due to funeral leave during the normal scheduled workweek shall be counted as hours worked for the purpose of computing overtime. Upon request of the company, you may be asked to offer valid proof of death before time off with pay is granted. You will not receive funeral leave pay unless days absent were scheduled work days. Nor will you receive funeral leave pay if you are on vacation or layoff.

In order for the employee to receive pay for funeral leave, the Department Supervisor must notify the Payroll Manager. Likewise, if the employee is a participant in the Employee Flower Fund, the responsibility for proper and timely distribution of the allocation rests with the Department Supervisor.

Sample Policy 7

A full-time regular or probationary employee may, upon written request, be granted a leave of absence for reasons determined to be valid by the company. Each case will stand on its own merits. A leave of absence will not be granted for other employment, except for employment arranged or agreed upon by the company.

A leave of absence is an authorized absence in excess of 14 consecutive calendar days during which you receive no payroll compensation for either services rendered or in the form of benefits from the Sick Leave or Salary Continuation Plans.

Approval should be obtained through your supervisor, section head, department head, and the human resources department. Request for approval must be made in writing and must state the duration of and reason for the leave of absence.

Any of the following conditions will result in changing your status from leave of absence to termination:

1. Accepting other employment while on leave without prior written approval from the company.

2. Failure to apply for reinstatement and/or refusal to accept an open position for which you are qualified when the leave terminates.

3. Unavailability of openings for which you are qualified at the time of application for reinstatement.

Nothing in this policy shall be construed to deprive the employee returning from military service of reemployment rights as provided by federal or state laws.

At the time of the leave, your human resources department will consult with you regarding the status of the various benefit plans.

The company may require you to be examined by a physician selected by the company prior to approving a leave of absence or prior to your return to work from a leave of absence.

Sample Policy 8

Unpaid personal leaves of absence for a period of up to thirty days may be requested by full-time regular and part-time regular employees who have completed three months of continuous service. You must request personal leaves in writing at least two weeks prior to the time you wish such leave to commence. If the personal leave request is necessitated by an emergency, you or a member of your immediate family must notify your supervisor or the head of your department as soon as is practicable; this should be followed up with a written explanation of the nature of the leave and the expected length of your absence. In such emergency situations, the written explanation must normally be submitted within three days of the beginning of your leave.

Personal leave may be granted for justifiable reasons (e.g., child care or to care for an ill family member) at the company's discretion, provided the leave does not seriously disrupt company operations. Personal leaves are not granted until all accrued unused vacation and personal days have been exhausted.

Reinstatement cannot be guaranteed to employees returning from personal leaves. However, we will try to place employees returning from personal leave in their former positions or positions comparable in status and pay, subject to budgetary restrictions, our need to fill vacancies, and our ability to find qualified temporary replacements.

Sample Policy 9

Our company may grant leaves of absence to employees who must be absent from work because of a nonoccupational disability, occupational disability, or military service. The company may reinstate such employees to their former positions or to like available positions, provided the company's circumstances have not so changed as to make it unreasonable to do so. In all cases, with the exception of military leave, leave of absence may be granted for a period of inactive employment covering thirty (30) or more calendar days, but not to exceed six (6) months. *To be eligible for a leave of absence, an employee must be "regular full-time" and actively employed continuously for a minimum of three (3) months.* (Parental/maternity leave may have some other time constraints.)

No leave of absence will be granted for "personal reasons." Giving a false reason for a leave of absence will result in an employee's immediate dismissal. *Furthermore, should an employee accept employment, including part-time employment, elsewhere during his/her leave of absence, his/her employment will be deemed to have terminated without notice as of the original date his/her leave was granted.* Proper and required forms, initiated by the employee and acquired through the company nurse, must be processed and approved for a leave to be approved and in effect. Normal company benefits (health, life insurance) would continue with the company's paying the normal premiums. For those requesting a parental related leave, separate notification requirements exist. The Human Resources Department can explain in more detail.

Sample Policies: Military Leaves of Absence _____

Sample Policy 1

A regular or probationary employee entering military service will be given a military leave of absence and have certain rights concerning a reemployment at the termination of the military service term, in accordance with applicable federal laws.

An employee called for military service should immediately inform his supervisor and determine whether a request for a leave of absence is appropriate.

If granted a leave of absence for military service, the employee should contact the Human Resources Department regarding the status of various benefit plans while on such leave.

Sample Policy 2

An employee entering the U.S. Armed Services will be expected to show orders to his or her supervisor as soon as they are received. Full-time employees who have completed service may return to work at their regular job or one similar to the one they left in accordance with applicable federal laws.

Sample Policy 3

Employees entering the U. S. Armed Forces are expected to show their orders to their supervisors as soon as the orders are received. Regular, full-time employees who have been on military leave for a period of up to four (4) years will be eligible for reemployment after completing military service, providing they have been honorably discharged and apply for reemployment within ninety (90) days after release from active duty.

Regular, full-time employees called to serve a tour of active duty training with a reserve or National Guard unit will be granted a leave of absence without pay for the time required. Employees desiring such leave should notify their immediate supervisors as far in advance as possible. Such leaves will not affect the employee's vacation.

Sample Policy 4

If you are a regular, full-time employee and interrupt your employment in order to serve with the United States Armed Forces, either on active or reserve training duty, you will be eligible for a military leave of absence. This leave of absence will be unpaid; however, you may elect to use any earned, unused vacation during this time. Please give your supervisor a copy of your military orders as soon as possible.

Sample Policy 5

If you are a member of a military reserve or National Guard unit and are called to serve a two-week tour of active duty, you will be granted military leave of absence with pay, reduced by your reserve pay for up to a maximum of two (2) weeks. Please give your supervisor a copy of your military orders as soon as possible.

Sample Policy 6

Members of the Armed Forces of the United States, including the Coast Guard, and members of the Armed Forces Reserves or the National Guard are entitled to certain rights regarding seniority, status, and pay if it is necessary to take a leave of absence for active duty. Three types of situations would require a leave of absence:

- Enlistment or induction into a regular branch of the Armed Forces for active duty for a period not to exceed four years

- Initial active duty for basic training in a Reserve component or the National Guard

- Periods of voluntary or involuntary active military training duty (in excess of four weeks)

When Leave Begins—When leave begins, the employee is entitled to the following:

- Salary due

- Unused vacation pay for the calendar year if the leave of absence becomes effective on or after the first Monday in January

- Unused personal holidays

Benefits—While on a military leave of absence, employees may elect to obtain continued medical and dental benefit coverage at their own expense for a maximum of 18 months.

Eligibility for other benefits, such as holidays, vacation accrual, and credited service, is suspended during the leave period but will be reinstated upon return to work.

Reemployment—Veterans returning from a military leave are entitled to reemployment without loss of seniority and in a job with status and pay equivalent to the job held immediately prior to the leave, provided application for reemployment is made within a specified period of time following release from active duty.

- In the case of *long-term enlistments,* reemployment application must be made within 90 days.

- Following *initial active duty for basic training,* application for reemployment must be made within 31 days.

- Following release from *short periods of active duty for training,* application for reemployment is not required, but the employee should return to work as soon as reasonably possible.

The company follows the legal requirements below:

- A returning veteran may not be discharged without cause by an employer within the first year of employment.

　　　　　© 1991 The Dartnell Corporation

- The minimum salary for returning veterans will be the salary they were receiving when they left the company. In addition to receiving at least the same salary as when they left, veterans returning to the company normally will benefit from any company-wide increases that may have been given employees during their absence.

- Veterans returning to jobs with a progression range (not based on merit) are entitled to the periodic increases they would have received had they continued working for the company.

- All employee benefits will be reinstated at the time of reemployment. Veterans retain the same seniority date that they had at the start of the leave.

Notification—Employees should notify their supervisor as much in advance as possible of the need to take a military leave of absence.

Sample Policies: Jury Duty ————————————

Sample Policy 1

If you are notified that your name has been drawn for jury service, inform your supervisor immediately so that it may be determined whether working conditions permit your absence from work. The company encourages employees to carry out their responsibilities as citizens in this regard whenever circumstances permit. Your supervisor will inform you about how your pay will be handled.

An employee called for jury duty should report for work during his or her scheduled working hours before and after such duty for assignment to available work. Time spent on jury duty shall not be considered as time worked for the purpose of calculating overtime.

Sample Policy 2

If you are a full-time regular employee who is summoned to jury duty, we will continue your salary during your active period of jury duty for up to a maximum of twelve (12) working days per calendar year. You are also permitted to retain the allowance you receive from the court for such service. If you are not a full-time regular employee, you are given time off without pay while serving jury duty.

All employees are allowed unpaid time off if summoned to appear in court as a witness.

To qualify for jury or witness duty leave, you must submit to your supervisor a copy of the summons to serve as soon as it is received. In addition, proof of service must be submitted to your supervisor when your period of jury or witness duty is completed.

We will make no attempt to have your service on a jury postponed except where business conditions necessitate such action.

Sample Policy 3

The company recognizes the fact that it is a person's duty to serve willingly on state and federal juries and wishes to cooperate fully. If you are requested to perform service as a juror, you shall be given time off while serving on the jury. At the completion of your service, you shall report the amount of juror's fees, and the company will pay you for the time of absence (the straight-time rate computed on the basis of straight-time scheduled work day for the number of days of jury service during the regular workweek), less the amount you received as juror's fees during such period.

Employees called for duty in (name of county) will be paid by the company for the first three days they serve as jurors. Starting the fourth day, the company will pay the difference between the amount paid by the county and the employee's regular rate of pay.

If you are called upon to serve for jury duty, you should give your supervisor as much advance notice as possible, as well as a copy of the jury service notice for payroll purposes.

There may be occasions when you are temporarily released from your duties because no juries are drawn. When this happens, you are expected to return to work if there is reasonable period of time left in the day.

Sample Policy 4

Jury duty is a civic responsibility which we should not avoid. We urge our employees to perform jury duty service whenever possible. You will be granted a leave of absence to serve jury duty, and you will receive differential pay for days served. Differential pay will be determined by subtracting the daily amount paid by the court for jury duty from the amount of your regular day's pay. You must provide your supervisor with a statement from the court indicating the days served and the amount paid by the court. We request that you notify your supervisor as soon as you receive your jury duty summons. Also, we ask that you report back to work any day in which you have been excused early or are not required to report for jury duty service.

Sample Policy 5

If you receive a summons to serve on a jury, please tell your supervisor as soon as possible so that he can arrange for another employee to work in your place during your absence.

In order to avoid any severe financial loss to you, the company will pay you the difference between any jury duty pay you receive and the amount you would have earned at your regular daily earnings. Time spent on jury duty will not be used to calculate overtime pay. Saturdays and Sundays are not considered scheduled workdays under this policy.

To be eligible for jury duty pay, you must deliver to the accounting office a statement from the court clerk indicating the time served on the jury and the amount received as jury duty pay.

When on jury duty, you are expected to report back to work on any day in which you are excused early or are not required to report for jury duty service.

Sample Policies: Educational Leave ———————————

Sample Policy 1

Under special circumstances, and at the discretion of the company, employees may take an educational leave of absence without pay for up to a maximum of 12 months to complete full-time study for an approved and required academic degree.

Eligibility—To qualify, employees must

- Have at least two years' regular, continuous service with the company

- Be accepted by an accredited college or university for study leading to an under-graduate, master's, or doctoral degree in a field applicable to and required for the employee's current job or for future advancement within the area or department.

Application and Approval—A written request for an educational leave must be submitted to the department manager at least three months before the start of the requested leave. The request for leave must be approved by the department manager, the appropriate area or functional Vice-President, the Personnel Director and the business sector Vice-President of Personnel.

Benefits—While on an educational leave of absence, employees may continue to apply for re-imbursement of eligible expenses under the company's Tuition Reimbursement program.

Employees may also continue life insurance and medical and dental coverage, provided they prepay all charges associated with the contributory portion of the plans. Eligibility for other benefits, such as holidays, vacation accrual, and credited services is suspended during the leave period but will be reinstated upon return to work.

Reemployment—Upon completion of study, employees may apply to their Personnel Director for reemployment. Reemployment, while not guaranteed, will depend upon the availability of a suitable job opening. If a suitable job opening is not available, the employee will be considered "resigned" effective the date the leave began.

Sample Policies: Sick Leave _____

Sample Policy 1

Medical (including pregnancy) leaves of absence for periods up to four months may be requested by full-time regular and part-time regular employees.

If you expect to be absent for more than five consecutive work days as a result of an illness, injury, or disability (including pregnancy), you must submit a written request for medical leave to your supervisor and the Human Resources Department as far in advance of your anticipated leave date as practicable. If your absence is due to an emergency, you or a member of your immediate family must inform your supervisor or head of your department as soon as is practicable; this should be followed up with a written leave request, normally submitted within three days of the beginning of your leave. All medical leave requests must be accompanied by appropriate medical certification from your physician, indicating the condition necessitating your leave request and your projected date of return to work.

If your leave request is granted, you are required to provide the company with additional physician's statements at least once every thirty days (or more frequently if requested), attesting to your continued disability and inability to work. You may also be required to provide the company access to your medical records or to submit to an examination at any time by a physician designated by the company at its discretion.

While on an approved medical leave of absence, you may be eligible for short-term disability, salary continuation, and/or long-term disability insurance benefits. (Please consult the statement of each of these policies in this handbook for further details.)

Before being permitted to return from medical leave, you are required to present the company with a note from your physician indicating that you are capable of returning to work.

All company benefits that operate on an accrual basis (e.g., vacation and paid sick days) continue to accrue only during the first thirty days of your medical leave. All company group health benefits (e.g., hospitalization and major medical insurance) continue during your leave.

Unless applicable state or local law requires otherwise, reinstatement cannot be guaranteed to any employee returning from medical leave. Employees are notified by the Human Resources Department regarding any such right to reinstatement prior to the commencement of their leaves. Our company will try to place employees returning from leave in their former positions or positions comparable in pay, subject to budgetary restrictions, our need to fill vacancies, and our ability to find qualified temporary replacements.

Sample Policy 2

The company's ability to serve its customers in a timely and efficient manner is of utmost importance. Regular attendance and promptness in reporting to work contributes a great deal toward a better team effort and better-served customers. Being here in accordance with your schedule is expected and is considered an important factor in overall employee performance.

We recognize that occasionally it may be necessary for you to be absent from work as a result of illness or to attend to matters of a personal nature. Therefore, beginning with your six-month anniversary as a regular, full-time employee, you will receive 2$\frac{1}{2}$ sick/personal days and, upon your one-year anniversary, another 2$\frac{1}{2}$ sick/personal days. Thereafter, beginning with your two-year anniversary, you will receive five sick/personal days each year.

Your sick/personal days are for your use as you see fit. However, if at all possible, we request that you schedule these days off with your supervisor as far in advance as possible so that arrangements can be made to take care of your work on the day(s) you are absent. Sick/personal days can be accrued up to a maximum of 12 weeks.

Sample Policy 3

Upon satisfactory completion of your orientation period, all regular full-time employees will be eligible for coverage under our sick leave program which pays benefits per week from the first day of accident or hospitalization or the fourth day of illness up to a maximum of thirteen (13) weeks. Pregnancy disability is also covered under the sick leave program.

In order to be eligible for benefits, you must be under the regular care of a doctor and may be required to submit a doctor's certificate at any time. You are required to come back to work as soon as your doctor certifies that you are physically able to return.

If you are not able to come back to work after thirteen weeks, you will be terminated from the active payroll and will be put on a preferential hiring list when your doctor certifies you are able to reenter the work force. While you are receiving sick leave benefits, your seniority will continue to accumulate for vacation purposes, and you will be eligible to receive pay for any observed holidays.

Continuation of your coverage under the group insurance plan will be maintained upon your authorization to deduct required premiums from your weekly benefit. Sick leave benefits will be paid at the same time as regular paychecks.

Sample Policy 4

We recognize that occasionally it may be necessary for you to be absent from work as a result of illness or accident. Therefore, beginning with the first of the month following the date of hire, all full-time employees will begin accruing one day of paid sick leave per month for a total of twelve days per year. Unused sick leave days along with unused personal leave days will accumulate indefinitely to provide you job protection should you have an extended illness or disability. This is an excellent job insurance protection for you; however, any unused disability leave days will not be paid upon termination of employment.

Paid disability leave will begin with the first day of hospitalization or illness. A doctor's excuse may be required to verify claims for disability leave. Should you be granted a personal leave of absence for more than twenty continuous workdays, the accrual of your disability days will be suspended until you return to work; however, your other benefits will continue.

Sample Policy 5

All "regular full-time" hourly and salaried (nonexempt) employees, after completing six months of continuous service, are eligible for paid sick leave benefits. These benefits are paid only when you are ill and unable to work because of non-job-related causes and are as follows:

Length of Service	Sick Pay Allowance Each Year	Waiting Period	Maximum Accumulation
First 6 months	None	N/A	N/A
6 months to 2 years	5 workdays	2 workdays	10 workdays
2 years to 5 years	5 workdays	1 workday	10 workdays
5 to 10 years	7 workdays	None	14 workdays
10 to 20 years	10 workdays	None	20 workdays
Over 20 years	15 workdays	None	30 workdays

Sample Policies: Funeral Leave

Sample Policy 1

In the event of the death of an employee's father, mother, brother, sister, husband, wife, child, father-in-law, mother-in-law, or a person living in the same residence as part of the same household as the employee, time off will be given, up to a maximum of three working days, without loss of regular straight-time pay during the period beginning with the day of death and up to and including the day following the funeral. Additional time off, without pay, will be granted whenever such additional time is reasonably required.

In case of the death of a son-in-law, daughter-in-law, brother-in-law, sister-in-law, grandchild, or grandparent, you will be given, upon request, one full day off without loss of regular straight-time pay on the day of the funeral to attend the services.

The provisions of this section covering absences for death in the family do not apply within the time limits of scheduled vacation or when an employee is off duty due to illness or injury or for other reasons.

Employees may serve as pallbearers when requested without loss of straight-time pay on the day of the funeral for the time necessary to perform this function.

Sample Policy 2

All regular full-time employees shall be entitled to receive time off with pay in the event of the death of a member of your immediate family. The immediate family is defined as father, mother, husband, wife, brother, sister, child, or mother- or father-in-law, grandparents, grandchildren, or any other relative living in the household of the employee. The period of absence may not exceed three work days for one cause.

Should more than three days be needed, they may be taken as personal days or vacation days or they may be taken without pay, subject to the discretion of your supervisor. For part-time or temporary employees, leave without pay may be granted upon the death of a member of the immediate family.

Sample Policy 3

If you are scheduled to work and you receive news of the death of a member of your immediate family, you may arrange for a bereavement leave in order to make necessary arrangements, attend the funeral, or handle other affairs immediately associated with the funeral.

You will be paid for time actually lost from your regularly scheduled work, up to eight hours per day, from the day of the death through the day of the funeral, but not to exceed two paid workdays.

The following are considered members of an employee's immediate family for purposes of providing up to two workdays off with pay: Mother, Father, Sister, Brother, Wife, Husband, Daughter, Son, and Mother or Father-in-Law.

Saturdays and Sundays are not considered scheduled workdays under this policy. Additional time off without pay may be requested through your immediate supervisor.

Sample Policy 4

Employees bereaved by the death of a relative will be granted time off from work without loss of pay according to the listed provisions which follow. All "regular full-time" employees are covered by this policy effective their first full day of active employment.

1. When a death occurs in an employee's immediate family, he/she will be compensated for the time actually lost from his/her regularly scheduled work on the day of the death and the days following it, but not to exceed three workdays (24 work hours). The immediate family of an employee is defined and limited to mother, father, wife, husband, daughter, son, sister and brother. Step-parents are considered immediate family.

2. Employees may be granted time off from work without loss of their regular pay upon the death of a relative who is not a member of their immediate family, but not to exceed one workday (8 work hours). For the purpose of this policy, a relative who is not of the immediate family is defined as sons- and daughters-in-law, aunts, uncles, nieces, nephews, grandparents, grandchildren, parents of spouse, brother or sister of spouse, and grandparents of spouse. Other relatives such as cousins, spouses married to brothers or sisters (of employee or spouse), etc., are not covered by this policy.

3. Any time off must be approved by the employee's immediate supervisor.

4. Compensation allowance will not exceed eight hours per day straight time at an employee's base salary rate.

5. Time paid for bereavement leave will not be counted as hours worked for the purpose of computing overtime.

6. Bereavement leave pay will not be paid in addition to allowable sick pay for the same day. The only exceptions to this will be when a death occurs in the family while an employee is on holiday or vacation, in which case additional days may be granted to compensate for any days used as bereavement leave.

7. Pay in lieu of taking bereavement time off is not permitted.

8. Leave must occur at the time of the relative's death. Leave after some time has passed will not be allowed.

4.06 Employee Benefits Administration

SESCO Observations and Recommendations
Health Care Benefits: Communicating Your Employee Health Care
Insurance Benefits and "Managing" Health Care Costs

Every new or revised employee handbook should contain your company's philosophy and mission statement relative to providing health care benefits to employees and their families. It is not unusual that group health insurance policies and procedures, eligibility, as well as the amount of covered expenses are provided in published "manuals" separate from the employee handbook. Nevertheless, it is recommended that your employee handbook make reference to the separately published group insurance manuals and, at the same time, provide employees and their families with a general overall policy and procedures statement highlighting your major health insurance benefits, wellness programs, health promotion and screening procedures, managed care, and employee assistance programs.

The following SESCO observations and recommendations can be beneficial in developing a new or revised health care policy and procedure statement and philosophy to be published in new or revised employee handbooks.

Not only do employers face a crisis of complying with the increasing amounts of legislation affecting benefits, but also we are faced with soaring health care costs. In a recently conducted survey by A. Foster Higgins & Company, Inc., the results showed that employer-sponsored health care plans soared 18.6 percent in cost per employee in 1988, after two consecutive years of annual increases averaging less than 8 percent. The national survey of more than 1,600 employers, representing 100 million workers and dependents found that the cost per employee hit a record high of $2,354, compared with the average of $1,985 reported in 1987.

Most employers have been fooled with unrealistic expectations of cost-containment measures which have been implemented in their health care plans. For example, most thought that mere cost-shifting would not only reduce cost during the current year, but also reduce the entire cost trend in future years. They expected that second surgical opinions would reduce the amount of surgery, but it just hasn't happened that way. Others expected that hospital utilization review programs, including precertification, would decrease admission rates and lengths of stay, and that has worked out in many cases, but the costs-per-stay have risen. The overall control of medical costs has continued to elude benefits managers. In recent studies of its 77 million subscribers, the Blue Cross and Blue Shield Association found that the number of out-patient visits per thousand people covered jumped 26 percent between 1981 and 1987. The cost-per-visit rose 88 percent. During that same period, the number of in-patient days fell 26 percent, but the cost-per-case rose about 77 percent, suggesting that hospitals have experienced sharp in-patient declines and have raised their prices to compensate for the loss of patients to out-patient facilities. These figures give increasing validity to the thought that health care providers are very quick to react to cost-containment provisions attached to medical plans. Therefore, such cost-saving provisions only experience a short-lived financial effect.

Survey reports also indicate that one of the major culprits of rising costs is the growing use of mental health and substance abuse benefits. Few companies have qualified utilization review of these products, but new numbers may force reluctant companies to review current measures. Cost of providing these benefits grew 27 percent in 1988 to an average of $207 per employee. The 1987 average was $163 per employee. Expenditures on these benefits now account for 9.6 percent of total medical plan costs. Effective marketing attempts by the many providers in the mental health/substance abuse market clearly have some effect on these figures.

Traditionally, most employers' reaction to rising health care costs has resulted in their dramatically raising employee contributions for health insurance coverage or the cutting back of medical health care benefits. Such actions may have compounded the rising health care cost problem by causing many employees to discontinue health care coverage which was either too costly or provided little coverage, resulting in the increase of indigent care cost for the general public. This increasing indigent care has resulted in as much as 30 percent to 40 percent increases in current hospital rates in most areas of the country.

Clearly the company's benefits objectives and philosophy play a great role in not only the benefits that are offered, but also the cost-containment/cost-sharing provisions that health care plans contain. Employee benefit plans, especially health care plans, are specifically instituted to perform a variety of services for the employer including attracting good employees, motivating employee productivity, and reducing turnover. One negative result of rising health care costs and increasing benefits legislation is that many small employers are considering termination of any employer-provided medical care plans. This drastic action could clearly result in increasing benefit costs for the remaining covered population and additional federal or state legislation mandating certain levels of employee benefits.

SESCO feels there are several alternatives that still remain open to employers in reducing the rising costs of health care and to control the utilization level of medical care plans. Surely a continuation of cost-containment provisions in medical plans is a necessity. However, these cost-containment provisions should be reviewed on at least an annual basis to determine their effect on the total cost-containment picture as well as on health care providers to these cost-containment provisions.

Preplacement Health Evaluations

One alternative facing employers is preplacement health evaluations. Several years ago, many employers utilized pre-employment physical examinations for applicants but have discontinued them for a variety of reasons. These physical examinations which would be required before the offering of employment or in a change of job have the following purposes:

- To identify preexisting medical conditions for which the employer wishes to limit liability

- To test the ability of the applicant to fulfill job requirements without danger to the personal health or safety of others

- To reduce the prospect of future injury or illness directly related to performance of duties

- To prevent the spread of communicable diseases

- To screen persons with addiction to drugs or alcohol

Case law interpreting statutes that guarantee equal opportunity in employment restricts the right to deny employment on the basis of physical conditions that do not affect job performance. The nature and extent of preplacement examinations should be determined by a systematic analysis of job requirements. The analysis should state in quantifiable measures, whenever possible, such details as the capacity to lift or climb, upper body strength, physical stamina and endurance, etc., and the nature of emotional stress the employee is expected to endure. If medical standards for employment are defined in very specific terms and related to objective job performance requirements, then inappropriate placements can be eliminated and defended successfully on appeal. Not only do preplacement health evaluations attempt to identify preexisting medical conditions which may be limited under health care plans, but also may identify certain other physical deformities or defects which could limit workers' compensation claims in the future.

Health Promotion and Screening

The second alternative which employers should consider is health promotion and screening. Since the lives and health of employees already on the payroll will change over a period of time, it is important to establish ongoing health screening and educational programs of potential health problems for employers. The purpose of health screening programs is to identify potential health problems early in their progression so they may be treated promptly and the cost of treatment can be reduced.

There is no magic formula in establishing either the frequency or the method of screening. Variables such as age, gender, occupation, cultural heritage, and genetic predisposition should be considered in determining the need and extent of screening programs. Periodical health monitoring should be targeted to those areas identified in the survey. Some employers may provide mass screening aimed at a single, common disorder (i.e., blood pressure tests, glaucoma), while others may provide screening for all body systems (multiphasic screening). Either approach can be used effectively. Screening can be done either individually or in groups.

An often-missed opportunity is for the employer to provide education to employees on specific high-risk diseases. These would include such areas as cancer detection, high blood pressure, diabetes, and other specific illnesses. Many local and county health organizations are available to provide free educational information and workshops for your employees. Of course, this could include such areas as nutritional weight reduction plans and smoking cessation programs.

Wellness

A third alternative, which is very closely linked to the second, is the idea of wellness in the workplace. It has been proven statistically that it is much more cost-effective to prevent illness or injury than it is to treat illnesses and injuries after they occur. Therefore, it is incumbent upon an employer to assist in promoting the general wellness of employees. A variety of approaches to promoting good health exists in U.S. industry today.

In addition to educating the workforce, promoting good health in the workplace can be approached in a variety of ways. These may include the following:

- Using attractive colors and interior design to enhance comfort and relaxation, with attention to lighting and noise control

- Eliminating cigarette, candy, and junk food vending machines

- Providing a smoke-free work environment

- Designing the workplace and equipment with sound ergonomic (i.e., human engineering) principles in mind

- Providing cafeteria menus that conform to fundamental nutritional principles

- Providing facilities for aerobic exercises, including showers and locker rooms

- Creating quality control circles or other comparable mechanisms to foster teamwork and to open pathways of communication between employees at every level who share interests and concerns

- Finding opportunities for organized sports and competitions with company sponsorship

- Scheduling periodic group discussions or seminars on a variety of general health or safety topics

Employee Assistance Programs

Employee assistance programs (EAPs) also provide an alternative to employers for controlling rising health and workers' compensation costs. Those engaged in research and practice in employee assistance programs are concerned with health problems that impair the performance of an employee at any level in the company. An EAP is defined as a company-sponsored assessment, treatment, and referral for early intervention in such problems as substance abuse, emotional stress, or situational crisis at home or at work. Program attributes include the following:

- Detecting deterioration in job performance possibly linked either to substance abuse or emotional distress and the avoidance of threats and confrontation

- Training supervisors to detect cases appropriate for EAP services in guiding early referral and follow-up

- Using documented evidence of poor performance to overcome denial and to offer constructive assistance in the face of a crisis involving job security

- Linking the employee with the appropriate resources while maximizing job continuity

- Assuring that the employee needing the treatment is sent to appropriate community-based providers that are competent and cost-effective

- Adopting a company policy that permits initial short-term rehabilitation in preference to discipline or removal of employees

Managed Care

Managed care delivery systems are now more important than ever in health care plans in controlling costs. This type of delivery system allows the review of high-dollar cases by trained professionals such as RNs or physicians to determine the most cost-effective and quality service for each patient. This allows the case manager to permit otherwise excludable services in light of the cost-effective nature of those services over more expensive alternatives. For example, out-patient home health care in contrast to an in-patient hospital bill.

Individual case management should be in every plan, not only because it is voluntary, but because in today's environment there are numerous cases of AIDs, cancer, and prenatal care. It is important to manage the cases from day one. In working with the family, the patient, and the providers, the intent is to use the most cost-effective mode of care. The four basic areas which should be assessed are the services, the resources, the appropriateness, and the facilities. Individual care management programs may last months on particular illnesses and cost quite a sum of money. These plans should be closely monitored between the employer and the provider.

Summary

To implement an effective health care cost management system, it is important to understand that the provider community must be involved. Without a "triangle effect" where the physician, the patient, and the plan sponsor/employer are involved, expectations of cost containment will not be met. It is very important to have a well-thought-out process of cost containment since everything you do is simply a piece of a bigger puzzle, and all the pieces must fit into an organized process. When medical inflation is running between 18 and 22 percent, you, as a health care plan sponsor, face few options other than the alternatives to implement effective cost-containment provisions in your health care plan.

4.06 Employee Handbook Development Checklist

Employee Benefits Administration

The following checklist can be used to help determine the various subjects to include in your handbook. Sample handbook statements covering many of the items in this checklist appear in this section. They can be used to help draft your personalized employee handbook statements.

Our Employee Handbook Should Include:

PAID VACATIONS

1. Length of vacations	Yes ___ No ___ Maybe ___
2. Eligibility and amount of vacation pay	Yes ___ No ___ Maybe ___
3. Scheduling vacation time	Yes ___ No ___ Maybe ___
4. Illness during vacation	Yes ___ No ___ Maybe ___
5. Extending, accumulating, or splitting vacation	Yes ___ No ___ Maybe ___
6. Military Reserve or National Guard Camp during vacation	Yes ___ No ___ Maybe ___
7. Effect of layoffs and absences	Yes ___ No ___ Maybe ___
8. Effect of discharge and resignation	Yes ___ No ___ Maybe ___
9. Part-time and temporary employees	Yes ___ No ___ Maybe ___

PAID HOLIDAYS

1. Number and name of paid and unpaid holidays	Yes ___ No ___ Maybe ___
2. Arrangements for Christmas and religious holidays	Yes ___ No ___ Maybe ___
3. Holidays falling on nonworking days	Yes ___ No ___ Maybe ___
4. Arrangements for long holiday weekends	Yes ___ No ___ Maybe ___
5. Eligibility requirements for paid holiday	Yes ___ No ___ Maybe ___
6. Amount of holiday pay and computation procedure	Yes ___ No ___ Maybe ___
7. Pay for worked holidays	Yes ___ No ___ Maybe ___
8. "Floating" holidays	Yes ___ No ___ Maybe ___

GROUP HEALTH INSURANCE

1. Health plan specifics   Yes ___ No ___ Maybe ___

   A. Type and amount of benefits provided   Yes ___ No ___ Maybe ___
   B. Kind of plan—self-funded, indemnity, HMO, etc.   Yes ___ No ___ Maybe ___
   C. Eligibility requirements for
       employees/dependents   Yes ___ No ___ Maybe ___
   D. Contributory or noncontributory plan—
       percentage contributions   Yes ___ No ___ Maybe ___
   E. Coverage—individual or family   Yes ___ No ___ Maybe ___
   F. Maximums—out-of-pocket, lifetime, etc.   Yes ___ No ___ Maybe ___
   G. Deductibles   Yes ___ No ___ Maybe ___
   H. Limitations and exclusions

2. Continuation provisions   Yes ___ No ___ Maybe ___

   A. Extended coverage   Yes ___ No ___ Maybe ___
   B. COBRA administration   Yes ___ No ___ Maybe ___
   C. Conversion privileges   Yes ___ No ___ Maybe ___

3. Dental insurance

   A. Coverage—individual or family   Yes ___ No ___ Maybe ___
   B. Maximums—out-of-pocket, lifetime, etc.   Yes ___ No ___ Maybe ___
   C. Deductibles   Yes ___ No ___ Maybe ___
   D. Limitations and exclusions

GROUP LIFE INSURANCE

1. Defining group life insurance   Yes ___ No ___ Maybe ___

2. Eligibility requirements   Yes ___ No ___ Maybe ___

   A. Employee   Yes ___ No ___ Maybe ___
   B. Dependents   Yes ___ No ___ Maybe ___

3. Amount of coverage   Yes ___ No ___ Maybe ___

4. Contributory or noncontributory plan   Yes ___ No ___ Maybe ___

5. Conversion privileges after termination   Yes ___ No ___ Maybe ___

6. Accidental death or dismemberment insurance rider   Yes ___ No ___ Maybe ___

7. Coverage of life insurance after employee's
   retirement   Yes ___ No ___ Maybe ___

GROUP ACCIDENT AND SICKNESS INSURANCE (Salary Continuance)

1. Employee eligible for coverage   Yes ___ No ___ Maybe ___

A. Nonexempt	Yes ___ No ___ Maybe ___	
B. Exempt	Yes ___ No ___ Maybe ___	

2. Type and amount of benefits provided — Yes ___ No ___ Maybe ___

3. Contributory or noncontributory plan — Yes ___ No ___ Maybe ___

4. Proof of disability — Yes ___ No ___ Maybe ___

5. Reemployment obligations for employee — Yes ___ No ___ Maybe ___

6. Insurance continuation during excused absences — Yes ___ No ___ Maybe ___

PROFIT-SHARING PLANS

1. Current profit-sharing plans — Yes ___ No ___ Maybe ___

    A. Cash plans — Yes ___ No ___ Maybe ___
       (1) Defining net profits for purposes of cash plan — Yes ___ No ___ Maybe ___
       (2) Defining the distribution formula — Yes ___ No ___ Maybe ___
       (3) Frequency of distributing profit-sharing earnings — Yes ___ No ___ Maybe ___

    B. Wage dividend plans — Yes ___ No ___ Maybe ___
       (1) Defining net profits for purposes of wage dividend plan — Yes ___ No ___ Maybe ___
       (2) Defining the distribution formula — Yes ___ No ___ Maybe ___
       (3) Frequency of distributing profit-sharing earnings — Yes ___ No ___ Maybe ___

    C. Production-sharing or cost-savings plans — Yes ___ No ___ Maybe ___

2. Deferred profit-sharing plans — Yes ___ No ___ Maybe ___

    A. Defining "profit" in plan — Yes ___ No ___ Maybe ___
    B. Eligibility requirements — Yes ___ No ___ Maybe ___
    C. Percentage of profits which will be distributed — Yes ___ No ___ Maybe ___
    D. Description of distribution formula — Yes ___ No ___ Maybe ___
    E. How and when benefits will be distributed — Yes ___ No ___ Maybe ___
    F. Contributory or noncontributory plan — Yes ___ No ___ Maybe ___
    G. Description of how plan will be administered — Yes ___ No ___ Maybe ___

RETIREMENT PLANS

1. Type of funding arrangement — Yes ___ No ___ Maybe ___

    A. Group annuities — Yes ___ No ___ Maybe ___
    B. Individual policy — Yes ___ No ___ Maybe ___
    C. Group life retirement plan — Yes ___ No ___ Maybe ___
    D. Uninsured or self-administered plan — Yes ___ No ___ Maybe ___
    E. Deposit administration plan — Yes ___ No ___ Maybe ___
    F. Self-administered or insured combination plan — Yes ___ No ___ Maybe ___

2. Contributory or noncontributory plan   Yes ___ No ___ Maybe ___

3. Employee eligibility requirements   Yes ___ No ___ Maybe ___

4. Retirement age requirements   Yes ___ No ___ Maybe ___

5. Amount of retirement benefits   Yes ___ No ___ Maybe ___

6. Description of retirement benefit formulas Yes ___ No ___ Maybe ___

7. Vesting rights of employees   Yes ___ No ___ Maybe ___

8. Death and disability benefits   Yes ___ No ___ Maybe ___

BONUSES

1. Discretionary year-end and Christmas bonuses   Yes ___ No ___ Maybe ___

2. Nondiscretionary productive-incentive bonus plans   Yes ___ No ___ Maybe ___

   A. Method of paying overtime compensation on
      production and incentive-type bonuses   Yes ___ No ___ Maybe ___
   B. Incentive standards   Yes ___ No ___ Maybe ___

OTHER BENEFIT PLANS

1. Severance pay plan   Yes ___ No ___ Maybe ___

2. Unemployment insurance   Yes ___ No ___ Maybe ___

3. Workers' Compensation   Yes ___ No ___ Maybe ___

4. Social Security benefits and payments   Yes ___ No ___ Maybe ___

5. Physical examinations   Yes ___ No ___ Maybe ___

EMPLOYEE SERVICES, RECOGNITION, AND PRIVILEGES

1. Length of service awards   Yes ___ No ___ Maybe ___

2. Employee discounts   Yes ___ No ___ Maybe ___

3. Employee loans and advances   Yes ___ No ___ Maybe ___

4. Credit union   Yes ___ No ___ Maybe ___

5. Employee food services   Yes ___ No ___ Maybe ___

6. Employee counseling   Yes ___ No ___ Maybe ___

7. Financial aid for commuting employees   Yes ___ No ___ Maybe ___

8.	Medical services on the premises	Yes ___	No ___	Maybe ___
9.	Safety shoes	Yes ___	No ___	Maybe ___
10.	Recreation programs	Yes ___	No ___	Maybe ___
11.	Employee charge accounts	Yes ___	No ___	Maybe ___
12.	Employee uniforms	Yes ___	No ___	Maybe ___
13.	Charitable contributions	Yes ___	No ___	Maybe ___

Sample Policies: Paid Vacations _____

Sample Policy 1

After one (l) year of continuous service, all full-time employees receive twelve (12) vacation days per year—or one (1) day per month of service.

After five (5) years of continuous service, all full-time employees receive eighteen (18) vacation days per year—one and a half (1.5) vacation days per month worked.

After fifteen (15) years of continuous service, full-time employees receive twenty-one (21) vacation days each year—one and three-quarters (1.75) vacation days for each month worked.

After one year of continuous service, part-time employees working a regularly scheduled shift operation receive one (l) working shift day's vacation for each month worked, regardless of length of service.

Employees must work with the company twelve (12) consecutive months before they are credited with twelve (12) days' vacation and are eligible to take the vacation time. If new employees terminate at any time within the first twelve (12) months of joining the company they will not receive any vacation pay.

Those employees with up to five (5) years' service will be allowed to carry over no more than fifteen (15) days' accrued vacation into each fiscal year starting April 1. Those employees with over five (5) years' service will be allowed to carry over no more than twenty (20) days' accrued vacation time into each fiscal year starting April 1.

Employees will forfeit their excessive accumulated vacation days if they do not take them within this time period.

Employees who have transferred from either part-time to full-time, or vice-versa, will have their vacation allotment determined and adjusted on an individual basis.

Desired multiple day vacation requests must be submitted to the department manager as soon as possible. Approval for vacations will be based upon the production needs of the individual's department on a first-come first-serve basis.

Single-day vacation requests must be submitted to the department manager and approved at least two (2) working days in advance of the desired vacation day. Same-day vacation requests will not be honored.

Employees are allowed to use their vacation in either full-shift or half-shift increments only.

To receive earned vacation pay in advance, approved time sheets covering the vacation period must be submitted to Accounting at least two weeks before employees take their vacation. Employees will then be paid the day before they start their vacation. The paycheck covering the last workweek before the vacation period will be paid on the first Friday following employees' return to work. Vacation pay will not be advanced to cover vacation days in the second pay period of a split-week vacation.

In the event a company holiday falls within a vacation period, the holiday will not count as a vacation day.

Sample Policy 2

A person is entitled to one full week of vacation after he or she completes one year of full-time service. A person is entitled to two full weeks of paid vacation after two years of service, three weeks of vacation after five years of service, and four weeks of vacation after fifteen years of service.

A person who has been with the company as a full-time employee for less than one year is entitled to one day's paid vacation for each 10 weeks of regular employment prior to May 1. After a person is eligible to receive at least a full week's paid vacation, he or she becomes eligible for the normal increase in the amount of vacation he or she receives as outlined in the paragraph above.

If an employee quits voluntarily without giving the company at least one week's notice, he or she is not entitled to any paid vacation. If a person is discharged by the company, he or she is entitled to payment of any accrued vacation time.

A maximum of up to one full year's accrued vacation time may be carried over from one year to the next. This permits each person to hold some "contingency" vacation to allow for possible time off due to sickness, slow work when time off might be assigned, or for other personal reasons.

Vacations do not have to be taken during any specific time of the year, but all vacations must first be cleared through the individual's department supervisor. The supervisor is responsible for assuring that overlapping of vacations within the department does not occur if this might in any way interfere with that department's ability to perform its required assignments during any period.

Sample Policy 3

All vacation pay is at the employee's regular straight-time rate.

A day's vacation is eight hours, and a week's vacation is 40 hours.

Only regular employees may actually take a vacation, though time spent as a full-time probationary employee counts toward eligibility for vacation.

Vacations are earned in one year and taken in the next year, except for: (a) a new employee; (b) an employee who passes a service anniversary year (7, 15, or 24) and becomes eligible for an additional week; (c) an employee who, not more than once every five years, defers all or part of his vacation to the next year.

Vacation pay (in weekly increments only) will be given prior to the vacation itself if the employee requests it at least ten calendar days before the vacation is to begin.

Vacation Entitlement:

Service Requirement in Year of Hire	Days of Vacation
Hired between January 1 – May 15	1 day for each month's service between January 1 and May 31
Hired after May 15	No vacation entitlement
In year after hire	1 day for each month's service between June 1 of year of hire and May 31 of year after hire. Maximum of 10 days, minimum of 5 days.
2 - 6 years of service	10 days
7 - 14 years of service	15 days
15 - 23 years of service	20 days
24 years service and over	25 days

Choice of Vacation Period:

You will be granted vacation at the time you desire as far as is practical; however, length of service, number of employees off duty at one time, and work load will be taken into account in scheduling vacations, and the company shall make the final determination of vacation schedules.

Vacations are not cumulative. Any vacation must be taken during the calendar year in which you are entitled to take it. However, at intervals of not less than five years, you may, upon written request and with the approval of management, forego a portion of or all vacation in one calendar year and carry it over to the next year.

If you are hospitalized during vacation, your status may be changed from "vacation" to "sick leave" if you have any sick leave to draw upon. If you have no sick leave entitlement, you can elect to remain on vacation status until your vacation entitlement is exhausted or you can be placed on "off duty without pay" status.

For entitlement purposes at the beginning of employment, parts of a month worked are either counted as a full month or not counted at all. The 15th of the month, regardless of the particular month, is the midpoint. Thus, if hired on or before the 15th of the month, you would have the month counted; hired on the 16th or later, you would not have that month counted.

Sample Policy 4

(Name of company) believes that each regular, full-time employee should have a time of rest and relaxation each year. Vacation with pay is one of the ways we show our appreciation for your length of service and good work.

Regular, full-time employees will accrue vacation in accordance with the following schedule:

Length of Service	Paid Vacation
After one year	One week (five 8-hour days)
After two years	Two weeks (ten 8-hour days)
After five years	Three weeks (fifteen 8-hour days)
After ten years	Four weeks (twenty 8-hour days)

Insofar as possible, your supervisor will honor your request for vacation dates preferred. Should there be more than one request in a department for the same period of vacation time, employee seniority will take precedence. Except in the case of personal emergency, we ask that you not request vacation time to be taken in January and February, as these are the busiest months of the year.

Once vacation is earned, you must take at least one week of vacation as time away from work, although you may split this vacation week into days if you wish, with your supervisor's approval. However, after you have been employed for at least two years and have earned at least two weeks of paid vacation, you may opt to receive pay in lieu of time off for a maximum of one week of vacation. Additionally, providing at least one week of vacation has been taken as time off, you may carry remaining vacation days forward to be used in subsequent year(s).

Employees who resign and give at least two weeks' notice will be paid for all accumulated, unused vacation days, providing they leave the company in good standing.

Sample Policy 5

Regular, full-time employees will accrue vacation in accordance with the following schedule:

Length of Service	Paid Vacation
Upon first day of month following date of hire through one year of continuous, full-time employment	3.33 hours per month (1 week per year)
After one year and through ten years of continuous, full-time employment.	6.66 hours per month (2 weeks per year)
After ten years or more of continuous, full-time employment.	10.00 hours per month (3 weeks per year)

You may accumulate and carry over a maximum of 15 days of vacation. The accumulation period will be based on the company's fiscal year from July 1 to June 30. At June 30 of any given year, no more than 15 days of vacation can be carried over to the next fiscal year.

Vacation time off will be scheduled on consecutive days and will be paid at your applicable straight-time rate or salary earned. However, vacations may be split if arrangements are approved in advance by your supervisor.

Insofar as possible, your supervisor will honor your request for preferred vacation dates. Should there be more than one request in a department for the same period of vacation time, employee seniority will take precedence. Department heads will report all vacation requests to the human resource office.

Sample Policy 6

If you are like most of us, you look forward to a time of rest and relaxation each year. Vacation with pay is one of the ways we show our appreciation to you for your length of service and good work. Management encourages all employees to take their accrued vacation time.

At (name of company), vacation time is accrued, and taken, on a calendar year basis. Calendar year is defined as the year beginning each January 1 and ending the following December 31. Vacation time accrued during one calendar year is to be taken during the next calendar year.

The number of vacation days you will accrue during your first calendar year of employment will be computed by multiplying the number of working days left in the year at the time you are hired by a factor of .0385. The result is the number of vacation days you may take during the next calendar year. Fractions of days are rounded to the nearest half day.

The number of working days used in this computation is determined by counting the number of full weeks left in the year at the time you start work here, and multiplying this by 5. Holidays and partial weeks are disregarded in this count. The factor of .0385 has been arrived at by dividing the number of work days in a full work year (260). The result, .0385, is the amount of vacation days an employee earns for each day of a full work year.

The following examples will help you understand the computation:

Example 1: The date of hire is April 1

$$
\begin{array}{rl}
39 & = \text{no. of weeks left in the year} \\
\times\,5 & \\
\hline
195 & = \text{no. of working days left in the year} \\
\times\,.0385 & \\
\hline
7.5075 &
\end{array}
$$

This would be rounded to 7½ for the number of vacation days for the next year.

Example 2: The date of hire is August 3

$$
\begin{array}{rl}
21 & = \text{no. of weeks left in the year} \\
\times\,5 & \\
\hline
105 & = \text{no. of working days left in the year} \\
\times\,.0385 & \\
\hline
4.0425 &
\end{array}
$$

This would be rounded to 4 for the number of vacation days for the next year.

During your second calendar year of employment, and for each year thereafter until you have been employed for five continuous years, you will accrue two weeks paid vacation per year.

After you have been employed at our company for five years, you will receive, in addition to the two weeks vacation each year, an additional day of vacation for each year of employment that is in excess of five. The maximum number of additional days you will receive in this manner is ten, for a total of twenty days vacation per year after you have been employed fifteen years.

If your employment is terminated for any reason, either voluntarily or involuntarily, you will be paid for those vacation days that you accrued the previous calendar year but which you have not taken. You will not be paid for any vacation days you have accrued in the current calendar year.

Our customers employ all of us. Therefore, we must be guided by customer demands when we schedule vacations. Vacations must be scheduled in such a way that we can maintain suffic- ient manpower to serve our customers' needs.

You should make certain to schedule your vacation with your supervisor at least two weeks in advance of your requested vacation date. In the event of conflicting vacation requests within a department, the employee with the greater seniority will get first choice.

The normal vacation period is from May 1 through September 30. This does not mean that all vacations must be taken during this period. Vacations shall be in consecutive days. Split vaca- tions will be permitted only for earned vacation days beyond the two weeks of "normal vaca- tion," or with written approval by the president of the institution.

Sample Policy 7

Every regular full-time employee shall be entitled to a vacation, using the following guidelines:

1. Each regular full-time employee on the active payroll shall be eligible for paid vaca- tion in accordance with the following schedule after serving one full year of continu- ous work as a full-time employee:

Length of Service	Paid Vacation
After 1 year of continuous employment	1 week
After 3 years of continuous employment	2 weeks
After 12 years of continuous employment	3 weeks

2. During the first year of employment, you will earn vacation time on a prorated basis, commencing with the third month of full-time active service.

3. Production employees will have one week of vacation during the week of July 4 when the plant shuts down. Employees will be paid for their earned vacation hours

during this period at their regular rate for their number of hours of earned vacation, up to one week.

4. Employees are required to schedule their vacations for their additional week or two weeks with their supervisor at least two weeks in advance.

5. Following your first year of employment, your date of hire (bonus date) will be used for the purpose of computing your vacation entitlement.

6. Vacation time will not be allowed to be carried forward from one year to the next.

7. Those employees who give at least a one-week notice, in the event of resignation, will be entitled to pay for any credited and unused vacation.

Sample Policy 8

Vacation eligibility is determined as of July 1 each year. All "regular full-time" employees earn vacation with pay after six (6) months of employment.

Vacation is accrued as follows:

Amount of Service Prior to July 1	Amount of Days Vacation Eligible
Less than 6 months	0
6 months but less than 1 year	5
1 year	10
5 years	15
15 years	20
25 years	25

Vacation time must be taken within the calendar year. Vacation not taken by December 31 will be forfeited.

Receiving pay in lieu of taking vacation time off is not permitted.

The amount of vacation an employee is entitled to may be affected by time off the job. If an employee is off the job for 60 days or more, the amount of vacation time and pay he/she is eligible for will be reduced pro rata the following year.

Normally, employees should schedule their vacation time between July 1 and December 31 of each year. With prior approval of the immediate supervisor and department head concerned, however, an employee may elect to schedule all or part of his/her vacation prior to July 1— even though, in effect, the vacation is not earned until July 1.

Not less than one-half day of time off the job may be designated as vacation time.

Any employee who is dismissed for misconduct will not receive any accumulated vacation benefits.

Employees who leave the company voluntarily (resign) and give two (2) weeks' notice will be paid for any accumulated vacation time due them. Employees who leave without giving two weeks' notice will not be paid for accumulated vacation.

Sample Policies: Paid Holidays ———————————

Sample Policy 1

(Number of holidays) holiday days will be observed during the year as days off with pay:

(List holidays.)

If any of these holidays fall on Sunday, the following Monday will be observed; or if any of these holidays fall on Saturday, the preceding Friday will be observed.

If you are a regular full-time employee, you will be paid for eight hours at your regular basic rate for each holiday, provided you worked your scheduled shift immediately preceding and your scheduled shift immediately following the holiday. Regular part-time employees will be paid for the hours they would have worked had the day not been a holiday. Temporary employees are not eligible for holiday pay benefits unless they work on a company-observed holiday.

Holiday time off is considered as time worked in the computation of overtime.

If you are required to work on an observed company holiday, you will receive your holiday pay plus double (2×) your hourly rate for all hours worked on that holiday.

Should a holiday occur during your vacation period, an additional day of vacation will be allowed.

Sample Policy 2

These paid holidays are granted to all regular, full-time employees each year after thirty (30) working days of employment:

(List holidays.)

An employee will receive holiday pay provided he/she works the full day before and after the holiday. When a holiday occurs during a regularly scheduled vacation, the vacation will be extended an additional day and the employee will receive the holiday pay.

Employees paid on a salary basis will receive their regular salary for any week in which there is a recognized holiday.

Sample Policy 3

At (name of company), we have seven (7) holidays which will be considered paid holidays as follows:

New Year's Day	Thanksgiving Day
Good Friday	Day after Thanksgiving
Memorial Day	Christmas Day
Labor Day	

If one of these holidays falls on a nonworking day, a day off before or after the holiday will be granted at management's discretion.

To be eligible for holiday pay, employees must have been continuously employed at least sixty (60) calendar days before the holiday and must have worked in full their last scheduled work day before and the first scheduled work day after the holiday, unless their absence on either of such days has been excused by the Director of Personnel.

Holiday pay for salaried and hourly employees will amount to eight (8) hours at your regular straight-time rate. If you should have to work a holiday, you will receive your regular rate in addition to your holiday pay.

Sample Policy 4

We have six paid holidays which we observe as follows:

New Year's Day	Labor Day
Memorial Day	Thanksgiving Day
Independence Day	Christmas Day

Employees who have completed 30 days of full-time, continuous employment prior to the holiday will be eligible for holiday pay. For all hours worked on a holiday, an employee will be paid time and one-half the regular rate of pay, or compensatory time off will be given.

If a holiday falls on a Saturday or Sunday, a compensating day off on the preceding Friday or following Monday will be observed, or at the convenience of the company and the employee.

Should a holiday fall during an employee's vacation period, an additional day of vacation will be given at management's discretion.

Sample Policy 5

The following days shall be recognized as holidays for regular and probationary employees:

New Year's Day	Labor Day
President's Day (3rd Monday in February)	Thanksgiving Day
Good Friday	Day after Thanksgiving
Memorial Day (last Monday in May)	Christmas Eve
Independence Day	Christmas Day

When any holiday (except Christmas Eve) falls on Sunday, the following Monday shall be observed. When any holiday falls on Saturday, the preceding Friday will be observed. Employees whose regular schedule includes Saturday and/or Sunday shall observe all holidays, regardless of the day of the week, on the actual calendar day on which the holiday falls.

Christmas Eve shall be observed on the day on which it falls, with the following exceptions: when it falls on Friday, it shall be observed on the preceding Thursday; when it falls on a Saturday or Sunday, it shall be observed on the preceding Friday; and when it falls on a Wednesday, it shall be observed on Friday, December 26.

Holiday pay is eight hours of regular straight-time pay, regardless of the employee's regularly scheduled number of hours in a workday. If a nonexempt employee works on a holiday, he will be paid, in addition to holiday pay, pay for hours worked at the applicable rate.

Sample Policy 6

Our company recognizes certain days of religious and historic importance as holidays and pays employees for time off on these days in accordance with its special eligibility rules. There are twelve (12) regular, paid holidays each year.

Each "regular full-time" employee on active payroll is entitled to the following paid holidays:

- New Year's Day
- Good Friday
- Memorial Day
- Independence Day
- Labor Day
- Thanksgiving Day
- Friday after Thanksgiving
- Day before Christmas
- Christmas Day
- Employee's Personal Day
- Floating Holiday (2)

Holiday pay is only received by those employees who work or are paid for the full day before and full day after a given holiday(s).

If a holiday falls on Saturday, the company may designate Friday to accommodate the paid work day off. Falling on a Sunday, the holiday may be designated as Monday. Whenever one of these conditions occur, you will be notified in advance to allow for proper planning.

Nonexempt employees working a scheduled designated holiday will be paid for the holiday—regular eight (8) hour rate—plus time and one-half for those actual hours worked. Exempt employees will be allowed a different day off with pay.

"Temporary" and part-time employees are *not* eligible for holiday pay. Each year the management committee designates what specific days will be taken as "floating holidays."

Sample Policies: Group Health Insurance _____

Sample Policy 1

(Name of company) is pleased to provide regular, full-time employees with one of the most comprehensive group insurance programs available today. Our program includes group life, accidental death and dismemberment, health, dental, and long-term disability insurance.

The company pays a significant portion of your group insurance coverage, with your portion being deducted from your paycheck on your written authorization.

Special brochures outlining the above plans will be made available to you. Your supervisor will discuss our group insurance program with you during your orientation program and will be available to assist you with enrollment material and determine your costs for your selected coverages.

You will be eligible to participate in the group insurance plans following a full calendar month of continuous employment.

Options for continued health insurance coverage under the COBRA Act are available for up to 18 months in the event of your resignation, reduction of hours, layoff, termination (except where termination results from gross misconduct), and for up to 36 months for your spouse and/or dependent children in the event of your death, divorce, or separation, coverage under Medicare, or a covered child ceases to be a dependent as defined in the plan. Should you or any covered dependent be disabled at the time of your termination (or reduction in hours), coverage would be extended to 29 months rather than 18 months. Also, if you or any covered dependent have a preexisting condition which would not be covered by a future plan, continuation coverage will still be available for the 18- or 36-month period as explained above, even though coverage under the new plan already exists. The cost of coverage would be the responsibility of the employee/spouse or dependent child. You will be notified of your rights for continued health coverage in the event you leave the company. You must notify us if an event occurs which would enable your spouse and/or dependent children to exercise their COBRA rights.

We will provide you with specific details of your rights under COBRA in a separate letter.

Sample Policy 2

All full-time regular and part-time regular employees and their eligible dependents are covered by our company's group hospitalization insurance program. Coverage for eligible employees is effective on the first day of employment.

Under our plan, semiprivate hospital accommodations are covered in full for 120 days.

Coverage includes, among other things, reasonable and customary charges for room and board; services, supplies, and equipment related to X-ray, laboratory, and pathological examinations; drugs and medicines for use in the hospital; and any additional medical services and supplies customarily provided by the hospital.

The cost to provide this benefit for you and your eligible dependents is currently paid completely by the company.

Hospitalization insurance coverage terminates on the date of your termination from the company's employ. (Please review company policy, set forth in this handbook, regarding continuing hospitalization benefits after termination of employment.)

For further details regarding hospitalization coverage, consult our insurance booklet entitled, "Your Hospitalization Benefits" or contact the human resources department.

Sample Policy 3

After six months of continuous, full-time employment, you will be eligible for coverage under our group health insurance and life insurance plans. The company pays for 50 percent of the cost of employee coverage, as well as 50 percent of the cost of dependent coverage; you may arrange to pay for the balance of individual or dependent coverage through a payroll deduction. Please see the Office Manager to enroll in the group insurance plans and to obtain additional information about your insurance benefits.

Sample Policy 4

Group health insurance for regular, full-time employees goes into effect the first day of the policy month after the employees have been with the company for thirty (30) consecutive calendar days since their last date of hire. The company pays the entire cost for health coverage for all full-time employees. Dependent coverage is available with the employee paying the entire added cost. Employees desiring dependent coverage should contact the personnel office so that the necessary application forms and payroll deduction authorizations can be completed.

Under certain circumstances, continued health insurance may be available to terminated or laid-off employees, employees whose hours are reduced below plan minimums, spouses and dependents of former employees, former spouses of employees, spouses of former employees who are eligible for Medicare, and dependent children who otherwise become ineligible for coverage under our group medical plan. In each case, the affected employee is responsible for the entire cost of this insurance, plus a two (2) percent administration fee. This coverage is not available to those who are discharged for gross misconduct, such as dishonest, disorderly, or disruptive acts. Additional details on the coverage available and required application materials are available from the personnel office.

Sample Policy 5

All full-time regular and part-time regular employees and their eligible dependents are eligible to participate in our group basic surgical and major medical insurance program. Coverage for eligible employees is effective on the first day of employment.

After a deductible of $150 per individual ($400 per family) per calendar year is satisfied, our plan pays 80 percent of reasonable and customary charges for the first $3,000 of covered expenses incurred for medical care and treatment, including surgery and prescriptions, and 100 percent of reasonable and customary charges for the balance of covered expenses incurred in that calendar year. Expenses incurred in a calendar year for, or in connection with, mental illness on an out-patient basis (e.g., visits to a psychiatrist) are reimbursed at the rate of 50 percent of actual expenses incurred to a maximum of $50 per visit.

The annual benefit maximum payable under our major medical plan for outpatient mental illness coverage is $1,500 per person. The lifetime benefit maximum payable under our major medical plan for all covered services—with the exception of out-patient mental illness benefits—is unlimited. The cost to provide basic surgical and major medical benefits for you and your eligible dependents is currently paid completely by the company.

Benefits under this plan terminate on the date your employment with the company terminates. (Please review company policy, set forth in this handbook, regarding continuing group health insurance benefits after termination of employment.)

For further details regarding basic surgical and major medical benefit coverage, see your insurance booklet or contact the Human Resources Department.

Sample Policy 6

Short-Term Disability Insurance—Our company provides employees with short-term disability insurance benefits, in accordance with applicable state laws. These benefits are funded by both employee and company contributions. Required employee contributions are automatically withheld from employees' paychecks.

Under this program, benefits are payable for non-work-related injuries or illnesses. They normally begin after seven days of disability and generally are payable for up to a maximum of twenty-six weeks. Payments to which you may be entitled through our salary continuation plan are reduced by any short-term disability benefits received. The amount of benefits payable under our short-term disability plan varies according to state law.

Please consult with our Human Resources Department for further details regarding short-term disability insurance benefits.

Long-Term Disability Insurance—Our company provides all full-time regular employees with long-term disability (LTD) insurance benefits. Coverage for eligible employees is effective on the first day of employment.

Under this program, employees who are disabled for more than 180 days because of injury or sickness (in accordance with the definition of "disability" specified in our insurance booklet regarding LTD and master insurance contract) are eligible to receive a benefit equivalent to 60 percent of their basic monthly earnings to a maximum benefit of $4,000 per month (less other income benefits). Benefits continue for as long as your qualifying disability continues in accordance with the maximum benefit periods specified in our master insurance contract.

The cost to provide LTD benefits is currently paid completely by the company.

Coverage under this plan normally terminates on the date your employment with the company terminates. If, however, you are receiving LTD benefits at the time of your termination, these benefits continue for as long as your qualifying disability continues, as previously noted.

For further details regarding LTD coverage, see your insurance booklet or contact the Human Resources Department.

Sample Policy 7

You are eligible for the medical plan if you are a full-time regular employee. If you wish, your dependents may also be covered. Your eligible dependents are your spouse and your unmarried dependent children until the end of the calendar month in which they reach age 23. "Children" includes legally adopted children, and foster and stepchildren who live in your home.

Coverage for a physically handicapped or mentally retarded child, incapable of self-support, may be continued indefinitely—if the child was enrolled for this coverage and the handicap or retardation existed before his or her 23rd birthday. To maintain this coverage for your child after age 23, you must submit satisfactory evidence of the child's incapacity through your personnel department to the claims paying agent for the Plan. Proof must be submitted no later than 31 days after the end of the month in which the child reaches age 23.

An individual who is eligible for the plan as an employee cannot also be covered as a dependent.

Cost—The company pays the full cost of these medical plan benefits for you. You contribute only $3 a month for your dependents' medical plan coverage—no matter how many dependents are enrolled. In addition, any dependents who are enrolled for medical plan coverage will be entitled to receive benefits under the dental plan as well.

How to Enroll—To join the plan, you will be asked to complete an enrollment form on which you:

- name your dependents; and
- authorize the company to deduct your contributions, if any, from your pay.

If you do not enroll yourself or your dependents on the date you are hired, you may enroll for benefits at a later date.

If you want to make any changes in the type of coverage you have, for example, to add a newborn child or a new spouse, you should notify the personnel department within 30 days from the effective date of change in status.

Sample Policy 8

The Group Insurance Program for all employees will be specified in detail in the applicable policies on life insurance, AD&D insurance, accident insurance, and long-term disability insurance. These insurances and coverages are subject to the terms, conditions, and limitations of the selected insurance carriers, and the original application and master contract. They are summarized as follows:

BASIC LIFE: Amount equal to annual base wage on November 1, each year rounded to the next even $5,000 (e.g., $25,000, $30,000, $35,000, etc.). This is effective on the first of the month following end of probationary period. Subject to reduction at age 65, which complies with the ADEA guidelines. Policy with carrier will include a disability waiver of premium benefit. Coverage terminates one month after the end of month of layoff, personal leave of absence, or termination. 100 percent paid by the company.

BASIC AD&D: Amount equal to basic life effective first of the month following end of probationary period. Subject to reduction at age 65. Coverage terminates at end of month of layoff, personal leave of absence, or termination. 100 percent paid by the company.

VOLUNTARY TERM LIFE: Amount available in $10,000 or $25,000 increments (according to the carrier requirements) up to $250,000 effective the first of the month following end of probationary period. Insurance carrier may require insurance to be contingent upon completion of underwriting information (medical questions, etc.) to the satisfaction of the insurance carrier. Policy effective upon acceptance by carrier. Spouse coverage available up to $100,000, child coverage up to $2,000. Policy with carrier will include a disability waiver of premium benefit. Coverage terminates at end of month of layoff, personal leave of absence, or termination. Employees on medical leave may pay for and retain voluntary term life coverage. 100 percent paid by employee.

VOLUNTARY AD&D: Amount available equal to $100,000/$150,000/$250,000 for employee, effective the first of the month following end of probationary period. Spouse eligible for 40 percent and child 10 percent of employee amount. Spouse without child eligible for 50 percent, child without spouse 15 percent of employee amount. Coverage terminates at end of month of layoff, personal leave of absence, or termination. Employees on medical leave may pay for and retain voluntary AD&D coverage. 100 percent paid by employee.

SHORT-TERM DISABILITY BENEFITS: Available to the employee only. Eligibility is the first of the month following completion of employee's probationary period. Limited to 66 percent of regular weekly base wages or monthly base salary for 40 hours up to a maximum monthly benefit of $3,000. Maximum benefit period will be 26 weeks. Eligible, covered employees will pay a contributory premium of one-half of one percent (1/2 of 1 percent) of the regular weekly wages for 40 hours. Benefits begin on the eighth day of disability (or upon the first day of hospitalization or surgical procedure if earlier).

LONG-TERM DISABILITY BENEFITS: Available to the employee only. Eligibility is the first of the month following completion of employee's probationary period. Limited to 66 percent of regular monthly base wages or salary for 40 hours to a maximum monthly benefit of $3,000. Maximum period of benefits will continue up to 65 years of age. The 180 days of disability is defined in the Insurance Contract. Eligible, covered employees will pay a contributory premium of one-half of one percent (1/2 of 1 percent) of the individual's regular weekly wages for 40 hours.

The details of the Healthcare Plan for all employees are specified in the official Plan Document (herein called the Plan) and is incorporated by reference to this labor agreement. The Healthcare Plan certifies that any employee or dependent who meets the eligibility requirements is eligible for coverage under provisions of the Plan Document covering benefits relative to medical; nervous and mental; alcohol and substance abuse; dental; vision; short-term disability; and Wellness Program.

ADMINISTRATION OF NEW GROUP HEALTH INSURANCE PROGRAM: The company shall arrange for administration of the new healthcare insurance program through the preferred provider organization and an employee assistance program. Eligibility for coverages of the healthcare benefits are described in the Plan Document. The benefits of the group health and group life insurance programs will be applicable only to the eligible employees and their dependents as described in the Certificate of Coverage issued by the insurance companies and the Plan Sponsor.

CONTRIBUTORY EMPLOYEE PREMIUMS: Effective the first pay period of the insurance plan year, eligible covered employees with dependents will pay contributory premium of one percent (1 percent) of their regular weekly straight-time wages or monthly base salary. Eligible single covered employees will pay a contributory premium of one-half of one percent ($1/2$ of 1 percent) of their regular weekly straight-time wages or monthly base salary.

Sample Policies: Group Life Insurance _____

Sample Policy 1
The company offers a contributory life insurance plan for each employee. For details of your life insurance coverage, please see the information provided you upon enrollment. Should you desire to change beneficiaries, please notify the Payroll Department.

Sample Policy 2
Every regular, full-time employee is given a life insurance policy, the entire cost of which is paid for by the company. This policy goes into effect the first day of the policy month after the employee has been with the company for thirty (30) consecutive calendar days since the date of hire.

Life insurance coverage is available to employees' dependents, provided the dependents are also covered by the company's group health insurance coverage. The entire cost of this dependent life insurance coverage is paid for by the employee.

The life insurance policy carries conversion privileges should an employee become separated from the company for any reason other than gross misconduct. At the time of separation, an employee may request the necessary forms to complete this transaction. Converting the insurance will be the employee's responsibility.

Sample Policy 3
The company makes available to all regular full-time employees life insurance for you and group medical insurance protection for you and your family. You will be eligible to participate from the first of the month following 60 days after the end of the month in which you were hired. The company shares in the cost of this coverage, and your portion of the required premium may be deducted from your paycheck upon your written authorization. Details of these benefits including deductibles, coinsurance, and conversion privileges in the event you terminate employment are available from Personnel when you become eligible.

Sample Policy 4
All full-time regular employees are eligible to participate in ABC's life insurance program. Coverage under this program is available for employees only; dependent coverage is not available. Coverage for eligible employees is effective on the first day of employment.

Under this program, you are covered by a life insurance benefit at twice your annual base salary. Additional coverage for the same amount is provided in the event of accidental death or dismemberment. Currently, the cost to provide this benefit is paid completely by the company. Life insurance benefits terminate on the date your employment with the company terminates.

For further details regarding life insurance benefits, see your group insurance booklet or contact the Human Resources Department.

Sample Policy 5

Your life insurance plan is designed to provide valuable financial protection for you and your family and is provided through a contract with an insurance company. You are automatically covered for Basic Life Insurance—at no cost to you—and can purchase an additional amount of Basic Contributory Life Insurance determined by your annual salary.

The Basic Plan also automatically provides Accidental Death and Dismemberment (AD&D) Insurance. This coverage pays benefits in addition to your Basic Life Insurance if your death is accidental or if you suffer loss of sight or limb. If enrolled in the Basic Contributory Life/AD&D program, you may also elect further coverage under the Supplemental Life Only program.

The company reserves the right to modify or cancel features of the life insurance plan from time to time, whether applicable to employees or retirees.

Insurance Amounts—The company provides Basic Life and AD&D insurance equal to your annual salary, rounded to the nearest higher thousand dollars or $10,000, whichever is greater, at no cost to you. You may elect to purchase, through payroll deductions, additional Basic Life and AD&D insurance. The total Basic Life and AD&D coverage, both noncontributory and contributory, will equal twice your annual salary rounded to the next higher thousand dollars. If you participate in the Basic Contributory Insurance, you may enroll in the Supplemental Life Only program for an additional one times your annual salary rounded to the next higher thousand dollars.

Annual Salary	Basic Life & AD&D (Paid by Company)	Basic Contributory Life & AD&D (Paid by Employee)	Supplemental Life Only (Paid by Employee)	Total Coverage
$ 8,235	$10,000	$ 7,000	$ 9,000	$26,000
	10,000	7,000	—	17,000
14,950	15,000	15,000	15,000	45,000
	15,000	15,000	—	30,000
25,000	25,000	25,000	25,000	75,000
	25,000	25,000	—	50,000
27,352	28,000	27,000	28,000	83,000
	28,000	27,000	—	55,000

If your salary increases make you eligible for more life insurance, the increased amount will be effective on the date your salary changes, if you are actively at work on that day. Otherwise, your coverage will change on the day you return to active work. This increase in coverage is applicable to your Basic Noncontributory Life/AD&D as well as your Basic Contributory Life/AD&D and your Supplemental Life Only coverage.

Cost—The cost of your Noncontributory Life and AD&D insurance is paid in full by the company. If you elect Basic Contributory Life/AD&D insurance, you pay, through payroll deductions, a rate for each $1,000 of additional insurance. If you are enrolled in the Basic Contributory plan, you may elect Supplemental Life Only coverage for an additional cost based on your age. Rates are based on the actual claims experienced under the plan(s); therefore, your contribution toward coverage may change in the future. If a change is to be made, notice of the contribution required thereafter will be given to all enrolled participants. You may obtain the current rates for the Basic Contributory Life/AD&D and Supplemental Life Only coverage from your local Personnel Department.

Sample Policies: Dental Insurance _____

Sample Policy 1

All full-time regular and part-time regular employees and their eligible dependents are eligible to participate in our group dental insurance program. Coverage for eligible employees is effective on the first day of employment.

After a deductible of $100 per individual ($300 per family) per calendar year is satisfied, our plan pays 80 percent of reasonable and customary charges for covered diagnostic and preventive services, including oral examinations, X-rays, cleaning and scaling of teeth and fillings, and 50 percent of reasonable and customary charges for covered major dental services, such as root canal therapy, crowns, bridges, and orthodontics.

The maximum annual benefit payable under our dental plan is $1,200 per person.

The cost to provide dental benefits for you and your eligible dependents is currently paid completely by the company.

Benefits under this plan terminate on the date your employment with the company terminates. (Please review our policy, set forth in this handbook, regarding continuing group health insurance benefits after termination of employment.)

For further details regarding dental coverage, see your insurance booklet or contact the Human Resources Department.

Sample Policy 2

Your dental plan is designed to encourage prevention of serious dental problems by helping you pay the cost of routine diagnostic and preventive care, as well as to help pay the expense of major dental repairs or replacement of teeth when needed. Moreover, you and your eligible dependents are covered by this valuable plan for the same low cost described under the medical plan.

Eligibility—You are eligible for this dental plan if you are a full-time regular employee. Your eligible dependents are also entitled to receive benefits under the dental plan, provided they are enrolled for coverage under the medical plan as well. Eligible dependents are your spouse and your unmarried dependent children until the end of the calendar year in which they reach age 23. "Children" includes legally adopted children and stepchildren who live in your home.

Coverage for a physically handicapped or mentally retarded child, incapable of self-support, may be continued indefinitely if the child was enrolled for this coverage and the handicap or retardation existed before his or her 23rd birthday. To maintain this coverage for your child after age 23, you must submit satisfactory evidence of the child's incapacity through your personnel department to the claims paying agent for the plan. Proof must be submitted no later than 31 days after the end of the month in which the child reaches age 23.

An individual who is eligible for this plan as an employee of the company cannot also be covered as a dependent.

Cost—The company pays the full cost of the dental plan for you. Any dependents who are enrolled for coverage under the medical plan are entitled to coverage under this plan. However, the company reserves the right to alter these as well as the other arrangements of the dental plan.

How to Enroll—If you are eligible, all you need to do is complete the enrollment card given to you by the Personnel Department.

When Coverage Begins—Coverage begins the first day of the month following or coincident with employment. If you are eligible for coverage and at work on the date coverage is effective, it begins immediately. If you are eligible but absent on the effective date, coverage begins on the first day you return to active employment.

Each dependent will be covered beginning with the latter of these dates:

- the day on which your coverage begins, or
- the date that person becomes a dependent as defined.

How the Plan Works—The dental plan will help pay the reasonable and customary charges of covered services provided in three broad categories:

- diagnostic and preventive services;
- other basic services; and
- major services . . . while covered and in connection with nonoccupational disease or defect, or expenses resulting from nonoccupational accident causing injury to teeth.

"Reasonable and customary" means the fee regularly charged patients for the same or similar procedure based on the prevailing rate in your area.

In each calendar year, the dental plan pays:

- 100% of the reasonable and customary charges for diagnostic and preventive services
- 80% of the reasonable and customary charges for other basic services, and
- 50% of the reasonable and customary charges for major services after you satisfy the deductible

Maximum Dental Benefits—The plan pays for you and each covered dependent a yearly maximum benefit of $1,000, with a total lifetime maximum benefit of $10,000 and separate lifetime maximum orthodontia benefit of $750.

The Deductible—No deductible is required for diagnostic, preventive, and other basic services.

A $25 deductible for major services, those covered by the 50 percent coinsurance feature, applies separately to you and each of your covered dependents once in each calendar year, with a maximum of 3 deductibles per family.

Sample Policies: Profit-Sharing Plans _____

Sample Policy 1

An excellent Profit-Sharing Plan is available to all full-time employees. You will automatically become eligible for profit sharing as of July in any year providing you were employed in the year prior and meet all normal qualifications. This plan will amount to tens of thousands of dollars for people who make (name of company) a career. The nice part is that it requires your best effort and not a dime out of your paycheck.

Sample Policy 2

(Name of company) prides itself on being able to provide employees with a share of the profits because our employees are the ones who make our business profitable.

At the end of each year, the company places a portion of its profits for the year into the profit-sharing fund. These profits are then allocated to the accounts of the participating employees in proportion to what they earned during the year.

Employees who participate in the company's profit-sharing/retirement plan accrue ownership of the profits in their accounts (a process called "vesting") with each year of service to the company. A complete copy of the vesting schedule and more information on the plan is available from the President of the corporation.

The growth of the profit-sharing/retirement plan depends on the efforts of all of the company's employees, including you. As you give more effort to accomplishing your work more quickly, more accurately, and with less waste, you make possible the growth of all participants' profit-sharing/retirement plan accounts.

Sample Policy 3

Your paycheck is only a part of your real income at our company. Your profit-sharing–retirement plan gives you a share in the profits of our business without your having to invest a single penny. Your profit-sharing plan will give you a substantial sum of money—up to many thousands of dollars if you remain with our company over a period of time. Your company contributes a part of its net profit each year which is credited to eligible employees in proportion to their earnings and years of service.

There is nothing mysterious about profit. We receive money for selling our tires and automotive services plus related accessories. Most of the money we earn is used to pay wages and salaries to our employees. We also use a lot of money we earn for new equipment, maintenance, and many other necessary expenses. What is left is *profit.* Then, a very large part of this profit is paid to our state and federal government in taxes.

The entire cost of your profit-sharing–retirement is paid for by your company. No employee is required to pay a single penny for the privilege of sharing in your company profits.

Sample Policies: 401(k) Plans _____

Sample Policy

We have established a 401(k) savings plan that is available to all regular employees who have completed a minimum of six months of employment. The purpose of the plan is to encourage eligible employees to save on a pretax basis and to build a financial reserve for retirement.

Under the plan, eligible employees may elect to have the company withhold between 1 percent and 15 percent of their gross compensation through payroll deductions (to a maximum of $7,000 per year adjusted by the IRS for inflation) and contribute that amount to the plan as a savings contribution. Employees may suspend their contributions at any time and may also increase or decrease the amount of their contributions as of the first day of any calendar quarter by completing a 401(k) contribution form, available from our Human Resources Department. Withdrawals from the plan are permitted once an employee has attained age fifty-nine and one-half or in the event of financial hardship as defined in the plan.

The money contributed by employees is held and invested by the plan's trustees. The value of each employee's account at retirement depends on a number of factors, such as how long an employee has been a member of the plan, how much the employee has contributed, and investment gains.

Once you are eligible to participate in the plan, you receive our booklet entitled "401(k) Savings Plan," describing the plan in more detail.

Questions regarding our 401(k) plan should be directed to the Human Resources Department.

Sample Policies: Unemployment Insurance _____

Sample Policy 1

The purpose of unemployment insurance is to provide financial assistance for workers who lose their jobs and remain unemployed through no fault of their own. An employee may also be eligible for payments through the company's Layoff Allowance Plan, which is described in your protection manual.

Sample Policy 2

Your company pays the entire cost of unemployment insurance. Its purpose is to provide temporary income for workers when, through no fault of their own, they have lost their jobs. They must have earned a certain amount in covered employment and be willing and able to work in order to receive unemployment benefits.

Sample Policy 3

The entire premium for this employment security insurance is also paid by the company. It provides a weekly income for those who may be laid off. The amount of this income varies with the individual and state in which he/she resides because it is based upon average earnings. The compensation is administered by your state government. For this reason eligibility and the amount of benefits that you may receive under this program are specified by state law.

Sample Policies: Workers' Compensation _____

Sample Policy 1

The company pays 100 percent of the premiums on insurance provided by the state Workers' Compensation Act. This law was designed to provide you with benefits for any injury which you receive arising out of your work with the company. Under the provision of the law, if you are injured while at work for the company, this injury must be reported at once to your supervisor, no matter how slight it might seem. The supervisor will then see that you receive proper medical services. It is for your benefit and also the company's benefit that all injuries be reported.

The company will pay for all time lost prior to the time that workers' compensation benefits take effect. Workers' compensation benefits are determined by law and are based on a percentage of your weekly wages.

Sample Policy 2

If you should be injured at work, we provide Workers' Compensation insurance to cover your accident or injury. Any on-the-job injury must be reported to your supervisor as soon as it occurs.

If, by a doctor's recommendation, you must miss work because of a work-related injury, notify your supervisor. You may be eligible to receive weekly Workers' Compensation payments and medical treatment at no cost to you.

Sample Policy 3

While you are working for (name of company), you are automatically covered by Workers' Compensation Insurance which is paid by the company. This insurance coverage provides benefits to any employee who may be injured as a result of employment requirements.

Under the rights and benefits established in the provision of the Workers' Compensation Act: IT IS ESSENTIAL THAT YOU REPORT TO YOUR SUPERVISOR PROMPTLY ANY INJURY, NO MATTER HOW MINOR IT MAY APPEAR AT THE TIME.

It is a law for your protection that the (state) Industrial Commission investigates any accident which causes time lost from work, and this commission must pass upon all benefits and make settlements that meet the requirements of the law.

You need no one to represent you to get what is due you under the law. You do not have to be involved in any expense to collect benefits provided for you under the Workers' Compensation Act. Your supervisor, upon request, will provide you with a copy of the law so that you may be fully informed of your rights and benefits.

The Safety Rules of our company are designed with the specific purpose of trying to help you avoid injury, suffering, and loss of time on the job, and to help you avoid having to call on Workers' Compensation Insurance. However, all accidents should be reported to your supervisor so that you may be assured of being properly covered in the event of emergency.

Sample Policy 4

To provide for payment of your medical expenses and for partial salary continuation in the event of a work-related accident or illness, you are covered by workers' compensation insurance. The amount of benefits payable and the duration of payment depend upon the nature of your injury or illness. In general, however, all medical expenses incurred in connection with an injury or illness are paid in full, and partial salary payments are provided beginning with the fourth consecutive day of your absence from work.

If you are injured or become ill on the job, you must immediately report such injury or illness to your supervisor, Human Resources, or the Medical Department. This ensures that the company can assist you in obtaining appropriate medical treatment. Your failure to follow this procedure may result in the appropriate workers' compensation report not being filed in accordance with the law, which may consequently jeopardize your right to benefits in connection with the injury or illness.

Questions regarding workers' compensation insurance should be directed to the Human Resources Department.

Sample Policy 5

In compliance with the Workers' Compensation Act, the company carries insurance which provides benefits to any employee who is injured or suffers an occupational disease in the course of and arising out of employment with the company. Income is also provided to help defray medical and hospital expenses, or a death benefit may be paid in the case of fatality occurring while at work. Disabilities are also compensated for in accordance with provisions of the Workers' Compensation Act. The cost of this protection is borne entirely by the company.

Sample Policy 6

You are automatically covered by workers' compensation insurance from the day you start to work. The company pays the full premium. The policy covers injuries resulting from accidents while on the job. Benefits include reasonable medical expenses, weekly benefits after seven (7) days, compensation for total or partial permanent disability, and death benefits.

Anyone who engages in any other employment while on leave for a work-related injury will be terminated.

Sample Policies: Social Security Benefits and Payments

Sample Policy 1

Under the federal Social Security Act, an amount is deducted from your pay each payday to cover Social Security benefits.

This money and an equal amount paid by the company is turned over to the federal government to establish a fund, which in some cases provides for family benefits if you die before age 65, or monthly payments to you upon reaching 65 (or later, if born after 1937), or upon becoming disabled. Your spouse, upon reaching age 65, would usually receive an amount equal to one-half of your benefits. These benefits are in addition to those available to you under the company's retirement plan.

Further information concerning the Social Security Act may be obtained from the local Social Security office and from your Human Resources Department.

Sample Policy 2

Federal Social Security provides a variety of benefits, including retirement income, death benefits, disability benefits, and monthly income payments for certain dependent survivors of covered employees. A percentage of your gross earnings is deducted as your contribution for this protection. The company contributes an amount established by federal law. Normally, you will be eligible to receive a monthly income from Social Security when you retire or in the event that you become totally or permanently disabled.

Sample Policy 3

The payment of Federal Retirement Benefits and Medicare Benefits under the Social Security Act is made by you and the company.

Normally, you will be eligible to receive a monthly income from Social Security when you retire at age 62 or older or become totally and permanently disabled.

The company matches your contribution to Social Security and Medicare dollar for dollar and thereby pays one-half ($1/2$) of the cost of your Retirement and Medicare Benefits under Social Security.

Sample Policies: Length of Service Awards _____

Sample Policy 1
The company recognizes years of service by presenting service awards to its employees. You will receive your first award after five years of employment. Successive awards are given on the anniversary of each five years of employment thereafter.

The service awards are available in several different forms of attractive jewelry and merchandise items. You will be given an opportunity to select the type you prefer.

Sample Policy 2
The company proudly recognizes the service our employees give to the company and our community each year. We are very proud of our employees, especially those who have been with us for a long time. So you may also convey to your friends and neighbors your years of service with the company, we give handsome service awards upon completion of 5, 10, 15, 20, 25, 30, and 35 years of service.

Sample Policy 3
The company recognizes the continuous service of its employees with appropriate awards. These awards are presented to employees upon completion of ten years of service and then upon successive five-year anniversaries.

For additional details about these benefits and other personnel policies, employees should check with their immediate supervisor who will review the appropriate Personnel Policy/Procedure with those concerned.

Sample Policies: Employee Loans and Advances _____

Sample Policy 1

The company strongly believes that each individual should be able to handle his or her own financial affairs. The company also recognizes, however, that emergencies do occur when a person may need a loan for a valid purpose. The company may, in infrequent instances, lend money to an employee who has a just cause for such a loan. All loans must be repaid through payroll deductions not to exceed 26 weeks.

Sample Policy 2

The policy of (name of company) prohibits making personal loans or advances. It disturbs fellow employees to be asked to loan another employee money. By asking for a loan from co-workers, the employee puts his/her co-workers in the position of feeling obligated to do so because they work side by side with the employee. In most cases, co-workers cannot make the loan and hard feelings develop. Because of this, (name of company) prohibits loan requests among employees.

Sample Policy 3

(Name of company) does not advance money to employees between paydays. The only exception is vacation check advances which are prepared for those employees requesting them.

Sample Policy 4

We are not in the position to grant cash advances; however, we understand that emergencies do arise. In an emergency situation, $20 company loans will be available. No more than one loan in a 90-day period will be permitted. You will be required to sign for any company loans. For your benefit, we have a Credit Union for greater needs.

Sample Policies: Credit Union

Sample Policy 1
One of the many advantages of working at our company is the opportunity to join the Credit Union, which is a means of saving and borrowing money at preferred rates. You may sign up for convenient payroll deductions for the amount you desire. The Personnel Department will provide you with information on the Credit Union and the necessary forms if you wish to join.

Our company provides the opportunity for employees to participate in a credit union at most facilities. Since the Credit Union may vary from site to site, information regarding specific services, hours of operation, etc., is available from your local Credit Union.

Sample Policy 2
Our employees' credit union is an employee organization. All employees are eligible for membership and are encouraged to save regularly through payroll deduction. Applications for loans are accepted from member employees after they have completed their tryout period. The employees' credit union is here to help you—not make a profit on you. The people who help operate the employees' credit union are experienced in financial and credit policies and can give you honest and impartial advice if you have a question or concern. You are invited to do all your savings and borrowing at your employees' credit union.

Sample Policy 3
While the employees' credit union is a nonprofit organization that maintains low-interest rates on loans, it also pays dividends on the savings of its members. Employees may apply for loans or arrange for savings accounts by calling the credit union office. Savings may be withdrawn as desired, although notice is required. Employee loans may be made on collateral such as your home, automobile, or upon the basis of cosigners from other company employees. Our payroll department will make deductions of stipulated amounts from paychecks and forward the money to your credit union.

Sample Policies: Employee Food Services ⸻

Sample Policy 1

Our company is proud to make available to its employees a convenient cafeteria which provides hot meals at reasonable costs. Vending machines are also provided for meal and break periods. Please keep these areas clean so everyone may continue to enjoy them. When you leave the cafeteria, please place your trash in the containers provided.

Sample Policy 2

In our company's effort to assist our employees in promoting wellness in the workplace, our vending machines will not contain junk foods or tobacco products. We will carefully monitor all vending machines to be certain they are kept fully supplied with fresh food products and a good variety of beverages that will meet the needs of a majority of our employees on all shifts.

Sample Policy 3

Our company is pleased to provide hot food cafeteria facilities for employees to use at meal and rest periods, as well as before the start of each shift. Beverages, sandwiches, hot meals, and pastries are available at less than cost because of our company's subsidizing this employee benefit service.

Vending machines have also been placed in the cafeteria for your convenience. These machines are intended to provide refreshments for employees during scheduled breaks and lunch periods. Please help maintain the cleanliness of our cafeteria and vending areas so everyone will enjoy their meal and rest periods.

Sample Policies: Employee Counseling ⎯⎯⎯⎯⎯⎯⎯⎯⎯

Sample Policy 1

You cannot be happy or do your best work if personal problems are worrying you. The company recognizes that professional counseling can help an individual through those difficult times of marital and family problems, financial or legal problems, stress, drug or alcohol abuse, emotional conflicts, and other personal problems. We therefore have an Employee Counseling Service available for all employees, spouses, and dependent children under 19 (25 if a full-time student).

The intent of the Employee Counseling Service is to provide employees with an opportunity to obtain help before problems affect their home life, interpersonal relationships, or job performance. The program is entirely confidential. Brochures containing additional information on this program are available from the Human Resources Department.

Sample Policy 2

The company recognizes alcoholism and drug dependency as illnesses for which there is effective treatment and rehabilitation.

Persons who suspect that they may have an alcoholism or drug dependency problem, even in its early stages, are encouraged to seek diagnosis. Follow through with the treatment that may be prescribed by qualified professionals, in order to arrest the problem as early as possible.

The company will become concerned and involved only when job performance, attendance, or job responsibilities are affected by behavioral/medical problems.

If you feel you have a problem or a potential problem, we will be pleased to talk to you in confidence and offer guidance in seeking professional help. Conversely, if we feel you have a problem, we will discuss it with you in private because we have your best interests at heart and must ensure a safe and efficient workplace.

Sample Policies: Recreation Programs ⸺⸺⸺⸺⸺

Sample Policy 1

The team effort which we all give to our company in our everyday work situation is also extended into our recreation time. We are proud to sponsor athletic teams and encourage our employees to join in these activities.

Sample Policy 2

Each year, during the summer months, our company sponsors an annual employee picnic. This special employee, family, and company gathering is usually held at a popular amusement park where children, as well as grownups, can have a great time together. Special food, games, and door prizes will be made available to all our employees and members of their families.

Sample Policy 3

Our company is pleased to sponsor a variety of sports programs for our employees. These include interdepartmental softball, golf, and tennis tournaments each year. Trophies, contributed by our company, are awarded at the end of each sports activity season to our winning employees.

Company-sponsored softball and bowling teams include providing uniforms and equipment. Please contact the personnel office if you're interested in participating in one or more of these sports. If you don't participate, turn out at one of our company-sponsored sports activities, and join the cheering section.

Our company-sponsored sports activities receives financial support from the profits of all vending machines in our facility.

Sample Policy 4

Our company provides and maintains recreation facilities and encourages you to participate in our athletic, cultural, and social activities. Administration of our social and recreational activities is the responsibility of the personnel office and the employees' recreation association. Call the personnel office for information about all company recreation activities, schedules, and facilities. Specific announcements concerning current special events and sports activities are announced in the employee newspaper and posted on our bulletin boards.

Our employees' recreation association assists in the administration of our recreational programs. All employees are automatically members of this association and are eligible to vote in the association's annual election of five board members.

Sample Policies: Employee Uniforms _____

Sample Policy 1

If your position requires you to wear a uniform and if you have three months' length of service, the company will pay one-half the rental fee for up to three clean uniforms a week.

Sample Policy 2

We supply and launder seven uniforms for each production employee. This provides three changes of uniforms each week. The system works as follows: An employee wears three uniforms during the week. These soiled uniforms are then collected and taken for cleaning. (Four uniforms are left.) The next week three more uniforms are used. At that time, these are picked up for cleaning, and the cleaned uniforms from the previous week are returned.

Size changes, repairs, and so forth should be written on the repair tags provided by the laundry service.

Sample Policy 3

(Name of company) provides uniforms to those production employees who wish to subscribe. (Name of company) will pay 50 percent of the cost of this service. The remainder will be paid by the employee in the form of a payroll deduction. This service is optional for all employees, except drivers, who are required to wear uniforms. (Name of company) will pay the full cost of the uniform service of those employees who are required to wear them.

Sample Policy 4

After one month of service, uniforms are provided by (name of company) to protect your clothing. Nine pairs of pants and nine shirts are issued so that uniforms can be cycled through the weekly cleaning service which we provide. If you leave employment, please return the uniforms issued.

Sample Policy 5

Some of our employees are required to wear uniforms. Uniforms provide a professional appearance to our stores and also save the employee's personal wardrobe. The company purchases these uniforms and makes them available to specified employees. If you are assigned uniforms, please make sure they are turned in for cleaning on the days specified by your supervisor. Upon separation of employment, your final settle-up pay cannot be determined until your uniforms have been turned in. For uniforms that are not returned, employees will be assessed the current cost at prevailing rates.

Some employees may also be required to wear steel-toe safety shoes. If you are required to wear safety shoes, you will be advised to do so by your supervisor. Such requirement takes effect following sixty (60) days of employment. For every pair of steel-toe safety shoes you buy for your personal use on the job, the company will reimburse you $25 upon presentation of a paid receipt.

4.07 Employee Handbook Development Checklist

Seniority, Promotions, Transfers and Layoffs

The following checklist can be used to help determine the various subjects to include in your handbook. Sample handbook statements covering many of the items in this checklist appear in this section. They can be used to help draft your personalized employee handbook statements.

Our Employee Handbook Should Include:

SENIORITY

1. Defining types or units of seniority   Yes ___ No ___ Maybe ___

2. Exceptions to seniority   Yes ___ No ___ Maybe ___

3. How seniority can be lost   Yes ___ No ___ Maybe ___

5. How seniority works   Yes ___ No ___ Maybe ___

    A. Layoffs   Yes ___ No ___ Maybe ___
    B. Recall   Yes ___ No ___ Maybe ___
    C. Promotions/demotions   Yes ___ No ___ Maybe ___
    D. Transfers   Yes ___ No ___ Maybe ___
    E. Overtime work distribution   Yes ___ No ___ Maybe ___
    F. Vacation scheduling   Yes ___ No ___ Maybe ___

6. Seniority lists   Yes ___ No ___ Maybe ___

7. Seniority by classification   Yes ___ No ___ Maybe ___

    A. Stewards and union officials   Yes ___ No ___ Maybe ___
    B. Supervision   Yes ___ No ___ Maybe ___
    C. Employees on strike   Yes ___ No ___ Maybe ___
    D. Military service veterans   Yes ___ No ___ Maybe ___

8. Job bidding procedure   Yes ___ No ___ Maybe ___

PROMOTIONS

1. Defining types of promotions   Yes ___ No ___ Maybe ___

2. Performance reviews   Yes ___ No ___ Maybe ___

3. Ability, skill, and length of service   Yes ___ No ___ Maybe ___

4. How promotion affects seniority   Yes ___ No ___ Maybe ___

5. How promotion affects pay   Yes ___ No ___ Maybe ___

© 1991 The Dartnell Corporation

TRANSFERS

1. Definitions of transfer	Yes ___	No ___	Maybe ___
2. Procedure for employee wanting transference	Yes ___	No ___	Maybe ___
3. Procedure for an employer initiating employee transferral	Yes ___	No ___	Maybe ___
4. Transfers within department	Yes ___	No ___	Maybe ___
5. Transfers outside department	Yes ___	No ___	Maybe ___
6. Transfers outside bargaining unit	Yes ___	No ___	Maybe ___
7. Transfers and bumping procedure	Yes ___	No ___	Maybe ___
8. How transfers affect seniority	Yes ___	No ___	Maybe ___
9. How transfers affect pay	Yes ___	No ___	Maybe ___

LAYOFFS

1. Definitions of temporary and permanent layoffs	Yes ___	No ___	Maybe ___
2. Reasons for layoff	Yes ___	No ___	Maybe ___
3. Advance notice of layoffs	Yes ___	No ___	Maybe ___
4. How seniority will be affected by short or prolonged layoffs	Yes ___	No ___	Maybe ___
5. Effect of layoff on employee benefits	Yes ___	No ___	Maybe ___
6. Layoff procedure	Yes ___	No ___	Maybe ___
7. Bumping procedure during layoff	Yes ___	No ___	Maybe ___
8. Recall procedure	Yes ___	No ___	Maybe ___
9. Income Assistance Plan	Yes ___	No ___	Maybe ___

Sample Policies: Seniority

Sample Policy 1

During your 60-day orientation period, you carry no seniority rights. If you are retained after the 60-day orientation period, you will become a regular employee and will be credited with seniority back to your date of hire.

Your seniority will mean your length of service at our company beginning with the date on which you started work after last being hired, plus any time spent as a former employee.

Seniority is important for you because it is taken into consideration for earning vacations, paying bonuses, providing length of service awards, and for layoff and recall purposes.

Sample Policy 2

During the first 90 consecutive days of full-time employment as a regular employee, you carry no seniority rights. Upon completion of these first 90 days, you will be credited with seniority back to your date of hire. Your seniority is measured by continuous employment at our bank—beginning with the date on which you started work after last being hired, plus any time spent in the Armed Forces of the country after your appointment as a regular, full-time employee.

Seniority is important for you as it enables you to continue your self-improvement, become more knowledgeable and comfortable with your job, and have greater participation in many of our benefit programs.

It is expected, however, that increased seniority will also be matched by increased performance ability. Seniority alone will not be the sole determining factor in consideration relative to promotions and compensation adjustments.

Sample Policy 3

At (name of company) we believe in recognizing your seniority and length of service. Seniority is a right given to employees through length of service which entitles them to certain privileges and considerations.

We recognize seniority between regular, full-time employees by job classification within a department if they are qualified to perform the type of work needed.

Your seniority is determined by a specific date. Usually this date is the day you were hired for the first time. However, if your seniority has been broken through resignation, dismissal, or extended layoff, then your seniority date becomes the last date you were hired following the break in seniority. Employees having the same date of hire will hold seniority in alphabetical order.

Your seniority is important to you in the following ways:

1. It represents an investment in time and money by the company in your training and experience. This gives you more job security and promotion possibilities as your experience increases.

2. Your seniority has a direct relationship to certain of our important employee benefits which are based upon length of service, such as paid vacations.

3. In case we should ever have a layoff, your seniority will give you more work opportunities, provided you have the necessary qualifications.

New employees are hired on a 90-calendar-day orientation period. During this orientation period, you carry no seniority rights. If you are retained after the 90-day orientation period, you will become a regular employee and will be credited with seniority. Your seniority will mean continuous employment at our company beginning with the date on which you begin work after last being hired, plus any time spent in the Armed Forces of this country after employment, or any other absence approved by the company.

You may lose your seniority rights and your length of service with our company for the following reasons:

1. If you voluntarily quit or resign.

2. If you are discharged.

3. If you retire or receive a settlement for total disability.

4. If you fail to report back to work within three workdays after a recall from layoff.

5. If you are laid off for a consecutive period of more than three months.

6. If you overstay an authorized leave of absence or vacation.

7. If you are on a sick leave longer than agreed, unless an extension is granted by your company.*

8. If you give a false reason for a leave of absence or accept employment elsewhere during an authorized leave of absence.

9. If you falsify information on your pre-employment or post-employment personnel form.

10. If you are absent without notification or acceptable excuse for a period of two consecutive workdays, you will be considered as having voluntarily quit your job.

*Profit-sharing eligibility and vesting requirements will be as stated in the plans.

Sample Policy 4

The company recognizes the principle of seniority between regular, full-time employees by job classification within a department for the purpose of job bidding, layoffs, recalls, and shift preference.

An employee's plant-wide seniority will mean continuous employment beginning with the date on which the employee began to work after last being hired plus any time spent in the Armed Forces of the U.S. while with the company, or any other company-approved leaves of absence. Employees having the same hire date will hold seniority based on the alphabetical order of their surname.

New employees will be hired on a ninety-calendar-day "tryout" period (probationary). During this probationary period, the employee will have no seniority rights and may be assigned to any work as determined by the company. At any time during the probationary period, the company will be the sole judge as to whether or not the employee is to be retained or dismissed. The probationary employee will have no recourse to the complaint procedure. Any employee retained after the ninety-day probationary period will become a regular employee and be credited with seniority as of his last date of hire. At such time he will be placed on the seniority list. There will be no responsibility or requirement for the company to rehire probationary employees if they are laid off or discharged during their probationary period for any reason.

An employee will lose all seniority rights and all other rights if any of the following occurs:

1. An employee voluntarily quits or resigns his job.
2. An employee is terminated.
3. An employee is retired or becomes permanently disabled.
4. An employee does not return to work within five work days after receipt of recall notice from layoff. Recall notice will be in writing to the last known address of employee by certified mail, return receipt requested. The employee is responsible for providing his or her correct address to the company for receipt of recall notices.
5. An employee is laid off in excess of six consecutive months will be considered permanently laid off.
6. An employee overstays an authorized leave of absence without written permission.
7. An employee who is absent without authorized leave for a period of three consecutive scheduled work days is considered as having voluntarily quit his employment with the company unless failure to request permission to be absent or failure to notify the company was due to circumstances beyond the employee's control.
8. An employee gives a false reason for a leave of absence or accepts employment elsewhere during a leave of absence.
9. An employee falsifies pertinent information on his pre-employment or post-employment personnel forms if discovered within three years from date of employment or longer if significant to his or her physical examination or job qualifications.

Restoration Rights: In cases of decrease in the workforce and subsequent recalls, an employee demoted in classification shall have first consideration when filling a regular vacancy in his or her former classification without regard to seniority. In cases of more than one employee with restoration rights, the most senior qualified person will have first priority, etc. In order to exercise restoration rights and the procedure as outlined below, an employee must sign the appropriate bid sheet. The signing of the bid sheet is necessary so that accurate records are maintained. This opportunity shall be applied one time only, and if not accepted, restoration rights shall be waived.

Sample Policy 5

Seniority and length of continuous service mean the same thing at our company. Your seniority is the amount of time on the payroll since your last date of hire. If your continuous length of service has been broken through resignation, not returning from an approved leave of absence, dismissal/termination, or extended layoff, then your seniority date becomes the latest date you were rehired. Employees having the same hire date will hold seniority by alphabetical order.

Having seniority is one valuable factor when considerations of transfers, upgrades/promotions, shift changes, overtime, or layoffs occur. Also, seniority is important for participation in and qualification for some benefit programs.

Sample Policies: Job Bidding ⸺⸺⸺⸺⸺⸺

Sample Policy

All employees may bid on any regular job opening that becomes available after they have completed a 90-day orientation period. If frozen by a downward bid, an employee will not be allowed to bid on any job for six months from the date he accepted the downward bid position.

To bid on a job classification, the employee should obtain the bid form from his supervisor and return the signed and dated form to the supervisor within the allotted time. If an employee refuses to accept a bid after being selected, he will waive the right to bid for six months.

The term *line of progression* is defined as a pattern of movement from one job to another normally (a) more favorable to an employee in respect to rate of pay, and (b) related to his former job in terms of the skill and knowledge required and job content.

Disqualifications for any reason shall occur any time before the first 30 days after the acceptance of the bid. In cases of disqualification, an employee may return to the position from which he bid. If disqualified after 30 days, he will be assigned to any job vacancy he is qualified to perform. If an employee is disqualified for any reason three times within a two-year period by the company, he will not be eligible to bid on future upgraded job vacancies for a period of two years.

Sample Policies: Promotions ——————————————

Sample Policy 1

It is the continuing policy of (name of company) that in the selection of employees for training, transfer, promotion, or upgrading, the basis for such action, without limitation or discrimination, will be qualification and seniority.

Promotions will be made primarily on the basis of your ability to perform and accept new and greater responsibilities. If all other requirements of a position are similarly met by two or more persons, seniority may be the deciding element. Seniority alone does not guarantee consideration for promotion.

The Personnel Division and Managers throughout the organization will be responsible for making employees aware of opportunities for promotion when they occur through the job posting and bidding system. To enable the managers and Personnel to accomplish this, employees are responsible for demonstrating positive interest.

Sample Policy 2

Our policies on promotion and transfer are based upon the following fundamental philosophies:

1. It is in the best interest of both (name of company) and our employees to promote from within, whenever qualified personnel are available within our organization.

2. An employee's work may be more meaningful and of better quality by permitting employees to transfer to jobs more suitable to their ability and interest. Such transfers require the approval of all department heads affected.

Filling of hourly paid job openings will be done by the bidding procedures on the basis of qualifications. The job posting will include a job description as well as special qualifications required. These jobs postings will be left up for a period of 72 hours, at which time the bidding will close.

Employees who wish to be considered should sign the job bid form, available in the Personnel section. Job bid forms should be signed within 72 hours from the posting of the notice.

Final selection will be made by the division or department manager, after consultation with the appropriate supervisor.

In the event an employee is chosen to fill a new position, a 90-calendar-day trial period for that position will begin. Extension of the trial period will be granted for vacation, illness, and leaves of absence in increments of not less than one week. If at any time during the 90-day period the employee is not performing satisfactorily, he or she may be terminated.

All personnel who bid on the job will be personally notified by the manager or the Personnel Department of the disposition of the opening. The name of the person who is awarded the job will be posted.

If the job is not filled through the posting process, management will hire someone to fill the position.

If an employee is assigned to a job due to lack of bids and has less than 90 calendar days of seniority, the employee will receive the three-month (90 calendar day) pay rate for that job.

Employees moving to a higher pay grade with one year seniority, or more, will be paid a percentage of the new grade, based upon the pay grade scale, dependent upon their experience and qualifications.

Sample Policy 3

It is the company's policy to fill vacancies, whenever practicable, by promotions from within. Ability, efficiency, attitude, job performance, physical fitness, leadership, experience, and length of service are some of the factors considered in making promotions. Your advancement is influenced by what you qualify yourself to do; by the way you have handled previous work assignments; and on the reputation you make for dependability, efficiency, loyalty to the company, and the ability to work congenially with others. The company believes in broadening the experience of its employees through training, thereby preparing them for future advancement.

In the development of its personnel, transfers within and between departments, divisions, and offices are made whenever they are in your interest and in the interest of the company.

Sample Policy 4

Here at our company, management tries its best to select the best-qualified person for every job. It is our policy to promote, whenever possible, from among present, qualified employees.

All jobs are grouped according to labor and salary grades based upon the difficulty of a given job and its skill requirements.

All nonexempt (positions paying overtime) job vacancies (other than entry level) will be posted on the bulletin board for three workdays to allow ample time for you to review the opening's requirements and position description.

If an employee believes he/she is qualified, he/she can express interest in being considered for the open position by "bidding"—that is, by completing the in-plant job application form. This position should be in a higher classification or a lateral classification which could lead to future promotions. Lateral transfers are granted at the sole discretion of management.

After the posting period, the Human Resources Department and the departmental manager where the opening exists will carefully review each application, conduct interviews where appropriate, and select the best-qualified candidate. The process includes consideration of outside candidates only after the posting/bidding process has been completed and no inside candidate has been found who possesses enough necessary job requirements.

Factors considered in the selection process include the following:

- Demonstrated skill and ability to perform the new position
- Prior and current work performance
- Past and current disciplinary record
- Past and current attendance record
- Cooperation with others and attitudes

When all these factors are considered equal in the opinion of management, your seniority will be the deciding factor.

Sample Policies: Layoffs _____

Sample Policy 1

We expect layoffs to be few and far between. However, if it is necessary because of economic or business conditions to cut back our force, each job will be carefully checked along with the employee's record. Because qualifications, past performance, and length of service of each employee will be the controlling factors, experienced personnel will have the best chance of avoiding a layoff.

Recalls from layoffs will also be based upon service needs. Positions to be filled will be recalled when needed. Those called back to work will be the most qualified followed by those less qualified. If qualifications are equal, seniority will be the determining factor.

Sample Policy 2

When conditions arise which are beyond the reasonable control of the company, temporary layoffs may be made for periods not to exceed ten (10) consecutive work days. Such temporary layoffs will affect only those employees whose jobs have been temporarily shut down due to unforeseen conditions, such as power failures, shortage in materials, or other interruptions in production. Bumping will not be permitted during temporary layoffs. In cases of temporary layoff, such layoffs shall be done by order of job classification seniority and if such a temporary layoff exceeds two workweeks, those affected shall be recalled and allowed to use their plant-wide seniority.

Sample Policy 3

When an indefinite layoff or reduction in force is necessary, the least senior employees, in the job classification affected within the department will be laid off first according to their plant-wide seniority. If not qualified to bump within the department, the displaced employee will be permitted to bump the least senior employee in any job classification in any other department of the plant, provided he is immediately and fully qualified and capable of performing the work without further training and provided he has more plant-wide seniority than the employee being displaced. Shift preference will not be permitted for bumping purposes during layoffs. It is management's responsibility to identify departments, shifts, and job classifications that have excess employees that need to be reduced. When a reduction in workforce is needed, probationary and part-time employees will be laid off first, provided there are other employees immediately qualified to perform their job duties.

During an indefinite layoff, employees will be assigned by seniority to the highest paid classification they are immediately qualified to perform, regardless of shift preference.

Sample Policy 4

In case of any type of layoff, the following procedure will be followed:

    a. All company tools and equipment will be turned in to the stock room.

      b. An inventory will be conducted of the above items and any item found missing will be itemized and the employee will be charged based on an estimated value.

Recall from layoff—Employees eligible to be recalled from reduction in force or layoff shall be returned to their job or work in reverse order. Employees eligible to be recalled from layoff will be notified by telephone and in writing by the company by certified mail sent to the employee's last known address as shown in the company records. If an employee does not report for work within five (5) work-days from the date of receipt of the notice of recall or the date agreed upon by the parties, not to exceed five (5) workdays, the employee shall be considered quit and lose all seniority rights. It is recognized that in emergencies and other immediate job openings that must be filled immediately, such job vacancies may be filled on a temporary basis.

When changes in job assignments are made due to job bidding, demotion, layoff, bumping, recall, or transfer, the company will not be required to assign an employee to a job for which he does not have the required skill, ability, or physical qualifications to perform the job, regardless of seniority.

An employee rehired after loss of seniority will have the status of a new employee. He will be required to complete a new employment application and other required personnel forms before he will be considered for rehire.

4.08 Conduct, Corrective Discipline, and Termination

SESCO Observations and Recommendations
A Positive Approach to Employee Discipline

Most employee handbooks contain a section dealing with standards of performance, "work rules," and progressive discipline procedures used to correct an employee for failing to perform the job satisfactorily or to management standards. It is highly recommended that any new or revised employee handbook clearly set forth "what the company expects from employees" in terms of their attendance standards, punctuality, on-the-job conduct, appearance standards, and other expected employee standards of conduct.

Some employee handbooks contain a detailed listing of personal conduct rules according to severity or seriousness, and then describe the progressive discipline. Other handbooks will place the listing "Rules for All of Us to Work by" in the appendix to the handbook and spell out the range of progressive discipline according to the offense and seriousness.

It is recommended that any new or revised handbook describe in a positive manner the employer's standards of performance covering health and safety, on-the-job performance, individual on-the-job conduct, business ethics, and other desired employee workplace behavior. This section will be of great value to the supervisor or human resource staff in the new employee orientation and training and will provide the employee with future reference as to what the company expects from him or her in on-the-job performance.

Traditionally, methods for maintaining discipline have been punitive in nature. The relatively new concept of a nonpunitive "positive discipline system" (PDS) is winning increasing acceptance, however, among many employers. Some commentators, such as Richard Grote and James Redeker, describe PDS as a "new wave in workplace discipline" that is now being used by such major companies as AT&T, GE, Union Carbide, Shell Oil, and Amoco.

To be effective, disciplinary action should emphasize correcting the problem rather than punishing the offender. It should maintain employees' dignity and self-respect. It should provide for increasingly serious steps if the problem is not resolved. And it should result in a change in employees' behavior and performance.

Like traditional approaches, the PDS approach involves a number of formal steps that increase in seriousness. But unlike punitive disciplinary systems, the positive approach emphasizes reminders of expected performance—not warnings or reprimands for misconduct.

Step 1: Oral Reminder—The first step in the PDS approach is a meeting between a supervisor and the employee to discuss the problem. The supervisor tells the employee the reason for the rule that has been violated, tells the employee the specific changes that are required, and expresses confidence that he or she will correct the problem and no further action will be needed.

Step 2: Written Reminder—If the problem continues, the supervisor again talks to the employee—seriously, but without threats. The supervisor tells the employee what is expected and asks the employee to confirm that he or she knows what changes must be made. At the end of the discussion, the supervisor tells the employee that a written summary of their conversation will be placed in the employee's file.

Step 3: Decision-Making Leave—In traditional discipline systems, the next step involves suspending the offending employee for several days. In the PDS approach, the supervisor tells the employee to remain at home the following day and to use that time to make a final decision as to whether she or he can meet the organization's standards. The employee is told that the organization wants to keep him or her as a productive member of the workforce, but that the decision is up to the employee—and future violations will result in termination. The employee is told to report back to the supervisor after the decision-making leave day to let the supervisor know his or her decision.

As a good-faith demonstration of the organization's interest in keeping the employee, he or she is paid for the leave day. This reduces the employee's hostility and anger, and in unionized companies, reduces the likelihood that the worker will appeal the action.

Some companies, using the PDS system, dispense with the traditional, "progressive" approach and simply operate as follows: the employee who is experiencing or causing problems is told to take the day off with pay to reflect on whether he or she really wants to or can keep working for the company, and if so, how the problem can be solved. When the employee reports for work the next day, the supervisor expects a positive commitment from the employee, backed by the understanding that failure to follow through will result in discharge.

Because this positive approach reduces conflict and fosters cooperation between supervisors and employees, it is gaining popularity.

Guidelines for Effective Employee Discipline
Effective Discipline Doesn't Just Happen

Every employer and supervisor must think realistically about the important area of employee discipline. A disciplinary policy and procedure should have three objectives: (1) the maintenance of a high standard of on-the-job conduct and productivity, (2) the maintenance of a desirable level of employee morale through rules that are fairly but firmly administered and the right to appeal disciplinary penalties to a grievance procedure, and (3) salvaging the employee to become a satisfactory and desirable worker rather than punishing the employee.

Many employers fail to establish an employee disciplinary policy. This invariably causes many unfavorable and costly experiences. Employees who know what they can and cannot do, or who know their rights and obligations, are more satisfied on the job. Employees respect impartial and firm discipline. They do not respect favoritism, unjust discipline, or inconsistency in discipline.

We recommend a sound disciplinary policy in writing, with a primary aim of prevention—not punishment. To accomplish this, it will be necessary to develop a program designed to salvage rule-breaking employees. Rules should be simple, clearly stated, and direct.

Why You Should Have Written Conduct Policies

1. Employees feel more secure when policies are spelled out. A secure employee is apt to be more productive on the job.

2. Unions are less likely to try to organize an employer who has satisfied employees—people who feel they are appreciated by their management—and who enjoy fair and equitable benefits.

3. Written policies save time for supervisors and make top management's job easier, less worrisome.

4. Good policies attract and hold employees, and they reduce costly turnover.

5. To avoid civil rights' complaints and to comply with EEOC guidelines on all aspects of an employment relationship, written policy statements are almost mandatory.

6. Consistent personnel policy administration can only be achieved if all supervisors and managers are "singing off the same sheet of music." This applies particularly to leaves of absence, layoffs, terminations, discipline, and promotion or transfer.

A Word About Progressive Discipline and Discharges

As a rule of thumb, in 85 percent of your discharge actions, the employee should not be taken by surprise. If you have fulfilled your responsibilities as a leader, if you have counseled progressively over a reasonable period of time in an effort to bring about a positive behavioral change in the employee, the possibility of discharge will be communicated well in advance of "D" day.

The role of a supervisor is to counsel an employee effectively to get the best possible job performance and job behavior. To the extent that either of these is not consistent with your desired work standards, it is a supervisory responsibility to counsel each employee to achieve this acceptable performance.

The first discussion with an employee about a job-related problem is not necessarily a formal write-up. However, there should be a written correction report routed to the employee's personnel file to substantiate the counseling interview. The purpose of this is to jog your memory of what took place.

If there is no acceptable improvement, the verbal discussion should be followed by a more formal corrective interview that is confirmed with a written correction notice. This notice should describe the inappropriate behavior and detail your concerns about the need for corrective action. A copy should be given to the employee, and a copy signed by the supervisor and employee should be placed in the personnel file.

If the unacceptable job performance continues, there should be further progressive discipline. With each application of discipline, a record in writing must be made. The number of corrective steps will depend upon the severity of the questionable performance and the degree of improvement.

How to Conduct a Disciplinary Interview

If an employee knows he has made a mistake and has learned by it, your words may only increase his embarrassment and serve no purpose. However, where a rule has been broken or misconduct has taken place, correction or discipline is in order. The following steps are recommended to correct an employee properly:

1. Don't talk about the problem standing up. Sitting down reduces the chances of either person becoming angry.

2. Sit opposite the employee but not behind the desk. This softens the atmosphere of confrontation.

3. Don't start with an accusation. Win the confidence of the employee by describing the problem as one that both of you have to work at solving.

4. Don't start with chit-chat. Your aim is to gather information by encouraging the employee to talk.

5. Don't deliver a sermon or make any wild promises. Try to influence by developing an emotional bond through honest discussion.

6. Avoid prejudging the problem from your point of view alone. Consider enlisting the help of an impartial third person to keep the situation from becoming too emotionally charged.

7. Never criticize, correct, or reprimand an employee in the presence of others. Discipline and correction is a private matter. You should find a quiet place where you can sit down and discuss the problem or mistake calmly, coolly, and objectively.

8. Never try to correct or reprimand an employee when tensions are high. Wait until matters have calmed down.

9. Listen. Listen quietly to your employee's point of view of what happened. He may see the situation more clearly than you do. Even if he has a distorted view, let him get it off his chest. You need to understand his point of view if you hope to work with him intelligently.

10. Share the blame if necessary. Accept your part of the responsibility for the mistake. Perhaps you didn't give your employee adequate training or preparation. Or maybe you didn't forewarn him that this type of problem or situation might arise. Your becoming a "center" with him helps ease the load and assures him that he is not alone.

11. Discuss the problem rather than the employee. Be concerned with correcting the mistake because it is a mistake. Don't focus on the person or his personality. To all of us, our person and personality are usually sacred ground.

12. Deal with "why" as well as "how." Many supervisors tell employees what they are doing wrong, but not why they should do something another way. Explain your recommendations fully. Make certain that you and the employee are shooting at the same target with the same kind of gun.

13. Find a better way. A correction or disciplinary interview is not a success unless there is agreement on a better way. No one likes to be told flatly that he is doing something wrong. He will dislike it even more if he is left up in the air with no solution to his problem. Through free give-and-take, try to settle on an approach that you both agree will be better.

14. Finish your correction and disciplinary interview on a high note. End on a note of optimism and confidence. Don't let your employee feel you have less confidence in him because the problem arose.

How to Prepare Written Warnings and Corrections

Written policies go a long way toward giving a supervisor a firm position in maintaining discipline. Once you have adopted and distributed agreed-upon work rules and rules of conduct, it may be necessary to give a written correction or warning notice for improper conduct or for violation of an established rule.

It is important to remember that formal written corrections are intended not only to maintain consistency in the enforcement of rules and regulations, but also to avoid costly discharges. Your company may be needlessly increasing turnover cost by firing potentially good employees who might be salvaged with skillful correction and proper supervision.

You may warn an employee verbally—keep a written record of all such verbal warnings. We recommend that all warnings be given in writing.

The following guidelines are suggested for preparing written corrections:

1. *Show the important facts.* Give the date, time, conduct, or actions involved which do not meet the requirement of the job.

2. *State whether the improper conduct violates an established company rule.* Quote the rule, rule number, or its pertinent part.

3. *State the employee's history of correction.* The written correction may also include any prior oral warnings, corrections, counseling, or cautioning within the past twelve-month period for the same or a similar offense. Clearly relate the dates, times, and material facts of such "prior corrections." Avoid general statements such as "on many prior occasions."

4. *State that this written form is a written correction for improper conduct or breach of rule.*

5. *State that this written correction gives the employee an opportunity to correct his improper conduct or action in the future.*

© 1991 The Dartnell Corporation

6. *State that the employee will be subject to further disciplinary action "if he fails to correct his conduct in the future."* Do not specify the future penalty—leaving flexibility to the supervisor and management.

7. *Give a copy of the written correction to the employee in private and file a copy in the employee's personnel file.*

To Minimize Wrongful Discharge Under "Employment-at-Will" Challenges

The following procedures are recommended as steps that employers can take to help minimize their liability in case of wrongful discharge and/or discrimination claims:

1. Review recruiting materials, advertisements, employment applications, and brochures, to avoid using words that create an implied "permanent" employment.

2. Train personnel staff to avoid pre-hire interview procedures which overstate job security or advancement opportunities.

3. Review employee handbooks and personnel policy manuals often to ensure that policies reflect actual practice.

4. Use language in all handbooks and manuals that clearly states that employment is on an "at-will" basis.

5. Refine employee evaluation systems to ensure honest and accurate appraisals of employee performance.

6. Utilize progressive disciplinary procedures to warn employees of unsatisfactory performance and to provide them with an opportunity to correct deficiencies.

7. Prepare written reasons for an employee's termination. After thoroughly discussing and explaining them, provide the employee the opportunity to review, comment, and sign the termination notice.

8. Avoid spur-of-the-moment terminations when emotions are running high by requiring at least one other supervisor or the personnel manager to participate in and/or review each discharge.

9. Be consistent in applying disciplinary and termination procedures. Avoid disparate treatment of employees in similar circumstances by appointing one senior officer to review all terminations.

10. Make sure the exit interview deals with any and all questions the employee may have.

Termination for Cause Checklist

When an employee continues to pay no attention to rules and disciplinary action, where an offense is repeated, or misconduct is serious enough for discharge on the first offense, decisive action must be taken. To help guide you through this area, we suggest you stop and review the following checklist very carefully, before any employee is terminated. Ask yourself these questions before you discharge an employee:

1. Is the company policy, which has been violated, a reasonable one?

2. Has the company policy or rule been properly communicated to the employee?

3. Have I been objective and have I treated this employee the same as another would be treated for the same offense?

4. Have I accumulated all of the facts accurately?

5. If it is a repeated offense, has the employee been properly reprimanded in the past and have written corrections been issued?

6. Is the employee guilty by his or her own actions or by association with another employee?

7. Am I taking action against the employee because he or she has "challenged my authority"?

8. Does the punishment fit the offense?

9. Have I considered the employee's past disciplinary record and length of service?

10. Was the employee's guilt supported by direct objective evidence, as opposed to suspicion or hearsay?

11. Has a top management official reviewed the facts and approved the discharge?

12. Should I try for a "voluntary resignation" instead of firing the individual?

13. Will the termination be a surprise to the employee? (If yes, repeat the discipline process.)

14. Should I suspend the employee first, to review all facts?

Remember, this recommended checklist is not very helpful after a discharge. If there is any question about facts or reasons for discharge, suspend the employee instead of firing, during an investigation of the facts.

When a discharge is found to be justified, proper documentation of the specific reasons for "separation of employment" is very important. Charges of discrimination may be filed following a discharge. Unless you can provide adequate proof to substantiate the discharge, the NLRB, EEOC, or Wage-Hour Division might find merit in a charge of discrimination and order you to reinstate the employee with back pay.

Employers frequently get into trouble when they take disciplinary action or discharge employees without documentation of the employee's poor work record. Government investigators do not make decisions based upon the statements or beliefs of supervisors and managers. Their decisions are based solely on documentation of warnings, reprimands, attendance, work record, etc.

Are your records adequate? As a test, select two or three employees whom you know to be marginal and review their personnel records. If the records indicate that the person is a good employee or, conversely, if they do not indicate that the person is a marginal employee, then you can be assured that you will have difficulty justifying and sustaining disciplinary action if a government agency becomes involved.

4.08 Employee Handbook Development Checklist

Conduct, Corrective Discipline, and Termination

The following checklist can be used to help determine the various subjects to include in your handbook. Sample handbook statements covering many of the items in this checklist appear in this section. They can be used to help draft your personalized employee handbook statements.

Our Employee Handbook Should Include:

CONDUCT AND CORRECTIVE DISCIPLINE

1. Conduct Rules   Yes ___ No ___ Maybe ___

   A. Misrepresentation or omission of facts in seeking
      employment   Yes ___ No ___ Maybe ___
   B. Clocking or altering the time card of another
      employee   Yes ___ No ___ Maybe ___
   C. Making or permitting a false or untrue record
      relating to any material or work   Yes ___ No ___ Maybe ___
   D. Defacing, damaging, or destroying property of
      the company or of another employee   Yes ___ No ___ Maybe ___
   E. Interfering with, obstruction of, or otherwise
      hindering the production or work performance of
      another employee   Yes ___ No ___ Maybe ___
   F. Engaging in horseplay, running, scuffing, or
      throwing objects on company property   Yes ___ No ___ Maybe ___
   G. Originating or spreading false statements
      concerning employees or the company   Yes ___ No ___ Maybe ___
   H. Assisting any person to gain unauthorized
      entrance to or exit from any portion of the
      company's premises   Yes ___ No ___ Maybe ___
   I. Fighting or causing bodily injury to another or
      other forms of disorderly conduct   Yes ___ No ___ Maybe ___
   J. Immoral or indecent conduct   Yes ___ No ___ Maybe ___
   K. Leaving work area without permission, wasting
      time, loitering, or sleeping during working hours Yes ___ No ___ Maybe ___
   L. Refusal to accept or follow orders or directions
      from proper authority or any other form of
      insubordination   Yes ___ No ___ Maybe ___
   M. Possession of or reporting to work or working
      under the influence of intoxicants or
      unauthorized drugs   Yes ___ No ___ Maybe ___
   N. Abusing company equipment or property or
      using any piece of equipment or property
      without being authorized to do so   Yes ___ No ___ Maybe ___
   O. Repeated tardiness or absence; failure to report
      to work without satisfactory reason   Yes ___ No ___ Maybe ___
   P. Theft, pilferage, or unauthorized removal of
      property of the company or others   Yes ___ No ___ Maybe ___

Q. Smoking in areas where it is prohibited   Yes ___ No ___ Maybe ___

R. Bringing in, possessing, or using weapons on company property without appropriate management approval   Yes ___ No ___ Maybe ___

S. Failure to meet quality and quantity requirements Yes ___ No ___ Maybe ___

T. Inefficiency or lack of application of effort on the job   Yes ___ No ___ Maybe ___

U. Abusive language to any supervisor, employee, or customer   Yes ___ No ___ Maybe ___

V. Contributing to unsanitary conditions   Yes ___ No ___ Maybe ___

W. Use of company facilities after normal working hours without authorization   Yes ___ No ___ Maybe ___

X. Violations of company policy on fair treatment, equal opportunity, and nondiscrimination   Yes ___ No ___ Maybe ___

Y. Gambling on company property   Yes ___ No ___ Maybe ___

2. Can conduct or safety rules be added, revised, or withdrawn at any time?   Yes ___ No ___ Maybe ___

    A. At management's discretion and judgment   Yes ___ No ___ Maybe ___

    B. If organized, after notifying the union   Yes ___ No ___ Maybe ___

    C. If organized, by joint agreement with the union   Yes ___ No ___ Maybe ___

3. How conduct and safety rules are to be publicized   Yes ___ No ___ Maybe ___

    A. Employee handbook   Yes ___ No ___ Maybe ___

    B. Bulletins and bulletin boards   Yes ___ No ___ Maybe ___

    C. Labor agreements   Yes ___ No ___ Maybe ___

    D. Employee publications   Yes ___ No ___ Maybe ___

    E. Special rule book   Yes ___ No ___ Maybe ___

    F. Individual meetings with immediate supervisor   Yes ___ No ___ Maybe ___

4. Type of discipline given employees for rule violations Yes ___ No ___ Maybe ___

    A. Penalty to be at the discretion of supervisor and immediate superior   Yes ___ No ___ Maybe ___

    B. Penalty determined by a disciplinary committee composed of management and employee or union representatives   Yes ___ No ___ Maybe ___

    C. Penalty determined by specific guidelines in writing according to seriousness of violation   Yes ___ No ___ Maybe ___

5. Type of disciplinary action   Yes ___ No ___ Maybe ___

    A. Oral reprimand—warning   Yes ___ No ___ Maybe ___

    B. Written reprimand—warning   Yes ___ No ___ Maybe ___

    C. Disciplinary layoff   Yes ___ No ___ Maybe ___

    D. Loss of special privileges   Yes ___ No ___ Maybe ___

    E. Demotion   Yes ___ No ___ Maybe ___

    F. Fine   Yes ___ No ___ Maybe ___

    G. Loss of seniority   Yes ___ No ___ Maybe ___

    H. Discharge   Yes ___ No ___ Maybe ___

6. If organized, shall the union have the right to appeal any disciplinary action taken by management?   Yes ___ No ___ Maybe ___

7. If not organized, does the employee have the right to appeal any disciplinary action taken through a nonunion grievance procedure?   Yes ___ No ___ Maybe ___

8. Shall disciplinary policy provide that after a period of time previous written reprimands or other disciplinary action on file will become void, giving the employee a clean slate for the future?   Yes ___ No ___ Maybe ___

DISCHARGE POLICY AND PROCEDURE

1. Description of misconduct that warrants the discharge of employees immediately without prior warning   Yes ___ No ___ Maybe ___

2. Policy providing employee to be suspended before a discharge is made final and effective   Yes ___ No ___ Maybe ___

3. Policy stating that management has the right to determine what is cause for immediate discharge   Yes ___ No ___ Maybe ___

4. Policy and procedure to be followed in issuing written warnings in less severe types of disciplinary action before discharge   Yes ___ No ___ Maybe ___

5. Requirements on documenting discharge without notice   Yes ___ No ___ Maybe ___

   A. To be given to employee   Yes ___ No ___ Maybe ___
   B. To be given to union   Yes ___ No ___ Maybe ___
   C. To be given to human resource office in employee's personnel file   Yes ___ No ___ Maybe ___

6. Policy on when termination of employment notice is to be given   Yes ___ No ___ Maybe ___

   A. Minimum period prior to discharge   Yes ___ No ___ Maybe ___
   B. At time of discharge   Yes ___ No ___ Maybe ___
   C. Within a specified period of time following discharge   Yes ___ No ___ Maybe ___

7. Type or form of termination notice—oral or written   Yes ___ No ___ Maybe ___

8. Contents of termination notice   Yes ___ No ___ Maybe ___

9. Policy providing that all discharges are subject to final approval and authorization of supervisor's immediate superior   Yes ___ No ___ Maybe ___

10. Policy on providing discharged employees with
dismissal or severance pay   Yes ___ No ___ Maybe ___

   A. Eligibility requirements for dismissal or
severance pay including reason for discharge Yes ___ No ___ Maybe ___
   B. Amount of severance or dismissal pay—
minimum and maximum   Yes ___ No ___ Maybe ___
   C. Policy statement providing inclusion or exclusion
of monies due employee from contributions to
benefit plans in determining maximum amount of
severance pay   Yes ___ No ___ Maybe ___
   D. Policy on making all necessary tax deductions
from severance pay   Yes ___ No ___ Maybe ___
   E. Policy on giving severance pay based upon
giving or not giving advance notice of
termination   Yes ___ No ___ Maybe ___

11. Policy on performing exit interviews   Yes ___ No ___ Maybe ___

12. Policy on discharges being subject to grievance
procedure   Yes ___ No ___ Maybe ___

13. Policy on reinstating employees if the employer is
found to be in error through grievance procedure Yes ___ No ___ Maybe ___

14. Policy on reinstated employee being eligible for back
pay for time lost   Yes ___ No ___ Maybe ___

15. Policy of COBRA extension of benefits
administration   Yes ___ No ___ Maybe ___

RESIGNATION POLICY AND PROCEDURE

1. Policy statement requiring or not requiring employee
notice of intent to resign   Yes ___ No ___ Maybe ___

   A. Verbal or written notification and time limit Yes ___ No ___ Maybe ___

2. Policy on a penalty provided for failure to notify the
employer of intent to resign   Yes ___ No ___ Maybe ___

   A. No recommendation   Yes ___ No ___ Maybe ___
   B. Loss of severance or dismissal pay Yes ___ No ___ Maybe ___

3. Policy on issuing letters of reference for terminated
employees   Yes ___ No ___ Maybe ___

4. Policy on providing employees who quit or resign
with a termination form describing reason for
termination   Yes ___ No ___ Maybe ___

A. Retaining copy of termination of employment
    form in personnel file   Yes ___ No ___ Maybe ___
B. Giving copy of termination of employment form
    to employee   Yes ___ No ___ Maybe ___

Sample Policies: Disciplinary Procedures ————————

Sample Policy 1

In order for (name of company) to have a consistent and fair disciplinary procedure, the following guidelines have been adopted. With the exception of unacceptable conduct which may be cause for more serious disciplinary action or for immediate dismissal, any employee whose employment is terminated will have gone through the following steps:

Step 1 Discussion—This is a verbal discussion in which the supervisor has a face-to-face conference with you to discuss your poor work performance or conduct and the need for correcting it.

Step 2 Assessment—If there is little or no improvement after the discussion, the next step is a written assessment. A report is completed by the supervisor in your presence and you have the right to read and discuss the report and comment in writing. A member of the Personnel Department staff must be present.

Step 3 Suspension—After step 2, if there is no marked improvement, you will be suspended for five days without pay. A written record of the suspension is completed by the supervisor in your presence. A member of the Personnel Department staff must be present. A suspension may take place only with approval of the supervisor, the department manager, and the Personnel Manager.

Step 4 Termination—After step 3, if there is no marked improvement, you will be eligible for termination.

Steps 1, 2, 3, and 4 will be followed consecutively if the incidents requiring these steps fall within a span of one year. If, however, there is a lapse of one year or more between any of the steps, the last step taken will be repeated without beginning over. If two years have passed after any step, the procedure will need to be initiated again.

Sample Policy 2

It is necessary, in order for the business to operate in an orderly and efficient manner, that you observe the rules governing our work environment. If you violate any of these rules, it will be necessary to take corrective measures in the form of disciplinary action.

(Name of company) follows a three-step disciplinary action procedure that is designed to be corrective rather than punitive. The company has two groups of work rules and regulations. Violation of any of the Group I rules will initially result in a verbal warning. A second violation of any Group I rule will result in a written warning. A third violation will result in further discipline up to and including discharge.

Group I Work Rules

First offense:	Verbal warning
Second offense:	Written warning
Third offense:	Discharge

1. Frequent tardiness.

2. Unexcused absence from work.

3. Leaving work before your scheduled shift is completed; leaving your department without permission; or loitering around the plant away from your work place.

4. Changing work clothes before quitting time.

5. Violation of the no solicitation/no distribution/no access rules.

6. Failure to punch your time sheet.

7. Excessive spoilage.

8. Making excessive personal telephone calls.

9. Failure to perform properly assigned work.

10. Littering or contributing to poor housekeeping, unsanitary or unsafe working conditions.

11. Tampering with or removing bulletin board notices without authorization.

12. Failure to keep the accounting department advised of pertinent personnel changes.

Group II Work Rules

First offense: Discipline up to and including discharge

1. Conviction of a criminal offense.

2. Fighting, threatening, or attempting bodily injury to another person on the company premises.

3. Stealing company property or personal property of another employee.

4. Malicious mischief which results in the injury of another employee or destruction of company property.

5. Intentional sabotage by an unauthorized stoppage and/or interference with the mechanical equipment or power supply of the plant.

6. Unauthorized removal of printed customer material from the premises.

7. Disorderly or immoral conduct on company premises.

8. Flagrant violation of safety rules or such carelessness regarding safety that it causes an accident to yourself or a fellow employee.

9. Insubordination, use of profane or abusive language, physical abuse to supervisory personnel.

10. Falsification of employment applications or falsification of production records, time sheets, or similar internal records.

11. Punching another employee's time sheet.

12. Neglect in the care and use of company property.

13. Reporting to work under the influence of illegal drugs or liquor. Possessing or bringing intoxicating beverages or illegal drugs on the company premises.

14. Moonlighting on another job without approval of your supervisor.

15. Unauthorized removal of company property.

16. Making false, vicious, profane, or malicious statements concerning any employee, the company, or its products.

17. Falsifying or withholding testimony when accidents other incidents in the plant are being investigated.

18. Sexual harassment.

19. Sleeping on the job.

20. Absent three consecutive work days without notification.

21. Making unauthorized long-distance calls.

Sample Policy 3

The greatest asset (name of company) has is an outstanding group of dedicated employees. Our employees contribute significantly to the successful operation of (name of company). Each employee's standard of living and security are closely related to the success of (name of company). Such a relationship creates mutual responsibility and mutual duty. (Name of company) is constantly seeking to establish and utilize fair standards for evaluating work performance and to reward outstanding employees for their achievements. (Name of company) also accepts the responsibility to help improve employees whose work performance and efficiency have fallen below established standards.

The work rules that follow in the next section of our handbook and the progressive discipline system in this section have been established to promote and improve efficiency and productivity.

We sincerely hope the procedures in this section will not have to be used, but we are prepared to deal with any significant employee problems. We believe that employees prefer to know the consequences of their actions and not be kept in the dark on such matters. We also believe that the only way to ensure fair and consistent treatment of each employee is to have a written policy that is known by all employees.

The Progressive Discipline System: The following disciplinary system will be imposed when an employee violates a company rule or policy or has a significant performance problem.

The progressive discipline system consists of four steps:

1. Correction: Oral warning

2. Reprimand: Written warning

3. Punishment: Suspension without pay

4. Termination

The first violation of a company rule or policy (unless classed as a highly serious violation) will result in an oral warning (step 1). A second violation within three months of the first violation will result in a written warning (step 2). A third violation within six months of the second violation will result in a suspension without pay (step 3). The length of the suspension will depend on the severity of the violation. Finally, a fourth violation within one year of the third violation will result in immediate termination of the employee without notice, severance pay, or accrued vacation pay (step 4).

The purpose of this progressive discipline system is to correct undesirable behavior and to motivate an employee to become more productive and efficient. This is why the first step is called "correction." The first step is to provide counseling to explain the problem to the employee and why and how the problem must be corrected. We feel that a mature person should respond positively to this action and not need additional discipline.

A general exception to the above procedures will occur if there is a very serious or highly serious violation of a company rule or policy. In this situation, steps 1 and 2 will be omitted and, depending on the severity of the violation, suspension without pay (step 3) or termination (step 4) will be imposed immediately.

As a guide, company rules have been divided into three classes: serious, very serious, and highly serious. These work rules and grounds for discipline or discharge are listed in the next section of this handbook.

Removal of Disciplinary Actions from Record: An employee may remove disciplinary actions from his or her record by achieving a good record for a certain number of months after a disciplinary action. An oral warning can be removed from an employee's record after a three-month period in which the employee does not violate any company rules. To have a written warning removed from an employee's record, the employee must have a period of six months with no violations. To have a suspension removed from an employee's record, a period of one year with no violations is required.

Sample Policy 4

It is our belief that the highest type of discipline is that which originates within the individual employee. Self-discipline in the employee group is the company goal; however, for those occasional instances where self-discipline and mutual cooperation do not prevail, supervisors will take corrective actions, subject to the employee's right of appeal.

Types of Disciplinary Action—It is the company policy to recognize and apply three forms of disciplinary action:

1. Written warning

2. Suspension, either (a) without pay and without work, or (b) with pay and with work (working suspension)

3. Discharge

Oral warnings may be given by a supervisor as a matter of information and training, but such warnings will not be considered as formal discipline.

Initial discipline for a particular offense is normally a written warning, followed by suspension without pay and, finally, discharge for recurrence of the same or a similar offense.

However, a working suspension may be given when the offense is failure to meet financial obligations which causes the company to become involved, as loss of pay would only make the situation worse. A working suspension may also be given for absenteeism, as a suspension from work would only result in the company being further deprived of the employee's services. There may be other circumstances in which the discipline would be a working suspension.

For the purposes of progressive discipline, for disciplinary record purposes, there is no difference between the two types of suspension listed above. Discipline may progress from either form of suspension to another suspension or to discharge, depending on the circumstances and the offenses.

Whether or not the employee has received any prior discipline of any kind, suspension or discharge may be imposed when the seriousness of an individual offense and/or the employee's accumulated employment record indicates that such action is required.

Generally, a suspension given as discipline will be of not less than three working days. In instances where it is appropriate for the employee to be off the company property immediately while the company investigates the incident, as in suspected theft, fighting, or gross insubordination, the employee may be suspended without pay for more or less than three days while investigation of the incident proceeds. After completion of the investigation, a final decision on discipline will be reached and the employee notified.

Sample Policy 5

We believe discipline is not meant to be punishment in any way. However, when it becomes necessary to change an employee's performance or behavior from unacceptable to acceptable, our Progressive Discipline Policy enables us to endeavor to do so in a fair and consistent way. When management determines disciplinary action is appropriate, actions will be taken according to (name of company) Progressive Discipline Policy.

Normal steps in the disciplinary process are outlined below. However, based on the seriousness of the offense, management may enter into any level of disciplinary action or termination.

1. VERBAL CORRECTION. The supervisor will provide a verbal correction to the employee. A written record of this correction will be placed in the employee's personnel file.

2. WRITTEN CORRECTION. If the employee does not correct his or her behavior, the supervisor will consult with higher management and prepare a written correction. The employee will be asked to sign, indicating receipt of a copy of the written correction, and a copy will be placed in the employee's personnel file.

3. SUSPENSION WITHOUT PAY. If the written correction does not correct the problem, the employee may be suspended without pay for a minimum of three days. This suspension without pay must have the approval of the President.

4. TERMINATION. When all other means of discipline have been used, or when the offense justifies such action, the employee may be terminated. The supervisor may recommend termination of employees. Recommendations will be reviewed by the management, who will determine the action to be taken.

   If the employee feels the termination is unfair, he or she may request a meeting with the President to discuss the termination. Based upon this discussion, the President will make a final determination in the case.

Management reserves the right to enter into any level of disciplinary action or termination based upon the severity of the offense requiring discipline and the employee's past work record.

Sample Policy 6

The company wants to provide a good work environment for all employees. This desire is expressed in many forms: safe working conditions, maintenance of facilities and equipment, equitable wage structures, and progressive benefit programs. In turn, it is reasonable to expect a good productive effort and the recognition of responsibility on the part of employees.

Each of us has the responsibility to our fellow workers to conduct ourselves according to certain rules of good behavior and conduct. In any business, some rules are needed to help everyone work together by letting them know what they can and cannot do. We expect our employees to follow our company rules and show good behavior and efficiency. For these reasons, we have included in our handbook a number of work rules. You are expected to read, understand, and follow these rules in your day-to-day work.

Disciplinary action, whether verbal or written, is given only for the purpose of correcting someone for doing something wrong. Having to dismiss an employee is distasteful for everyone, and we try to work with our employees to avoid such action. However, failure to follow our work rules is against the best interest of our other employees and our company and usually leads to dismissal. In every case where disciplinary action is being considered, you will be given every opportunity to explain your side of the story. Should you have any questions at all concerning any work rule listed, please see your supervisor.

In order to be absolutely fair, we have what we call a "washout" period for certain disciplinary actions. We believe that a person's mistakes with the company should not haunt them for years afterwards unless there is a consistent pattern of similar or related problems. Therefore, after an employee's having made a "mistake," we will "wipe the slate clean" if no more rule infractions occur within twelve months from the date of the last rule violation.

Our rules are basically common sense, requiring conduct acceptable to a customer-service-oriented employment environment. When these common sense practices are violated, disciplinary action may be taken. While the following list is not all inclusive, some of the violations which can result in disciplinary action, including discharge, are as follows:

(List of Rules)

Violations of company policies outlined within other sections of this handbook or habitual offenders of various company rules will be dealt with by written correction to dismissal, depending upon the frequency and nature of the offense.

Should you ever be considered for disciplinary action, you may be assured that your case will be fully investigated and reviewed before final action is taken. In certain serious cases, a supervisor may suspend an employee from work pending review and final determination of the circumstances involved.

Sample Policies: Personal Mail _____

Sample Policy 1
The handling of personal mail is not a company responsibility.

Should mail be received that is specifically addressed to an employee, the company would release it to the employee. However, since it is sometimes difficult to distinguish personal mail from business mail, the company reserves the right to open any and all mail received. Should the employee not be at work to receive his or her personal mail, the company reserves the right to open such unclaimed mail on the premise that it could contain a business communication.

The company cannot and will not assume any responsibility for the contents of personal mail.

Sample Policy 2
The handling of personal mail is not a company responsibility. The company cannot and will not assume any responsibility for the contents of personal mail.

Since we use a postage meter for outgoing mail, we do not have postage stamps available for any employee to purchase. On special occasions personal first class mail on which you have affixed the correct amount of postage may be placed in the outgoing mail in the shipping department.

Sample Policy 3
All personal mail should be received by the employee at his/her home. In the normal operation of business, however, incoming mail is frequently addressed to individual employees. While this practice is not desirable, every effort will be made to deliver the mail to the proper party. It should be remembered, however, that all business mail is opened upon receipt.

Sample Policies: Visitors _____

Sample Policy 1

Visitors are not allowed in the plant without special permission from management. All visitors must be registered at the reception desk and must prominently display a visitor's badge with which they will be furnished. It shall be the responsibility of departmental supervisors to see that no visitors are permitted in their departments without displaying a visitor's badge.

Sample Policy 2

We like to be friendly, hospitable, and cooperative with people who wish to visit our plant and "see" how things get printed. That includes outside groups such as clubs, school classes, and so forth—and it also includes small parties of friends and relatives of our employees.

However, for the safety and convenience of everyone concerned—as well as for the efficiency of plant operations—we must follow certain guidelines relating to visitors:

1. No visitors are permitted in production areas or beyond the front office without the explicit approval of management and without an escort provided by or authorized by the company.

2. If an employee (or outsider) wishes to host or escort a tour group in the plant, he or she must contact management as far in advance as possible to allow for adequate preparation and a minimum of disruption to normal operations.

3. An employee bringing visitors into the plant must do so on his or her own time and must escort them personally (unless other arrangements have been approved in advance by the management).

4. An employee escorting personal guests in the plant will be responsible for the visitors' safety and for the control of children.

5. Any visitors who create a disturbance or who act in any way which endangers their own safety or that of others will be asked to leave the plant immediately.

6. All visitors must enter through the front office. The employee plant entrance and the shipping/delivery entrance are for use only by employees and authorized service personnel.

Unplanned visits or emergencies:

All visitors, including employees' family members, who wish to see an employee during working hours, either for personal or business reasons, must first check in at the front office. Depending upon the circumstances of the visit, office personnel will either deliver a message to the employee or arrange for a personal meeting outside of the production area.

If a visit involves an emergency, the employee will be notified immediately, and both the employee and the visitor will receive all possible cooperation from management and appropriate company personnel.

Sample Policy 3

We encourage members of your family to visit our plant during the week and to tour the facilities. If you desire to take your family through the plant, you may conduct a tour during normal business hours, before or after your regularly scheduled shift or on Saturday when the plant is open. Please be sure that all visitors register with the receptionist in the lobby and are issued visitors' passes.

All visitors, including customers and salesmen, are required to register in the office lobby and receive permission to enter the plant, generally accompanied by an escort. Occasionally groups tour the plant but always with the prior approval of management, which also provides a guide. Entrance at unauthorized doors or times is not allowed.

Company tours are available through the personnel department for printing industry related groups.

Sample Policy 4

Employees are expected to remain in their work area during working hours, and the visiting of other employees, except on company business, is discouraged. Visits to employees by persons outside the company for nonbusiness purposes during working hours, except when absolutely necessary, is also discouraged.

Our visitors, no matter how much we like them, do disrupt business. Remind your friends and relatives that unless there is an emergency involved, they should not disturb you while you are working. Former employees, or those employees on leave of absence, are requested not to disrupt bank operations by disturbing employees while they are working.

Sample Policies: Radios, Televisions, and Newspapers

Sample Policy 1

Radios are allowed in certain plant areas where the type of work makes it practical. Radios must be tuned to music only and volume is to be kept down so as not to disturb people.

Personal headset-type radios are not to be used. They could present a safety hazard by distracting an employee from concentrating on his or her duties.

At no time are sporting events allowed to be broadcast over plant radios. This rule applies to all departments and to all shifts. Management reserves the right to prohibit all radios if the privilege is abused.

Sample Policy 2

(Name of company) expects its employees to devote their full attention to the successful execution of their job duties. Because of this, radios and televisions will not be permitted in the plant except in unusual cases with the specific authorization of management.

Newspapers and magazines (other than trade publications) will be allowed only in the lunch room and may be read during those times when the employee is allowed to be in the lunch room. Pornography will not be allowed in the plant under any circumstances.

Sample Policy 3

Customers' impressions of our work areas and habits may determine future continued business from them. For this reason, it is important that there should be no distractions from the work at hand.

1. No radios or other sound systems are permitted.

2. No newspapers or other reading matter will brought in or read in the production area.

Sample Policies: Rumors ⎯⎯⎯⎯⎯⎯⎯⎯⎯⎯⎯⎯⎯⎯⎯⎯⎯⎯⎯⎯

Sample Policy 1

Rumors are always destructive to all concerned—they benefit no one. For information about the company or about things that are being done that you think will affect your job, ask your supervisor. Please feel free to do this. Don't depend on rumors; get the facts.

You are expected to discourage the practice of starting or spreading rumors and to refrain from being a party to such actions.

Sample Policy 2

Whenever large numbers of people are working together, there are those who like to listen to rumors. Most rumors are misleading and become increasingly inaccurate as they pass from person to person. (Name of company) follows the policy of promptly notifying all personnel of information of general company interest. Please be careful to avoid spreading rumors, and contact your supervisor if you hear information which you wish verified.

Sample Policy 3

During the course of anyone's employment, much information travels through the grapevine. (Name of company) is no exception. Traditionally, this information is more misleading than informative, often causing employees to become upset unnecessarily. To avoid this, always obtain accurate information from your supervisor, manager, or Personnel Department about any rule or job-related issue. If you have a question, please ask management. If we don't know, we'll find out for you. Accurate information is important and useful. Misinformation is useless and can lead to unnecessary problems.

Sample Policies: Discharge Procedures ——————————

Sample Policy 1

Discharges are always unpleasant and costly, so you can be sure that they won't be considered lightly. If, however, discharge becomes necessary, advance notice may or may not be given depending on the circumstances surrounding the termination. No unused vacation or personal leave credits will be paid in the event of termination of your employment. If you believe that you have been treated unfairly with regard to your termination, you have a right to an interview with the Personnel Officer, Supervisor, or the President.

Sample Policy 2

If an employee's performance is unsatisfactory due to lack of ability or failure to fulfill the requirements of his job, he will be notified of the problem and his supervisor will work with him to correct the situation. If the employee's failure is due to a mismatching of person and job, every effort will be made to find a more suitable job.

If this does not succeed, the employee will be dismissed. If you are dismissed, and we certainly hope nothing like this ever happens, a full explanation of the reason will be given to you by your supervisor. We will take all steps necessary to work with an employee to correct or rectify a situation before taking the step of dismissal. If you believe you have been treated unfairly, you have a right to an interview with the President. Advance notice is not given in discharge cases or to those employees terminated during their orientation period.

Sample Policy 3

It is the policy of (name of company) to process termination of employees according to standardized personnel procedures to ensure consistent and equitable treatment.

A. Voluntary Termination

In the event of resignation, advance notice of two weeks for hourly employees and four weeks for salaried employees is requested. Resignation for good cause can be allowed with less notice.

B. Involuntary Termination

Should it be found necessary to terminate your employment because of a permanent reduction in personnel needs or your inability to do your job successfully, you will be given advance notice of at least two weeks for hourly employees and four weeks for salaried employees, or the equivalent in termination pay.

Neither advance notice nor termination pay will be granted if you are discharged for an infraction of employer's rules or policies. The termination pay provisions are applicable only to employees who have completed one year of continuous employment.

Any vacation or personal time due you upon the date of notification of termination will be allowed. Your insurance benefits will be paid by (name of company) until the end of the month during which your termination is consummated.

All terminating employees, whether voluntary or involuntary, will have a scheduled exit interview, if at all possible, with the Personnel Director. The purpose of this interview is to be certain that the reasons for the employee's termination are not founded on a misunderstanding or erroneous situation. Also, Personnel wants to get any information that may improve future working conditions at (name of company). This interview will also be used to detail exactly what compensation the employee will receive or has coming and when termination of benefits will occur.

Sample Policies: Resignation Procedures ——————————

Sample Policy 1

You will receive pay for the vacation time due to you when you leave the company if you are released through no fault of your own and have six months service, or you give at least two weeks notice and have six months service. An employee giving less than two weeks notice forfeits all vacation money.

On the last day of employment, you should report to the Personnel Department to return any company property you may have and to receive an explanation of your status as it relates to company benefits. Final pay arrangements will be discussed at that time.

Sample Policy 2

An employee desiring to terminate his employment must give his supervisor two weeks written notice in order to receive accrued vacation pay. All other benefits are terminated on the last day of employment.

If an employee terminates his employment with (name of company) and at a later date wishes to rehire, he will be treated as a new employee.

Sample Policy 3

Occasionally, personal affairs result in an employee's decision to change jobs. In such cases, you are expected to give your supervisor at least two weeks notice. Advance notice will allow us time to adjust working schedules and secure a replacement. This act of courtesy will be entered favorably on your employment record. Employees who leave in good standing are given consideration if they wish to return to work at a later date.

Sample Policy 4

Sometimes personal affairs force a change in jobs. Should you decide to resign, you are expected to notify your supervisor at least two weeks in advance. This courtesy will allow time for adjustment of work schedules and will be acknowledged in future references and rehiring decisions.

Sample Policy 5

Those employees who resign and fail to give and work out proper notice (two weeks) forfeit all accumulated vacation benefits which may be due.

Exit Interview—An exit interview may be conducted for anyone who leaves our company. This exit interview is held for your advantage because we want to give you complete information on how you can protect your group insurance benefits. Also, we will want to have your honest opinion on our company policies—comments which may lead to improvements.

Your final paycheck will be ready and mailed to you on the next regular payday for the immediate past period worked.

4.09 Complaint and Grievance Procedures

SESCO Observations and Recommendations
Solving On-the-Job Complaints with Formalized
Complaint/Grievance Procedures

A formal grievance procedure is an effective way for an employer to keep workers content in their jobs—it acts as a "safety valve" for both management and employees.

Good employee relations are based on employees' belief that their employer gives them a fair deal—not only in pay, hours, and benefits but also through reasonable work rules, consistent discipline, unbiased supervision, and appropriate treatment on the job. As a wise executive, you strive to establish policies and practices that emphasize the employer's *fairness*. But the managers and supervisors who administer the policy to the rank and file can't always be perfectly impartial. Errors in judgment, misunderstandings, and other human shortcomings are bound to enter the picture. The result is real or imagined injustices from your employees' point of view.

And remember, it doesn't matter whether an employee actually suffers an injustice or only *thinks* so. Goodwill is damaged either way unless there is a chance to air the complaint and seek relief from higher management. A formal grievance procedure guarantees your employees a fair shake by providing a channel for appeal that goes all the way to the top.

The goal of a grievance procedure is not to eliminate grievances but to provide for a prompt, friendly, and mutually satisfactory settlement of differences between management and employees. If your grievance system meets these criteria, you can be sure it will pay off your investment of effort many times over.

Publish Grievance Procedures in the Employee Handbook

It is not necessary to create an elaborate grievance or complaint-handling procedure, but it should be in writing as a benefit to supervisors and employees. Use your employee handbook or bulletin boards to explain *what* it is, *why* it is beneficial, and *how* it works.

The number of steps in the formal grievance procedure is important. A good system provides for orderly appeal up through successive levels of management.

Step 1 involves informal discussion of the problem between the employee and his or her supervisor. If agreement is not reached, the grievance is reduced to writing and progresses to the next step.

The number of succeeding steps will depend on your organizational structure. Typically, there are two or three steps, with the president, owner, or senior administrative person making the final decision.

Be sure to set a time limit within which a grievance must be filed and target dates for action at each step. Otherwise, long-forgotten complaints may be revived to plague you, or there may be undue delays in progress toward a mutually satisfactory conclusion.

© 1991 The Dartnell Corporation

The key to the effective adjustment of employee problems lies in the attitude of the supervisors as they reflect the attitude and philosophy of their employer. If a supervisor is willing to listen to an employee's complaint and take action, when it is legitimate, grievances will not be too much of a problem.

Guidelines for Supervisors

1. An employee has the right to talk to his or her supervisor about a problem, real or imagined, and the supervisor is responsible for listening with interest and attention.

2. When an employee has a justified complaint, the supervisor should take immediate remedial action. If such an action cannot be taken, an acceptable explanation should be given.

3. A supervisor should never promise action and not follow through. An employee who is left in a state of uncertainty is likely to be one whose grievance will grow and fester.

All grievance machinery—even the most elaborate—is based upon these simple maxims. They are a practical application of the Golden Rule.

No nonunion grievance procedure will work unless it has the wholehearted backing of top management. It must be clearly understood that the successful resolution of employee complaints is an integral part of each manager's job duties.

Train the Managers

SESCO suggests that the following points be included in training managers to settle employee complaints and grievances effectively and to promote more harmonious employer-employee relationships:

1. To an employee, a grievance, whether real or imaginary, is a grievance in any case and requires fair, open-minded, patient, and considerate treatment.

2. The immediate supervisor of the employee is the first person to whom a grievance should be taken.

3. The grievance procedure allows an employee to appeal or take a grievance to a higher supervisory level if it is ignored, neglected, unfairly handled, or if the request is refused by the immediate supervisor.

4. Every employee should know that there is a right to state a grievance and that your personnel procedures assure this right.

5. When employees have complaints or grievances, the supervisor should listen sincerely, get the employee's explanation or view of the fact, withhold immediate judgment or snap decisions, discuss the grievance in private, and take prompt action on the problem.

6. In dealing with an employee complaint or grievance, the supervisor should discuss, not argue; be friendly, not antagonistic or defensive; and avoid any implication or threat of retaliation because the employee has voiced a complaint or grievance.

7. Whether or not the grievance is justified, the employee should receive a timely decision and explanation of the basis of the decision.

8. If someone is at fault or has made a mistake, it should be frankly admitted, and action taken to make amends.

9. Don't pass the buck in accepting a grievance, in acting on a grievance, in explaining the decision, or in saying "no" when justified by proper review. If you lack the proper authority to handle the grievance, get the answer from one who does have the authority.

10. Give a fair hearing: judge the employee's story objectively. If a past action of yours has been unintentionally unfair, admit it, and set the situation straight. You will gain the respect of the employees by doing so.

Maintain a file of grievances and complaints and document all final answers and solutions made in settlements. Review this file periodically and take action to remove or correct all possible areas of vulnerability to overall job satisfaction and high morale.

Following is a very basic complaint procedure. You will have to substitute appropriate titles in the steps to apply to your own operation.

Our Complaint Procedure—If You Have a Problem

Your complaints or problems are of concern to us. It will always be our policy to let an employee tell his or her side of the story and give full consideration to the problem or complaint. If you follow these steps, no one will criticize or penalize you in any way. Remember, the only way we can help you answer your questions or solve your problems is for you to tell us about them.

1. If you have a complaint to make or if you feel that any action by your employer or supervisor is unjust, go to your immediate supervisor about it. That person knows more about you and your job than any member of management and is in the best position to handle your complaint properly and quickly. Be sure to talk with your supervisor within two consecutive workdays. If the problem or complaint you have is with your supervisor, you may omit Step 1 and go directly to Step 2.

2. If you have not received a satisfactory answer or settlement from your immediate supervisor, you will be allowed five days to refer your problem in writing to your department manager. You may obtain assistance from the Personnel Office in preparing the written presentation of your problem, and you may then present your problem to the department manager who will give you an answer with five days of your presentation.

3. If you are not satisfied with the recommendation provided by your department manager, you will have an additional five days to request an appointment for a

personal interview with _____, who will discuss the problem with you and review all aspects of it thoroughly. The _____ will respond within five days of the personal interview. Any decision rendered by the _____ must be regarded as final and binding.

Please remember that the only purpose of our complaint procedure is to give us an opportunity to clear up any problems or complaints of any kind. In order for this complaint procedure to work, you must want it to work and use it. It is for your benefit. When things go wrong, we would like to have a chance to correct them if we can.

4.09 Employee Handbook Development Checklist

Complaint and Grievance Procedures

The following checklist can be used to help determine the various subjects to include in your handbook. Sample handbook statements covering many of the items in this checklist appear in this section. They can be used to help draft your personalized employee handbook statements.

Our Employee Handbook Should Include:

1. Defining the term *grievance*   Yes ___ No ___ Maybe ___

   A. What is a grievance?   Yes ___ No ___ Maybe ___
   B. What is not a grievance?   Yes ___ No ___ Maybe ___

2. Steps to be followed in the grievance procedure   Yes ___ No ___ Maybe ___

   A. Number of steps or levels in the procedure   Yes ___ No ___ Maybe ___
   B. Defining the parties involved at each step of the procedure   Yes ___ No ___ Maybe ___

3. Defining time intervals for each step of the procedure in which a decision is to be made and between each step of the procedure   Yes ___ No ___ Maybe ___

4. Policy stating that a grievance will be considered settled if not presented to next higher step within established time limits   Yes ___ No ___ Maybe ___

5. Policy requiring grievances to be written out   Yes ___ No ___ Maybe ___

   A. Recommended form and number of copies   Yes ___ No ___ Maybe ___
   B. Type of information to be included in written grievance   Yes ___ No ___ Maybe ___

6. If organized, policy statement defining union representatives who have the right to investigate and assist in the settlement of employee grievances at various steps of the procedure   Yes ___ No ___ Maybe ___

7. Policy statement on establishing grievance sessions during workday or after working hours   Yes ___ No ___ Maybe ___

8. Policy statement on how employees are paid for time spent in processing grievances   Yes ___ No ___ Maybe ___

9. Payment for time spent in processing grievances to apply under which situations?   Yes ___ No ___ Maybe ___

   A. Grievance sessions during working hours   Yes ___ No ___ Maybe ___

    B. Grievance sessions after working hours   Yes ___ No ___ Maybe ___

    C. Grievance sessions at specific steps of the
       grievance procedure   Yes ___ No ___ Maybe ___

    D. Grievance session called only by management   Yes ___ No ___ Maybe ___

10. Policy statement requiring employee union
    representatives to obtain prior approval of supervisor
    in charge of department when representatives wish
    to investigate the grievance   Yes ___ No ___ Maybe ___

Sample Policies: Complaint Procedures

Sample Policy 1

It is our purpose to provide an effective and acceptable means for employees to bring problems and complaints concerning their work and their well-being at work to the attention of management. For that reason, a formal grievance procedure has been established for the benefit and use of (name of company) employees.

1. Definition of Grievance

   A grievance is any condition of employment that the employee feels is unjust or unfair, or thinks should be brought to the attention of company management. To assure prompt attention, grievances should be submitted within five working days of the event prompting the grievance.

2. Procedure

   a. Any grievance must first be given orally or in writing to the employee's immediate supervisor. The employee should submit the grievance personally but may ask a fellow employee to appear with him/her.

   b. If the grievance was not written out by the employee, it should be written by the supervisor for permanent record. Grievances must be signed by the supervisor and the employee.

   c. The employee's supervisor will attempt to resolve the question and must respond within two working days in writing, describing the steps taken to correct the problem. If the employee's supervisor cannot settle the grievance, the supervisor will submit a written response to the Personnel Manager for review. The Personnel Manager will follow the grievance through to a final solution, taking it to the President of the company for final arbitration if necessary.

   d. If the employee does not feel comfortable submitting the grievance to his/her immediate supervisor, the employee may submit the grievance directly to the Personnel Manager after receiving the supervisor's permission. The Personnel Manager will then write out the grievance and discuss it with the employee's supervisor before taking it to a final solution.

Sample Policy 2

The following equity procedure is established to provide a means of appeal from a decision, company policy, personal treatment, etc., (name of company's) long history of fair dealings with employees, as well as the existence of these formal steps, assures fair and equitable consideration of all complaints or grievances that may arise within a reasonable amount of time.

Follow the sequence outlined below to take advantage of the procedure:

Step 1   Discuss the situation with your immediate supervisor. If you feel the problem is of such a nature that you cannot do so, take the matter to the Director of Personnel.

This should be done at a time which will cause no disruption to the flow of work. In most instances, you will receive an answer within three working days. All decisions come through the supervisor involved and not the Director of Personnel. If you consider the decision unreasonable or unfair, you may discuss it further with the Director of Personnel. Most problems are settled through this initial step; but if you are still dissatisfied, you may appeal the decision through Step 2.

Step 2 Make an appointment, through the Director of Personnel, to discuss the matter with your supervisor's immediate superior, who will consider it and give an answer within three working days. If the problem is still not resolved, you may follow the procedure as outlined in Step 3.

Step 3 All complaints taken beyond Step 2 must be in writing and signed. If you need assistance, the Director of Personnel or your supervisor will prepare a written summary of the situation and give it to you for your approval and signature. The Director of Personnel will submit the matter to the member of the management committee responsible for your area of work, who will review the situation and discuss it with you and render a decision within three working days.

Step 4 A final appeal may be made to the President of the company if there is a question of discrimination, legality, or company policy. The Personnel Department will submit the matter to the President of the company, who will review it and deliver in writing a final decision within ten working days. If you wish at this point to discuss the matter with the President personally, arrangements will be made by the Director of Personnel for you to meet with him as soon as it is mutually convenient.

The company is anxious to take care of complaints before they become major problems for either you or (name of company). For this reason, we urge employees to bring any disturbing matters to management's attention through the equity procedure as outlined.

Sample Policy 3

Management intends that you shall receive fair and equal consideration of problems or misunderstandings that may arise in connection with your job. If you are a regular nonexempt, nonsupervisory employee not represented by a union, the following paragraphs outline the action you should take in order that your problem or misunderstanding will receive proper attention.

FIRST: If you have a problem or misunderstanding that affects your job, take it up with your supervisor within five working days of its occurrence. Your supervisor will give you an opportunity to discuss the matter fully and will give you an answer within three working days following the discussion. The majority of such problems will be of such a nature that they can be settled between you and your supervisor with mutual satisfaction.

SECOND: In case the problem or misunderstanding cannot be settled satisfactorily between you and your supervisor, you should describe your problem in writing and submit it to your department head within three working days thereafter. Your department head will meet with you within three working days following receipt of your request and will give you a written answer within three working days following the meeting.

THIRD: If further review is needed, the written grievance should be submitted to your Division or Plant Manager or General Office Department Head, whichever is appropriate, within five working days following the receipt of the reply in the second step. Your Manager or General Office Department Head will meet with you within five working days following receipt of your request and will give you a written answer within five working days following the meeting.

FOURTH: If the problem or misunderstanding cannot be satisfactorily resolved by the Division or Plant Manager or General Office Department Head, you may submit it to the President within five working days following the third step answer. The President or a designated representative will meet with you within ten working days following the receipt of your request, and will provide you with a written answer within five working days following the meeting. The object of the procedure is to obtain a complete understanding of the problem and to try to reach a settlement at the lowest supervisory level.

Sample Policy 4

Your complaints or problems are of concern to us. It is our purpose to provide you an effective and acceptable means of bringing your problems and complaints concerning your well-being while at work to our attention. For your benefit, we have established a Complaint Procedure to be used by all employees.

It will always be our policy to let employees tell their side of the story and give full consideration to their problem or complaint. There will be no discrimination against anyone for presenting a complaint or discussing a problem with supervisors or anyone in our management. If you follow these steps, you will not be criticized or penalized in any way.

Please remember that the only purpose of our complaint procedure is to give you, our fellow employees, and the company an opportunity to clear up any problems or complaints of any kind. *In order for this open-door complaint policy to work, you must want it to work and use it. It's for your benefit. Our door is always open.* When things go wrong, we would like to have the chance to fix them if we can.

Steps to Take

Step 1: If you have a complaint to make or if you feel that any action by the company or supervisor is unjust, go talk to your supervisor about it. Your supervisor knows more about you and your job than any other member of management, and is in the best position to handle your complaint properly and quickly. Be sure to talk with your supervisor within five consecutive workdays. Your supervisor will make every effort to satisfy your problem or complaint within three working days. If the problem or complaint you have is with your supervisor, you may omit Step 1 and go directly to Step 2.

Step 2: If you feel your supervisor has not answered your complaint to your satisfaction, you should refer your problem in writing to your department manager within five days. Your department manager will provide you with an answer within five working days of your presentation.

Step 3: If you feel your department manager has not answered your complaint to your satisfaction, you will have an additional five (5) days to request an appointment for a personal interview with the President, who will discuss the problem with you and review all the aspects thoroughly. The President will respond within five days of the personal interview. Because the responsibility for the operations of the association is the President's, any decision rendered in a problem situation by the President will be final and binding.

Sample Policy 5

Your complaints and problems, large and small, are of concern to us. For this reason we have provided for you an effective means to bring your problems and complaints to the attention of company management. This "Problem-Solving Procedure" is described below.

It will always be our policy to let you tell your side of the story and give full consideration to your problem or complaint. There will be no discrimination against you for your part in presenting a complaint or in discussing a problem with your supervisor with any other member of management. If you follow the steps outlined below, no one will criticize you or penalize you in any way. The sole purpose of this Problem-Solving Procedure is to help you work out any complaint or problem you have to the satisfaction of both you and the company. Remember, the only way we can help you answer a question or solve a problem is for you to tell us about it.

Problem-Solving Procedure

Step 1:

If you have a complaint or if you feel that any action by the company or company management is unjust, talk to your immediate supervisor about it. Your supervisor knows more about you and your job than any other member of management. He or she is in the best position to handle your complaint or problem properly and quickly. If you are concerned about a specific action or situation, you should discuss the problem with your immediate supervisor within two consecutive workdays of its occurrence. (If your complaint or problem involves your supervisor, you may skip Step 1 and begin with Step 2.)

Step 2:

If the response which you receive from your supervisor is not satisfactory to you, you may then take your complaint in writing to the Production Manager. You should do so within two working days of receiving your supervisor's response. The Production Manager will make every effort to give you a satisfactory answer within two working days after receiving your written complaint.

Step 3:

If the response which you receive from the Production Manager is not satisfactory to you, you may then take your complaint to the Plant Manager. You should do so within two working days of receiving the Production Manager's response. The Plant Manager will make every effort to give you a satisfactory answer within two working days after receiving your written complaint.

Step 4:

If, after receiving an answer from the Plant Manager, you are still not satisfied, notify the company President. The President will review your problem carefully and will give you an answer within five working days after receiving it. This answer will be final.

Please remember that the only purpose of the problem-solving procedure is to give you, your fellow employees, and the company an opportunity to clear up any problems or complaints. In order for this problem-solving policy to work, you must want it to work and use it. It is for your benefit. When you feel that things have gone wrong, we would like to have the chance to fix them if we can.

Any employee desiring assistance with this problem-solving procedure is invited to contact the Personnel Manager.

Sample Policy 6

When you perceive things going wrong or when you have a question or a problem, you can expect to receive fair and objective consideration and answers without reprisal in an attempt to resolve your specific concern. This includes questions or problems concerning safety, compensation, fair treatment, supervision, discipline, policies and practices, or working conditions.

The formal procedure for seeking a solution to your complaint is as follows:

1. First, consult with your immediate supervisor. Most employees find personal concerns can be resolved satisfactorily by discussing them with their supervisor.

2/3. You should find your supervisor's answers to your complaint or problem completely satisfactory. However, if you are not satisfied that your supervisor has considered all the facts in your situation, you may choose to discuss the matter further. You may request a meeting first with your department head and then with the appropriate management committee member.

4. If you are not satisfied with the decision from your department head and management committee member in Steps 2 and 3, you are to contact the Human Resources Manager. He/she will then arrange a meeting with you. At this meeting your complaint or problem and its circumstances will be reduced to writing. Then a determination will be made concerning whether or not the previous solutions or decisions given to you were fair and proper.

5. If you are still unsatisfied, a meeting will be arranged for you with the company president. The decision reached in this meeting will be final.

Please remember that the purpose of this complaint procedure is to give you and our company an opportunity to clear up problems or misunderstandings of any kind. It is a formal way of assuring you proper treatment. In order for this procedure to work, you must want it to work and use it when an informal method hasn't worked.

The complaint procedure is not intended for use by any employee after he/she has terminated employment. Employees who are discharged for any reason may not use this policy.

To ensure fair treatment, *dismissal* will not occur until the immediate supervisor has discussed and gained approval for action with his/her chain of command, including the management committee member and the Manager of Human Resources.

Only active "regular full-time" employees may utilize this complaint policy.

4.10 Employee Handbook Development Checklist

Employment Expenses and Reimbursement

The following checklist can be used to help determine the various subjects to include in your handbook. Sample handbook statements covering many of the items in this checklist appear in this section. They can be used to help draft your personalized employee handbook statements.

Our Employee Handbook Should Include:

RELOCATION

1. Management relocation   Yes ___ No ___ Maybe ___

2. Nonmanagement relocation   Yes ___ No ___ Maybe ___

3. New-hire relocation   Yes ___ No ___ Maybe ___

4. Premove expenses   Yes ___ No ___ Maybe ___

5. Sale of old residence   Yes ___ No ___ Maybe ___

    A. Company purchase   Yes ___ No ___ Maybe ___
    B. Company assistance—real estate firm   Yes ___ No ___ Maybe ___
    C. Closing costs   Yes ___ No ___ Maybe ___

6. Purchasing of new residence   Yes ___ No ___ Maybe ___

    A. Bridge load   Yes ___ No ___ Maybe ___
    B. Mortgage differential   Yes ___ No ___ Maybe ___
    C. Closing costs   Yes ___ No ___ Maybe ___
    D. Miscellaneous allowance   Yes ___ No ___ Maybe ___

7. House-hunting trips   Yes ___ No ___ Maybe ___

8. Temporary living expenses   Yes ___ No ___ Maybe ___

9. Household moving expenses   Yes ___ No ___ Maybe ___

10. Use of personal automobile   Yes ___ No ___ Maybe ___

11. Explanation of tax liability   Yes ___ No ___ Maybe ___

12. "Gross-up" procedure   Yes ___ No ___ Maybe ___

13. Authorization required   Yes ___ No ___ Maybe ___

14. Expense reports   Yes ___ No ___ Maybe ___

15. Receipts required   Yes ___ No ___ Maybe ___

BUSINESS TRIPS

1. Travel advance   Yes ___ No ___ Maybe ___

2. Travel authorization   Yes ___ No ___ Maybe ___

3. Rental automobile   Yes ___ No ___ Maybe ___

4. Personal automobile   Yes ___ No ___ Maybe ___

5. Spouse/family travel   Yes ___ No ___ Maybe ___

6. Meal allowance   Yes ___ No ___ Maybe ___

7. Air travel   Yes ___ No ___ Maybe ___

8. Nonallowable expenses   Yes ___ No ___ Maybe ___

9. Travel expense report   Yes ___ No ___ Maybe ___

10. Receipts required   Yes ___ No ___ Maybe ___

OTHER EXPENSE SUBJECTS

1. Payment of employment expenses   Yes ___ No ___ Maybe ___

2. Temporary assignment expenses   Yes ___ No ___ Maybe ___

3. Automobile usage   Yes ___ No ___ Maybe ___

4. Customer entertaining   Yes ___ No ___ Maybe ___

5. Meal reimbursement   Yes ___ No ___ Maybe ___

6. Membership in clubs and civic organizations   Yes ___ No ___ Maybe ___

7. Participation in trade and professional associations   Yes ___ No ___ Maybe ___

Sample Policies: Relocation Expenses

Sample Policy 1

When an employee is required to transfer from one company location to another at the company's request, all reasonable travel and out-of-pocket expenses connected with the transfer will be paid by the company. This includes lodging, meals, transportation for the employee and dependents, as well as the moving expenses of the employee's furniture and household goods.

Sample Policy 2

If you are requested to transfer to a different company location, we will make every effort to help you and your family make this relocation with a minimum of inconvenience. Please discuss our moving and transfer policy with your department manager. Our company will pay the following moving and relocation expenses:

1. All your living expenses up to a maximum of 30 days if you cannot find permanent living quarters immediately.

2. Car transportation expenses for you and your family.

3. All moving expenses for your household goods, including storage charges up to a maximum of 30 days.

Our company will not pay for any losses you may incur under a lease of a house or an apartment or any loss in the sale of your personal real estate during the transfer.

Sample Policy 3

Employees transferred to another company location at the company's request will be eligible for moving and living expenses as follows:

1. Packing, shipping, and unpacking charges of personal and household goods up to a maximum of 8,000 pounds including weight of crating plus insurance on household goods.

2. Cost of transportation of the employee and family to the new location, either by plane or surface. If the employee elects to drive his own vehicle, he will be allowed 27¢ per mile for most direct mileage from point of origin to the destination. Mileage allowance will be permitted only for one automobile per employee family.

3. Actual and reasonable meal expenses and lodging for the employee and immediate dependent family will be allowed regardless of the method of transportation. Actual and reasonable expenses for motels, meals, and out-of-pocket expenses will be allowed for the employee and dependents upon arrival at the new company facility for a period not to exceed 10 days in which to locate suitable living quarters.

    If suitable living quarters are not obtained at the end of 10 days, a special cost-of-living per diem allowance may be approved for a period not to exceed an additional 15 days.

All moving, lodging, and meal expenses will be submitted by the employee to the immediate supervisor for approval and reimbursement at the end of each month.

Sample Policies: Business Trips _____

Sample Policy 1

You are reimbursed for expenses incurred by you in the conduct of company business, as authorized by your supervisor. Such items as transportation, telephone, and rooms, as well as meals under certain conditions, are included. Full information concerning the rules governing payment of such expenses can be obtained from your supervisor.

Sample Policy 2

When employees must travel on company business, the company intends to provide for their comfort and well-being and to receive the best value for the money spent on business travel expenses.

In general, the company will pay all reasonable business travel expenses. Employees are expected to live normally while on company business without experiencing any personal financial loss. At the same time, employees are asked to spend the company's money with the same care and judgment that they would use with their own funds.

The following guidelines are intended to summarize the company's practices in several key areas. Specific details about these and other aspects of business travel are available from department managers and the Personnel and Finance Departments.

Air Travel—The destination and duration of a flight will determine the class of travel that may be used. As a general rule:

- Economy class should be used for all flights within the U.S.

- Business class may be used for all intercontinental and transcontinental flights and for travel within continental Europe, where appropriate.

- First-class ticketing may be permitted in exceptional cases and only after approval by the General Manager or Vice-President of Administration.

Automobile Transportation—When driving is the most convenient and economical means of transportation, employees may rent a car to reach their destination or to use during the business trip. Employees should decline the collision damage waiver and personal accident insurance offered in the car rental agreement since the company provides this insurance.

Employees who want to use their personal automobile for a business trip may do so under the following conditions:

- They must obtain their supervisor's approval in advance.

- Use of their automobile is the most economical and convenient form of transportation to the business site.

- They carry personal automobile insurance for both bodily injury and property damage.

Reimbursement for expenses associated with the use of a personal automobile includes mileage at the prevailing corporate rate and tolls. The maximum amount the company will pay for a trip during which an employee uses a personal automobile will be the amount that would have been reimbursed if the employee had taken an economy class flight or train.

Business Entertainment Guidelines—Employees who travel on company business may be obliged to entertain business associates in the normal course of a business trip. The amount of the expenses incurred should reflect good business practice and judgment. All entertainment expenses should be well-documented to include the time, place, business purpose, names, and business relationships of the people involved.

Company-Approved Travel Agencies—Employees should use a travel agent designated by the company in order to obtain the most economical prices for air fare, car rentals, hotels, and other related expenses. The company's designated travel agent will ensure that employees receive the most advantageous arrangements to accommodate business and personal needs.

4.11 Union-Free Policy Statements

SESCO Observations and Recommendations
Guidelines for Drafting and Publishing Union-Free Policy Statements

Since 1947, the National Labor Relations Act, as amended by the Taft-Hartley Act, has provided covered employees with the right to engage in union activities, to join a union, or to refrain from engaging in union activities and the right not to belong to a labor union under Section 7:

> Employees shall have the right to self-organization, to form, join, or assist labor organizations, to bargain collectively through representatives of their own choosing, and to engage in other concerted activities for the purpose of collective bargaining or other mutual aid or protection, and shall also have the right to refrain from any or all of such activities except to the extent that such right may be affected by an agreement requiring membership in a labor organization as a condition of employment as authorized in Section 8(a)(3).

Under Section 8(c) of the National Labor Relations Act, an employer has the right to express his opinion, verbally and in printed form, of his preference that his organization operate union-free.

> The expressing of any views, arguments, or opinion, or the dissemination thereof, whether in written, printed, graphic, or visual form, shall not constitute or be evidence of an unfair labor practice under any of the provisions of this Act, if such expression contains no threat of reprisal or force or promise of benefit.

Most union-free employee handbooks contain policy statements explaining the company's reasons why it prefers to operate free of unionization. In addition, such union-free policy statements explain in some detail the advantages to employees and their families of not being represented by a labor organization for the purpose of collective bargaining.

Important NLRB Case on Handbook Union-Free Policy Statements

The National Labor Relations Board (NLRB) has ruled for the first time that an employee handbook statement confirming an employer's union-free policy violated Section 8(a)(1) of the National Labor Relations Act (NLRA). La Quinta Motor Inns, Inc. (1989) 293 NLRB No. 6, 130 LRRM (BNA) 1338 (1989) CCH NLRB 15, 411 1988-89.

Until the board's decision in La Quinta Motor Inns, an employer's union-free policies have been protected under the constitutional guarantees of "free speech" and Section 8(c) of the Act (see above). Section 8(c) protects an employer's right to communicate with employees regarding unions, as long as threats of reprisal or force or promises of benefits are absent.

La Quinta operates a chain of motor inns. The company revised its employee handbook in 1983, which was distributed to all new hires and included several paragraphs under the title "Company Position on Labor Unions":

La Quinta's position on labor unions is something you should know.... It is our belief that direct interaction between our employees and management is essential for the continued maintenance of good employee relations. We are committed to protect the personal rights and independence of our employees from outside interference from any union or agent.

The page following the union-free policy in the handbook was an acceptance form that employees were asked to sign, acknowledging receipt and understanding of the handbook. Like many employers' acceptance forms, La Quinta's form also stated that the employee agreed to abide by the policies and procedures contained in the handbook. Continued employment was conditioned on adherence to the employer's rules.

During an organizing drive, the Hotel, Bartenders and Restaurant Workers Union filed an unfair labor practice charge with the NLRB against La Quinta. The union alleged that the union-free policy contained in the handbook interfered with employees' Section 7 rights to organize, form, or join a union.

Agreeing with the union, the administrative law judge (ALJ) found that the combined message of the union-free policy statement and the handbook acceptance form was "reasonably coercive." The policy, followed by a request for the employee's signature, "created the impression that, as a term of employment, employees must agree not to engage in activities in support of a labor organization."

On appeal, the board affirmed the ALJ's reasoning and found that La Quinta employees could infer that adherence to the employer's policies and procedures, as required by the acceptance form, would also require supporting the union-free policy statement.

There was nothing coercive found by the NLRB in the union-free statement cited above. However, it was the location of the union-free statement on the last page of the handbook, next to the employee acceptance receipt page that led the NLRB to rule the union-free statement was "coercive." The union-free statement was published in the last section of the handbook entitled, "Other Policies," which also contained policy statements on No Solicitation Rule, Attendance and Punctuality, Hours of Work, Break Periods, Overtime, etc. The union-free statement was the last item in this section and was immediately followed by the perforated "employee acceptance" page containing language to the effect that the employee agreed to "abide by the policies and procedures contained herein.... I understand that continuance of my employment is contingent on my so abiding by these rules."

The ALJ ruled that by the company's placing the union-free policy in the "Other Policies" section of the handbook, then putting the "employee acceptance" form perforated page immediately thereafter, that the employer was threatening to discharge anybody who didn't comply with the company's union-free policy statement.

The NLRB concluded that *the company made no effort to convey clearly to its employees that its position on labor unions was merely a statement of opinion and not a policy covered by the scope of possible discipline contained in the employee acceptance form.*

According to the NLRB, *the positioning of the policy and the acceptance form as the last two pages of the handbook—and the requirement that all employees sign the acceptance form*—also led employees to believe that failure to execute and abide by the "acceptance" could lead to discharge.

Caution on Publishing Union-Free Statements in Handbooks Distributed to Unionized Employees

In 1989, the United Food and Commercial Workers Union (UFCW, Local 23) filed unfair labor practice charges against an employer, Heck's, Inc. (293 NLRB No. 132, 1988-1989 CCH NLRB, 15,517). The union alleged the employer had violated the act (NLRA) by interfering with, restraining, or coercing employees in the exercise of their rights to belong to the union [Section 8(a)(1)].

The "proof" offered by the union was the employer's handbook which contained a union-free policy statement. The handbook also contained a receipt page in which the employer required employees in the bargaining unit to acknowledge with their signature that they agreed to live up to and comply with the personnel policies outlined in the employee handbook.

The NLRB investigated the charges and held the employer in violation of the act because in requiring employees to sign the receipt page that contained the requirement that employees agree to be bound by the employee handbook policies and procedures, the employer was giving the impression to employees that they would be subject to employee discipline if they failed to comply with all personnel policies contained in the handbook. According to the NLRB, the employer was violating the act because he was requesting employees to refrain from their right to unionize and bargain collectively.

It is important to note that the NLRB did not rule that the company violated the act by merely publishing their union-free policy statement in the handbook. It was a violation of the act because the company was requesting employees to "promise in writing" to be bound by that union-free policy statement. Furthermore, the NLRB concluded that by requesting employees represented by a union to promise in writing to comply with the company's union-free policy was an attempt to "undermine" the union as the exclusive bargaining agent of employees in the appropriate bargaining unit.

Although these two NLRB cases are important for future compliance with the NLRB's guidelines by union-free employers, the cases should not discourage employers from continuing to draft, publish, and distribute union-free policy statements in future employee handbooks. The following employer recommendations and guidelines should be followed to protect their continued right to communicate to their union-free employees the company's preference to operate their business in a union-free environment.

SESCO Recommendations

1. Review current employee handbook union-free policy statements regarding their *content and location* in your employee handbook. Place future

union-free policy statements in the introductory section of the handbook dealing with the company's history, employee relations policies, etc.

2. Rewrite and republish the employee handbook receipt or acceptance pages that are usually found at the back of the handbook, perforated, and acknowledged by new and present employees. Draft the revised "acceptance" or "acknowledgement" form so that present or newly hired employees are confirming that they have read or will read the employee handbook and the policies contained therein without requiring employees "to agree to abide by the policies."

   It is not necessary to require an employee to agree in writing to follow all personnel policies or to comply with them, in order to protect the company. Should a former employee sue an employer alleging "wrongful discharge" or that there was some "guarantee" on the basis that the employee handbook was a "contract" between the former employee and employer, acceptance/receipt form wording requiring employees to abide or comply with all personnel policies of the handbook may persuade a judge to rule that a "contract" was created in the employee handbook.

   If a union-free employer desires to continue language in the acceptance/receipt page of future handbooks stating that employees will agree to comply with all handbook policies, then the employer should clearly separate and distinguish between company "work rules" and "personnel policies." The employer would require only that the employees agree to abide by company "work rules" on the receipt page. An alternative way of protecting the employer is to specifically exclude the union-free policy statement from the acceptance/receipt page language of the handbook.

3. Another employer option is simply to avoid any requirement that employees sign and acknowledge any acceptance or receipt statements in the employee handbook. However, the advantages of having a copy of the acceptance/receipt form in the employee's handbook can be of importance to employers in future administration of personnel policies and benefits when it can be proven the employee did receive the employee handbook and was aware of the company's personnel policies, work rules, etc. (See Section 3.05 for sample acceptance/receipt pages.)

4. Draft, publish, and distribute union-free policy statements but do not include them in future employee handbooks. They can be posted on bulletin boards, distributed in a special handbook supplement, and distributed to new employees in the induction and orientation process.

4.11 Employee Handbook Development Checklist

Union-Free Policy Statements

The following checklist can be used to help determine the various subjects to include in your handbook. Sample handbook statements covering many of the items in this checklist appear in this section. They can be used to help draft your personalized employee handbook statements.

Our Employee Handbook Should Include:

1. Do we want to draft and publish a union-free policy statement? Yes ___ No ___ Maybe ___

2. Should the policy statement refer to past unionization attempts? Yes ___ No ___ Maybe ___

3. Should the policy statement refer to federal and/or state labor law rights of employees to join or not join a labor union? Yes ___ No ___ Maybe ___

4. Should the policy statement spell out employee advantages in working in a union-free company? Yes ___ No ___ Maybe ___

5. Should the policy statement point out disadvantages of unionization for employees and their families? Yes ___ No ___ Maybe ___

6. Should the policy statement describe the percentage of decline of unionization in U.S. and our industry? Yes ___ No ___ Maybe ___

7. If a policy statement is included in the handbook, will employee "acknowledgement and receipt" statements be free of the requirement that employees "comply" or "abide" by the policy as a condition of employment? Yes ___ No ___ Maybe ___

8. Does the company presently have a union-free policy statement in an employee handbook? Yes ___ No ___ Maybe ___

9. Does the company presently have a union-free policy statement in its corporate personnel policies and procedures manual? Yes ___ No ___ Maybe ___

10. Has the present, existing union-free policy statement in the employee handbook or revised handbook been reviewed by labor counsel? Yes ___ No ___ Maybe ___

Sample Policies: Union-Free Statements _____

Sample Policy 1

(Name of company) provides a union-free work environment by maintaining an open-door policy under which each employee has the right to deal directly with members of management with reference to all working conditions. Talking face-to-face, without third parties, is the best way to achieve mutual goals—an enjoyable and profitable workplace.

When a union organizes a company, sides are taken, and it becomes a "we/they" situation. This is contrary to the strong team spirit that is necessary in order for us all to prosper. (Name of company), like all other companies, will have problems. We feel our success in finding solutions to those problems, however, is the result of cooperative efforts based on confidence in each other and mutual respect. With this in mind, union representation becomes unnecessary, and we share in our success directly with one another.

Sample Policy 2

Union membership is not a requirement for employment in your job with (name of company). There is always a chance, however, that in the future a labor union organizer will try to persuade some of our nonunion employees to sign union membership authorization cards. For this reason, it is important that you understand our position concerning unions.

To say it simply and clearly, while you have the legal right to join a labor union, you also have the legal right *not* to join a labor union. We prefer to work with our employees informally, personally, and directly, rather than through third-party outsiders intervening between us. Furthermore, we accept our responsibility to provide good pay, benefits, and working conditions, to the best of our ability under sound business practices. You do not need a third party to obtain these benefits. A third party could only deplete your spendable income.

Sample Policy 3

(Name of company) is an open shop or nonunion company. We operate on the principle that employees have the freedom to speak for themselves and discuss directly with management their complaints, comments, suggestions, and problems without third-party interference. As a result, we believe employees have no need for a union.

A union, despite promises, cannot create jobs or increase a company's income so that higher wages can be paid. Only a competitive, aggressive, and productive company can generate the sales needed to make jobs secure and to raise wages and improve benefits. Outside intervention may reduce a company's competitive position, resulting in possible loss of business, which may lead to loss of jobs and wages. Because we believe a labor union could not serve the best interest of (name of company) employees, the company will oppose any attempt of union organization, by every legal means.

This open-shop philosophy should not be interpreted as an attack on labor unions; instead, this policy reflects our belief that the interest of all (name of company) employees will be best served by working directly with each other, rather than through outsiders. (Name of company) has operated as a nonunion company since it was founded in (date) and we see no logical reason, or any need, for a situation to arise where a third party, under outside direction and influence, should stand between you and the company.

Sample Policy 4

(Name of company) does not require individuals to join or to affiliate with a labor organization in order to work at our company. In fact, the federal law guarantees the right to employees not to have to join any union in order to hold a job. It is therefore not necessary for you or any other employee to have to join or to have to pay dues or other union fees to any union to work at our company.

It is the policy of our company to pay wages that compare favorably with other wages in other industries in our area, to give the best possible working conditions we can, to deal with our employees fairly and honestly, and to treat each employee as an individual. Even more important is our intention of doing everything possible to furnish excellent opportunities for employees who want to work at our company and to provide them with the best possible job satisfaction.

Under these policies and conditions, we do not feel that a union could help our employees.

In the best interest of our employees and our company, we will oppose by every moral and legal means any attempt by any union or any other outside organization to disturb or break up the fine relationship we enjoy with our employees here.

Sample Policy 5

In our company we believe in dealing with people directly as individuals rather than through a third party. This does not mean that we do not have problems on occasion. However, we are able to work them out without the intervention of outsiders. No organization is free from day-to-day problems, but we believe that our policies and practices serve to help us resolve these problems. We recognize and accept our responsibility to provide the best working conditions, pay, and benefits that we can afford. It is not necessary for you to pay union dues to receive fair treatment, and we encourage you to bring your problems to your supervisor or anyone else you feel can help you; and we, in turn, promise to listen and give the best possible response we can. Unions have never found anybody his job and they have never caused anybody to keep his job. You are an individual and we respect the right that you have to speak for yourself. All of us, working together, will make this a healthy, successful organization for each of us and our families.

Sample Policy 6

We want our employees to clearly understand that we desire a union-free operation.

We believe a union is not necessary for our employees to receive fair and equitable treatment. Regardless of whether or not our employees are represented by a union, we will maintain pay and benefits which are comparable to the industry in this area.

You have the right to engage in union activities as described in the National Labor Relations Act. Likewise, you have the right not to join a union. You may be asked by a union organizer to sign an "authorization card." Signing an authorization card generally means that the signer would like a particular union to become his bargaining agent or representative. Because we believe that a union is unnecessary, we ask that you do not sign any authorization card. However, it is your individual decision. You have the right to sign or to refuse to sign the card.

If someone attempts to threaten you or your family into signing a union authorization card, you have the right to report this fact to the NLRB (National Labor Relations Board), Atlanta, Georgia. Union coercion, union intimidation, or union threats are prohibited by federal law. Any employee or our company can file federal unfair labor practice charges against any union for this unlawful conduct. We will not interfere with your right under the law; however, our company will stand up for any employee and support all legal steps to protect our employees and their families from any union coercion, union intimidation, or union threats.

Also, we understand that problems may arise simply because we're all human. Therefore, we have an effective policy for resolving employee problems and differing supervisory practices. (See section on Grievance Procedure.)

We intend to be responsive to your needs and recognize that your questions deserve timely answers.

Sample Policy 7

(Name of company) is a 100 percent nonunion company. This means that all our employees are at liberty to deal directly with the company management—without any third party intervening or coming between us. We consider this a high compliment to us and to our employees indicating that they do not feel the need for third-party representation.

Experience shows that where there are unions there is often trouble, strife, and discord. It is therefore our positive intention to oppose unionism by every proper means and in particular by fair and square treatment of our employees.

It is quite possible that from time to time our employees may be approached by union representatives who will try to sell them on unionism. In such approaches or contacts, they often make false promises and claims and very frequently distort the facts with respect to matters affecting employees' working relationships with the company. They also hold out many promises which they actually cannot live up to. We sincerely trust that if and when you may be approached by union organizers, you will obtain all facts on all sides, and we invite you to seek information from your supervisor if at any time questions arise on these matters.

It is also important for you to keep in mind that any person who might join or belong to any union will never get any advantages or any preferred treatment at (name of company) of any sort over those who do not join or belong to a union. Also, if anyone at any time should cause any of our employees any trouble at their work or put them under any sort of pressure to join a union, our employees should let the company know about it, and we will see that it is stopped. Everyone should also know that no person will be allowed to carry on union organizing activities on the job and that anyone who does so, and thereby neglects his or her own work or interferes with the work of others, will be subject to serious disciplinary action.

Sample Policy 8

[A large employer that has both union and nonunion employees has printed a small "supplement" consisting of two pages, 5″ × 7″ in size, that is distributed to new employees in their nonunion locations.]

Working Nonunion

This is a nonunion location. None of the employees here are represented by a union.

If you worked at a union location before you came here, you may wonder what it is like to work nonunion. If you worked at a nonunion location before you came here, you may know little about unions.

Unions are organizations to which employees pay monthly dues to represent them in their dealings with management. A union serves as a go-between, a third person between the employee and his supervisor and the other members of management.

Here at this location we do not feel that employees need or want someone outside to represent them. They can speak for themselves. It is not necessary for them to pay union dues or to risk strikes in order to receive competitive wages and benefits or to be treated fairly. As a matter of fact, employees here receive the same wages and benefits and have the same working conditions as do union employees in the same job at other company locations.

As for fair treatment, that is the responsibility of your supervisor and the other members of management, with your doing your part as well. We encourage you to discuss with your supervisor any working problems that may arise, and also to discuss with him any other problems that you care to bring to him. Above all, if something is bothering you, tell us. Don't keep it bottled up inside.

In the Employee Handbook and Handbook Supplement that were given to you, we have spelled out many of the things that we will do for you. We expect you to carry out your obligations, those shown in these two booklets and those conveyed to you otherwise. If you don't think we are carrying out our obligations, talk to your supervisor. You also have access to the nonunion grievance and arbitration procedure shown in the Employee Handbook.

We want to stay nonunion here. Your fellow employees apparently feel the same way, as evidenced by the fact that there is no union here. If you worked nonunion before, we think you'll see even more advantages to working here. If you worked union before, we think you'll enjoy the different atmosphere in a nonunion location.

Welcome aboard. Good luck on your new job. You do your part and we'll do ours, all contributing toward providing essential electric power to the communities we serve.

Sample Policy 9

Often new employees ask how we feel about labor unions, as some of our plants do have unions.

Our plant, like many others within the company, does not. In fact, we do our best to operate this plant in such a way that people here never feel the need to pay dues to have any outside organization represent them. This handbook, for example, spells out our personnel practices and procedures for everyone to know and understand. Our managers, supervisors, and foremen are committed to the fair and consistent application of these practices. They are further committed to the voluntary payment of rates that are proper in this community and to treating each of us with respect. We believe most employees recognize that they already have as much or more than unionization could provide—without union dues.

While we recognize that problems can and will arise in any organization, we are sincere in our desire to make every effort to minimize problems and treat employees fairly. In the past we have had unions attempt to organize our workforce, but our employees have turned them away. You should feel free to discuss this matter with your supervisor because, presumably, unions will return again seeking new members and new sources of monthly union dues.

We believe, and apparently most employees agree, that unionization means more than damaged relationships and lost dues. Strikes and violence have all become synonymous with unionization; and even many disheartened union members at some of our other locations would tell you so, following the bitter 100-day strike the company experienced several years ago.

In short, we feel that unionization offers no advantage to employees here and would represent, in our opinion, a threat to our success. We intend to do the right thing because it just makes good business sense to do so. With the confidence and assistance of every one of us, we should have no need for a union.

4.12 Health, Safety, and Security

SESCO Observations and Recommendations
How to Maintain a Drug-Free Workplace

It is absolutely essential that new or revised employee handbooks contain the employer's policy statement, philosophy, and workplace standards pertaining to maintaining a drug-free workplace and rules prohibiting substance abuse. The challenging and costly problem of drugs in our society has presented some of the most difficult management challenges in working with employees and supervisors in all industries. It is an insidious problem that involves as many as one in five workers using illegal drugs on the job. It is estimated that up to 73 percent of drug abusers hold full-time jobs.

In addition to the unacceptable risk to personnel, employers are picking up the costly tab for lost productivity, absenteeism, and skyrocketing health care expenses and uncontrolled health care insurance premiums. It is estimated that the loss and the cost to American employers in terms of on-the-job accidents, insurance, medical bills, and lost productivity is approximately $100 billion a year.

Employers in the process of revising employee handbooks are responding to this costly people management problem by developing and publishing their substance abuse policies in their handbooks in much detail. Some handbook policy statements remind employees of the following tragic facts:

- 10 percent to 23 percent of all U.S. workers use dangerous drugs on the job.

- An estimated 73 percent of drug abusers hold full-time jobs.

- Drug use has the following effects on employees:
  — 10 times greater absenteeism
  — 4 times greater accident rate
  — 30 percent lower productivity
  — 5 times greater worker's compensation cost
  — 3 times higher health insurance costs
  — 50 percent of accidents reported by companies are drug/alcohol related
  — Male employees tend to be more prone to chemical substance abuse use than female employees
  — Over 5.8 million people use cocaine at least monthly

Handbook Substance Abuse Policy and Drug Testing: Issues and Risks

Legal Considerations: Employers must ensure their substance abuse policies and drug testing procedures do not run afoul of a federal or state law, a local ordinance, a state constitutional provision, or a common-law theory of liability.

In 1988, the federal government recognized the costly, harmful effect illegal drugs have on employees, their families, job performance, and the untold cost to industry by requiring federal government contractors and recipients of federal funds to establish a drug-free workplace. Congress passed the Drug-Free Workplace Act of

1988 (DFWA) as part of the broader Omnibus Drug Initiative Act of 1988. Federal contractors and grantees are required by the DFWA to develop, distribute, and communicate drug-free policies and procedures that effectively deal with the workplace drug problem.

Employers are covered by the DFWA if they have federal government contracts of $25,000 or more, provide goods or services, or obtain grants of federal financial assistance, regardless of value. Covered government contractors and recipients of federal financial assistance are required by the DFWA to certify to the federal government that they have developed and distributed substance abuse policies to prevent, correct, and remove abusive drug use in the workplace. The required substance abuse policy must communicate to all employees that "the unlawful manufacture, distribution, dispensation, possession, or use of a controlled substance is prohibited" in the workplace.

There is nothing in the DFWA regulations that requires drug testing. Surprisingly, DFWA regulations are weak here compared to the drug-free requirements enforced by the Department of Transportation (DOT).

Challenges to drug testing have been based on the following:

- Fourth Amendment—Protection from unreasonable search and seizure by the state (applies to public employees)

- Fourteenth Amendment —Protection from invasion of privacy by state action (applies to public employees)

- Federal and State Handicap Discrimination Laws —Protects alcohol and drug abusers, but employers are not required to employ them if they cannot properly perform the job or if they present a threat to safety (applies to public and/or private employers)

- Collective Bargaining Agreements—Previous rulings imply that the adoption of drug-testing policy constitutes a mandatory subject of bargaining under NLRB.

- Protections Under Common Law—Includes defamation, intentional infliction of emotional distress, negligence, invasion of privacy, wrongful discharge in breach of implied covenant of good faith

- Negligence Law—Employers have a duty to provide a safe workplace for employees and the public at large and face liability for impaired employees' acts.

Medical Considerations:

- Accuracy of drug tests
  - Initial test of choice: Enzyme Multiplied Immunoassay Test (EMIT) (May be prone to producing false positive results)
  - Confirmatory test of choice: Gas Chromatography/Mass Spectrometry (CG/MS)

- Reliability of drug tests
  - Chain-of-custody procedure: Protects against switching, adulterating, or mislabeling of samples

- Professionalism of laboratory

  Professional expertise and procedures of the medical facility processing the drug tests are key factors in enhancing an employer's defensibility. In choosing a facility to perform drug testing, it is recommended the following questions be asked:
  - What methods of screening and confirmation does the lab use?
  - Does the lab use documented chain-of-custody procedures?
  - Does the lab use internal and/or external quality assurance programs?
  - Can the lab provide negative results within 48 hours and confirmed, positive results within 96 hours?
  - Will the lab provide an expert witness if the lab results are challenged?

Recommendations for Developing a Policy:

1. Utilize the task-force approach to policy development, involving those with related expertise and those who have a stake in the outcome. Receive input from your consultant, medical and legal counsel, and those involved in safety, security, and supervision within your organization.

2. Provide employees advance, clear, written notice of the company's philosophy, rules, and consequences regarding substance abuse at work. It is recommended your employee handbook policy cover the following important areas:

   a. Types of substance abuse prohibited under your policy

   b. Types of disciplinary and/or rehabilitation procedures to be taken against employees who violate the substance abuse policy

   c. Drug-free awareness and education information

   d. The availability of an employee assistance program (EAP) for employee counseling provided by the company

   e. Obligations of employees and supervision under the substance abuse policy

3. Provide supervisors with training so they will have a general understanding of chemical dependency and how to undertake intervention in a nonconfrontational way. While supervisors are not to become diagnosticians, they are in a position to refer employees to assistance programs.

4. Base the requirement for drug screening on business necessity, related to safety, security, or job performance, rather than on arbitrary considerations.

5. Ensure the collection, transportation, and analysis of specimens meet high legal, technical, and ethical requirements; use only a reputable lab with high regard for chain-of-custody procedures to ensure proper identification of the specimen.

6. Validate positive tests. When a routine test, such as the enzyme multiplied immunoassay test is positive, follow up with a confirming test such as the gas chromatography/mass spectrometry test.

7. Provide individuals the opportunity to explain or rebut positive test results.

8. Maintain records in strict confidence, divulging test results only to those with a business need to know.

9. Provide employees whose first-time confirmed tests are positive the opportunity to undergo treatment or rehabilitation before disciplinary measures are taken.

10. Ensure your company's policy applies to all levels in the company "from the tool room to the boardroom." Endorsement and practice of your company's policy must come from the highest level of management within your organization.

Pre-employment Documentation: To give fair notice to new applicants and present staff alike and to provide your organization with documentation protection, the statement on page 268 is a suggested model for inclusion in your personnel system.

Intervention and Rehabilitation

Identifying an Impaired Employee: Many substance abuse manifestations are not readily detectable. Additionally, drug use is further masked by substantial denial on the part of the user. In many cases, there are telltale early warning signs, however subtle, that might identify a potentially impaired employee. These indications include the following:

- Blatant signs such as intoxication

- Bizarre behavior

- Redness of the eyes

- Short-term memory loss

- Reoccurring huddling of employees

- Behavior reflecting hyperactivity, overanxiousness, and intenseness

- Frequent mood swings

- Failure to maintain concentration

- Boisterous, assaultive, or irrational behavior

Employee Authorization: Substance Screening

By my signature below, I voluntarily and knowingly agree to the following:

a. I consent to take any physical or medical examinations, including blood and urine or other tests for alcohol and drugs, requested by the company in connection with the processing of my application for employment, and further agree to take any such physical or medical examinations requested by the company during my employment if I am offered and accept a job. I understand that such an examination is needed in order to determine my competence to perform the job or work for which I was hired or to identify any physical or mental condition bearing on my job performance. I understand that refusal to submit to any physical or medical examination ordered by the company is grounds for rejection for employment or for disciplinary action up to and including immediate discharge. I further understand that any information obtained through such exams may be retained by the company and is exclusively the company's property. I also understand that the examinations will be performed by medical personnel, clinics, or laboratories qualified to do the necessary work and that costs for such examinations will be borne by the company.

b. I consent to submit to and cooperate in any questioning, any searches of my assigned vehicle, locker, or storage area, or bags or other belongings on or in the company's property that the company in its discretion may request, and I understand that the refusal to submit to or cooperate in these procedures is grounds for disciplinary action up to and including immediate discharge.

c. I acknowledge that I have read, understand, and will abide by the above notice, that a copy has been furnished to me, and another copy is made a part of my personnel file.

_____   _____

(Employee Signature)   (Date)

- Accidents

- Higher incidence of coughing

- Reduced motivation and energy

- A tendency to frequent hideaway locations—i.e., washrooms, parking lots, and the like

- Signs of paranoia and anxiety

- Signs of lethargy, lack of motivation

- Marked behavior change

- Impaired motor coordination

In confirming that an employee may be unfit for duty, a supervisor should first observe the behavior. A second opinion from another supervisor should be obtained. Next, approach the employee away from the job duties and focus on the unusual behavior. If an explanation is not appropriate, intervene with suspension from job duties, with a mandate or immediate medical assessment. *Caution: Make no attempt to accuse the individual of a chemical wrongdoing.*

Why Provide Opportunity for Rehabilitation?

- Rehabilitation is cost effective. It is often less expensive to treat impaired employees than to terminate them and to recruit, hire, and retrain new employees.

- Rehabilitation opportunities increase employee loyalty and morale.

- A rehabilitation program enables employees to view substance abuse policies as constructive, rather than exclusively punitive, with the welfare of both company and employee of concern.

EAPs (Employee Assistance Programs)

- EAPs are job-based strategies for the identification, motivation, and treatment of impaired employees in which company-authorized professionals provide assistance in returning such employees to a productive position within the workplace.

- Internal EAPs are in-house programs in which professionals in the areas of medicine, psychiatry, and/or social work are employed or retained by the company for its employees' rehabilitation.

- External EAPs are programs in which employers rely on professionals in private practice, in-patient facilities, out-patient facilities, and/or professionals in public agencies to provide treatment and/or counseling.

Resources for Treatment and Consultation

- Local comprehensive mental health centers

- Alcoholics Anonymous

- Narcotics Anonymous

- Al-Anon Family Groups

- Telephone book Yellow Pages:
  - "Alcohol Information and Treatment Centers"
  - "Drug Abuse and Addiction"

- National Institute on Drug Abuse

Substance Abuse Intervention Effectiveness
Ten Essentials for Effectiveness in Intervention and Treatment

1. Early Intervention—Intervention needs to occur at the earliest possible point. The problem seldom improves when left alone. Protection of a substance abuser usually supports chronic use and a drop in employee morale and productivity.

2. Involve the Employee's Family—Denial, projection, and avoidance of treatment are basic to the substance abuse process. Success is very dependent upon the involvement of all members of the employee's support system.

3. Be Certain—It is essential to be certain that there is a problem involving substance abuse. The employee will often admit the problem when faced with specific evidence of behavioral and performance deficits.

4. Be Firm—When it has been established that there is a substance abuse problem, it is essential that there be very specific and definite expectations for treatment. Follow up on every detail of the agreement. It is what you inspect that will determine success; never, what you expect.

5. Treatment Takes at Least One Year—The substance abuser's prognosis is very dependent upon extended treatment. Total abstinence is essential during and after treatment.

6. Treatment Should Include the Family—Substance abuse is a problem for the abuser's whole family. High expectations for results requires that the entire family make changes.

7. In-patient and Out-patient Treatment Work—Success rates are more determined by the quality of the treatment program than by where or how treatment is provided. Use the most cost-effective form.

8. The Employee Should Share in the Cost of Treatment—There is less resistance to treatment when costs are shared.

9. Confidentiality Is Important—While others may know that there is a problem, discussion should be restricted to the relationship between management and the employee. The employee's family involvement should be with the employee's permission.

10. Optimism—Positive expectations are important and should be maintained. Good employees are worth the investment. However, we must remember that addiction is powerful and that toughness and active follow-up are the foundations of success.

Sample
Substance Abuse Policy Consent Form

If we are to continue to fulfill our responsibility to provide reliable and safe service to our customers and a safe working environment for our employees, employees of our company must be physically and mentally fit to perform their duties in a safe and efficient manner. Therefore, no employee shall work or report to work while under the influence of alcohol, illegal drugs, or drugs that affect his/her ability to perform the job in a safe and efficient manner. No employees shall consume, display, or have in their possession alcoholic beverages or illegal drugs while on company property.

Should an employee be required to take any kind of prescription or nonprescription medication that may potentially affect job performance, the employee is required to report this to his/her supervisor. The supervisor will determine if it is necessary to temporarily place the employee on another assignment to ensure his/her safety and the safety of other employees and the public. A letter from a physician may be required to confirm it is safe to continue working while on medication.

Intoxication at work is grounds for disciplinary action, including immediate discharge. As used in this policy, intoxication means being under the influence of drugs or alcohol, or physical evidence which indicates that drugs or alcohol have been consumed. If any employee is suspected of being intoxicated or obviously impaired at work, he/she will be suspended pending investigation.

The company reserves the right to test applicants and employees for the presence of drugs or alcohol, and a refusal to take such a test is grounds for refusal to hire or discharge. When urinalysis and/or blood tests are requested or necessary, samples will be taken under the supervision of an appropriate health care professional.

To protect the best interests of employees and the public, management at XYZ Services, Inc., will take whatever measures are necessary to determine if alcohol or illegal drugs are located or are being used on company property. Measures that may be used will include, but will not be limited to, searches of people and of personal property located on company premises. Searches may be conducted by law enforcement authorities or by management. The aforementioned searches and drug tests will not be conducted if an individual refuses to submit; however, refusal to submit will result in immediate suspension and may result in termination.

Employees experiencing problems with alcohol or other drugs are urged to voluntarily seek assistance to resolve such problems before they become serious enough to require management referral or disciplinary action. Successful treatment will be viewed positively, but it will not prevent normal disciplinary action for a violation which may have already occurred nor will it relieve an employee of the responsibility to perform assigned duties in a safe and efficient manner.

As a condition of employment, each of the company's employees, including management, must acknowledge by signature that he/she has received and understands this policy.

I certify that I have read and fully understand the company's drug policy which is set forth above, and I agree to be bound thereby.

Employee's Signature: _____

NOTE: This sample policy is provided as a guide; counsel should be consulted before final policy development and implementation.

Technical Assistance on Workplace Substance Abuse Programs
National Resources

The National Clearinghouse for Alcohol and Drug Information (NCADI) is a toll-free service funded by the federal government. NCADI's information specialists will help you find information on all aspects of substance abuse— from videos and prevention materials, to specific program descriptions, resources in your state, and the latest research results. Many publications and educational materials are available free from NCADI (1-800-729-6686) P. O. Box 2345, Rockwell, MD.

The Drug-Free Workplace Helpline is a toll-free service funded by the federal Government to provide individualized technical assistance to business, industry, and unions on the development and implementation of comprehensive drug-free workplace programs (1-800-843-4971).

Demand Reduction Coordinators (DRC) from both the Drug Enforcement Administration (DEA) and the Federal Bureau of Investigation (FBI), and the **Law Enforcement Coordinating Committee** (LECC) **Coordinator,** U.S. Department of Justice, offer a variety of technical assistance services to employers on workplace substance abuse. Contact your local DEA, FBI, or U.S. Attorney's office to locate the nearest coordinator.

Alcoholics Anonymous World Services, P. O. Box 459, Grand Central Station, New York, NY 10163, (212) 686-1100.

Cocaine Anonymous, 1-800-347-8998 toll-free.

Narcotics Anonymous, P. O. Box 999, Van Nuys, CA 91409, (818) 780-3951.

National Council on Alcoholism and Drug Dependency, 1-800-NCA-CALL toll-free.

National Institute on Drug Abuse Hotline, 1-800-662-HELP toll-free.

American Council on Alcoholism Helpline, 1-800-527-5344 toll-free.

Al-Anon/Alateen Family Group Headquarters, P. O. Box 862, Midtown Station, New York, NY 11018, 1-800-356-9996 toll-free.

Nar-Anon Family Group Headquarters, P. O. Box 2562, Palos Verdes Peninsula, CA 90274-0119, (213) 547-5800.

State and Local Resources

The National Association of State Alcohol and Drug Abuse Directors (NASADAD) coordinates and encourages cooperative efforts between the federal government and state agencies on substance abuse. Through its Drug-Free Workplace Project, NASADAD is working through state substance abuse agencies to provide technical assistance to small businesses developing substance abuse programs and policies. NASADAD serves as a resource on state drug programs and can provide contacts in each state (NASADAD, Drug-Free Workplace Project, 444 N. Capitol Street, NW, Suite 642, Washington, DC 20001, 202-783-6868).

State drug and alcohol program offices exist across the country. To find your state's office, you can call your state government, consult your local phone directory, or contact NCADI and NASADAD, listed above.

Community organizations are available to provide help with drug or alcohol problems. Check your local telephone directory under headings such as Alcohol/ Drug Abuse Information, Treatment, or Counseling. Be sure to look in the blue pages (government listings and public service section), the yellow pages, and the community service section of your directory.

4.12 Employee Handbook Development Checklist

Health, Safety and Security

The following checklist can be used to help determine the various subjects to include in your handbook. Sample handbook statements covering many of the items in this checklist appear in this section. They can be used to help draft your personalized employee handbook statements.

Our Employee Handbook Should Include:

<u>ALCOHOL/DRUG ABUSE</u>

1. Possession of drugs/alcohol on company property   Yes ___ No ___ Maybe ___

2. Requirements of duties   Yes ___ No ___ Maybe ___

3. Definitions—drugs, etc.   Yes ___ No ___ Maybe ___

4. Training for management   Yes ___ No ___ Maybe ___

5. Referral to employee assistance program   Yes ___ No ___ Maybe ___

6. Disciplinary procedures   Yes ___ No ___ Maybe ___

7. Searches and investigations   Yes ___ No ___ Maybe ___

8. Drug testing   Yes ___ No ___ Maybe ___

     A. Pre-employment   Yes ___ No ___ Maybe ___
     B. Promotion/transfer   Yes ___ No ___ Maybe ___
     C. Company physicals   Yes ___ No ___ Maybe ___
     D. Investigations   Yes ___ No ___ Maybe ___
     E. Random testing   Yes ___ No ___ Maybe ___
     F. Chain-of-custody requirements   Yes ___ No ___ Maybe ___

9. Procedure if drug tests are positive   Yes ___ No ___ Maybe ___

10. Exams/testing after first tests   Yes ___ No ___ Maybe ___

11. Prescription medication   Yes ___ No ___ Maybe ___

12. Employee education program   Yes ___ No ___ Maybe ___

<u>AIDS</u>

1. Company philosophy   Yes ___ No ___ Maybe ___

2. Group insurance coverages   Yes ___ No ___ Maybe ___

3. Legal responsibilities of company   Yes ___ No ___ Maybe ___

4. Accommodation measures for affected employees   Yes ___ No ___ Maybe ___

5. Education of employees   Yes ___ No ___ Maybe ___

6. Confidentiality of information   Yes ___ No ___ Maybe ___

7. Refusal of nonaffected employees to work with
    AIDS-affected employees   Yes ___ No ___ Maybe ___

8. Company and community resources for treatment
    and counseling   Yes ___ No ___ Maybe ___

9. Requirement for medical certification of
    AIDS-affected employees   Yes ___ No ___ Maybe ___

EMPLOYEE ASSISTANCE PROGRAM (EAP)

1. Purpose of EAP   Yes ___ No ___ Maybe ___

2. Who provides services (company vs. outside
    agency)   Yes ___ No ___ Maybe ___

3. Guidelines for availability   Yes ___ No ___ Maybe ___

    A. What problems are covered?   Yes ___ No ___ Maybe ___
    B. How to receive help—whom to contact   Yes ___ No ___ Maybe ___
    C. Who is covered—employee, family, etc.   Yes ___ No ___ Maybe ___
    D. Cost to employee/family   Yes ___ No ___ Maybe ___
    E. Coordination with group health plan   Yes ___ No ___ Maybe ___

4. Responsibilities of employees   Yes ___ No ___ Maybe ___

5. Responsibilities of immediate supervisors   Yes ___ No ___ Maybe ___

6. Responsibilities of EAP coordinator   Yes ___ No ___ Maybe ___

7. Confidentiality of information   Yes ___ No ___ Maybe ___

8. Coordination with disciplinary policies   Yes ___ No ___ Maybe ___

9. Effect upon other company policies/procedures   Yes ___ No ___ Maybe ___

10. Education of managers/supervisors   Yes ___ No ___ Maybe ___

11. Education of employees/families   Yes ___ No ___ Maybe ___

HEALTH AND SAFETY

1. Is there a dispensary or first-aid station?   Yes ___ No ___ Maybe ___

A. Company operated	Yes ___ No ___ Maybe ___
B. Outside source	Yes ___ No ___ Maybe ___
C. Nurse in attendance	Yes ___ No ___ Maybe ___
D. Physician in attendance	Yes ___ No ___ Maybe ___
E. Ambulance service available in case of emergency	Yes ___ No ___ Maybe ___
F. Accurate records made of employee contacts:	
1. Health	Yes ___ No ___ Maybe ___
2. Accident	Yes ___ No ___ Maybe ___
3. General	Yes ___ No ___ Maybe ___
G. Request employees to use dispensary when necessary?	Yes ___ No ___ Maybe ___
2. Are there arrangements for medical services?	Yes ___ No ___ Maybe ___
A. Entrance physical examination	Yes ___ No ___ Maybe ___
B. Periodic physical examination for all workers	Yes ___ No ___ Maybe ___
C. Medical examination for employees returning to work from:	
1. Brief absence	Yes ___ No ___ Maybe ___
2. Long or repeated illness	Yes ___ No ___ Maybe ___
D. Vaccination and inoculation services	Yes ___ No ___ Maybe ___
E. Distribution of vitamin preparations	Yes ___ No ___ Maybe ___
F. Distribution of salt tablets	Yes ___ No ___ Maybe ___
G. Visiting nurse services	Yes ___ No ___ Maybe ___
3. Is there a safety and accident prevention program?	Yes ___ No ___ Maybe ___
A. Safety engineer	Yes ___ No ___ Maybe ___
B. Committee	Yes ___ No ___ Maybe ___
C. A specific written program	Yes ___ No ___ Maybe ___
D. Are records kept of all accidents	Yes ___ No ___ Maybe ___
1. Analyzed to determine causes?	Yes ___ No ___ Maybe ___
2. Analyzed by department and shift?	Yes ___ No ___ Maybe ___
3. Is the cause analyzed to determine methods to prevent recurrences?	Yes ___ No ___ Maybe ___
4. Is a report made to top management showing:	
a. Accidents and causes?	Yes ___ No ___ Maybe ___
b. Progress in accident prevention program?	Yes ___ No ___ Maybe ___
E. Is a periodic check made on all safety devices?	Yes ___ No ___ Maybe ___
4. Are safety rules and practices explained to new employees as they apply each particular job?	Yes ___ No ___ Maybe ___
5. Does company make use of first-aid training?	Yes ___ No ___ Maybe ___
A. Have any employees taken courses in first aid?	Yes ___ No ___ Maybe ___
B. Is first-aid practice provided for in the establishment?	Yes ___ No ___ Maybe ___
6. Is the health and safety program designed to make all employees "good health and safety" conscious?	Yes ___ No ___ Maybe ___

7. Do we insist that workers must not wear bracelets, rings, and other jewelry around machines? Yes ___ No ___ Maybe ___

8. Do we require workers to wear safe wearing apparel and hair covering? Yes ___ No ___ Maybe ___

OSHA—HAZARD COMMUNICATION STANDARD

1. Notices to employees—where, etc. Yes ___ No ___ Maybe ___

2. Inventory of all chemicals Yes ___ No ___ Maybe ___

3. Identification of hazardous substances Yes ___ No ___ Maybe ___

4. Material Safety Data Sheets (MSDS) Yes ___ No ___ Maybe ___

    A. Availability to employees Yes ___ No ___ Maybe ___
    B. Availability to others Yes ___ No ___ Maybe ___

5. Labeling requirements Yes ___ No ___ Maybe ___

6. Training requirements Yes ___ No ___ Maybe ___

7. Hazardous substance spill clean-up procedures Yes ___ No ___ Maybe ___

8. Coverage of contractors (subcontractors) Yes ___ No ___ Maybe ___

9. Record retention requirements Yes ___ No ___ Maybe ___

10. Fire plan policy and procedures Yes ___ No ___ Maybe ___

11. Hearing testing program Yes ___ No ___ Maybe ___

12. Smoking Yes ___ No ___ Maybe ___

Sample Policies: Alcohol/Drug Abuse _____

Sample Policy 1

It is the policy of our company to create a drug-free workplace in keeping with the spirit and intent of the Drug-Free Workplace Act of 1988. The use of controlled substances is inconsistent with the behavior expected of employees, it subjects all employees and visitors to our facilities to unacceptable safety risks, and it undermines the company's ability to operate effectively and efficiently. In this connection, the unlawful manufacture, distribution, dispensation, possession, sale, or use of a controlled substance in the workplace or while engaged in company business off our premises is strictly prohibited. Such conduct is also prohibited during nonworking time to the extent that, in our opinion, it impairs an employee's ability to perform on the job or threatens the reputation or integrity of the company.

To educate employees on the dangers of drug abuse, the company has established a drug-free awareness program. Periodically, employees will be required to attend training sessions at which the dangers of drug abuse, our policy regarding drugs, the availability of counseling, and the company's employee assistance program will be discussed. Employees convicted of controlled substance-related violations in the workplace (including pleas of no contest) must inform the company within five days of such conviction or plea. Employees who violate any aspect of this policy may be subject to disciplinary action up to and including termination. At its discretion, the company may require employees who violate this policy to successfully complete a drug abuse assistance or rehabilitation program as a condition of continued employment.

Sample Policy 2

It is the company's goal to establish and to maintain a work environment that is free from the effects of alcohol, illegal drugs (marijuana, cocaine, etc.), or drugs taken for nonmedicinal purposes. The company requires employees to report for work in condition to perform their duties. The company recognizes that an employee's off-the-job or on-the-job involvement with alcohol or drugs can have an impact on the work environment. The following clearly states the company's position regarding the use or possession of drugs and/or unauthorized use or possession of alcohol:

1. Any employee on the job or on company premises who is found to be involved in the manufacture, distribution, dispensing, possession, or use of a controlled substance or is under the influence thereof will be suspended from work immediately pending further investigation. Also, any employee on the job or on company premises who is involved in the unauthorized possession or use of alcohol or is under the influence thereof will be suspended from work immediately pending further investigation. In either case, if the initial finding is substantiated, disciplinary action, up to and including discharge, will be imposed.

2. An employee who is convicted of a violation of any criminal drug statute, where such violation occurred on the job or on company premises, must notify the local Human Resources Supervisor no later than five days after such conviction.

3. Off-the-job use of alcohol or drugs which adversely affects an employee's job performance or jeopardizes the safety of himself/herself, other employees, company equipment, or where such usage adversely affects the public trust in the ability of the company to carry out its responsibilities may also be cause for disciplinary action, up to and including discharge.

4. Employees who are undergoing prescribed medical treatment with a drug or controlled substance which may alter their physical or mental ability will be required to advise the Human Resources Supervisor of such treatment before or at the time the treatment begins. This will enable the Human Resources Supervisor, in conjunction with the employee's physician, to determine whether it will be necessary to change the employee's job assignment while he or she is undergoing treatment.

Supervisors shall enforce this policy by reporting any violation of items 1–4 above to the Human Resources Department. Through discussion with that department, an appropriate course of action will be determined.

Especially because of the nature of the electric utility industry, the use of drugs or alcohol may subject employees to serious injury or worse. Employees using such substances are not only endangering themselves, but they are also endangering other employees who work with them. In view of this, employees are expected to protect their own welfare and to participate in the company's efforts to provide a safe working environment by notifying their supervisors of apparent violations of this policy on drug and alcohol abuse.

Sample Policy 3
No persons in our employ shall work or report to work while under the influence of alcohol, illegal drugs, or drugs which would affect their ability to perform their job in a safe and efficient manner. No employees shall consume or have in their possession alcoholic beverages or illegal drugs on company premises. To do so would create a bad public image and possible safety hazard and is a prime cause for dismissal.

Sample Policy 4
(Name of company) has a responsibility and strong commitment to its employees to provide a safe and secure work environment. The bank is concerned only when safety, job performance, or attendance is affected. We have no desire to intrude upon the individual's private life. However, when off/on duty activities affect an employee's ability to satisfactorily perform his/her duties or affect the condition in which an employee reports for work, then the bank is rightfully concerned. It is the bank's expectation that maintaining satisfactory performance is the responsibility of all employees and the decision to acknowledge substance-abuse-related problems and seek assistance is also the employee's responsibility.

Also, we recognize that substance abuse is a treatable problem, and we are willing to provide referral assistance to those who want to understand and correct their problem before it impairs their performance and jeopardizes their employment.

Substance abuse is the misuse or illegal use of drugs or controlled substances such as marijuana, barbiturates, etc., or alcohol.

The bank will provide referral assistance to those who want to understand and correct the problem.

Possession or distribution/sales of alcohol, drugs, or controlled substances during work hours or on bank premises or being under the influence of drugs, alcohol, or controlled substances while on bank premises will lead to disciplinary action up to and including dismissal.

To preserve the safety of all employees and maintain satisfactory performance, all employees whose "fitness for duty" is questionable will be subject to a drug/alcohol screen by medical personnel without prior notice. Examples of being unfit for duty include irrational or erratic behavior, carelessness or disregard for the safety of others, and damage to bank equipment or property.

Additionally, should you be required to take any kind of prescription or nonprescription medication which will affect your job performance, you are required to report this to your supervisor. Your supervisor will determine if it is necessary to temporarily place you on another assignment or to take other action as appropriate.

Sample Policy 5

Our policy regarding drug and alcohol abuse does not permit the employment of persons who use drugs or chemicals which may impair sensory, mental, or physical functions (hereinafter collectively referred to as "drugs/alcohol"). In furtherance of this policy, the company has adopted a drugs/alcohol testing program that will be applied as follows:

1. Any prospective employee will be required to submit to a drugs/alcohol test. Any prospective employee whose drugs/alcohol test is confirmed positive will not be offered employment.

2. Existing employees will be required to submit to a drugs/alcohol test under the following circumstances:
   a. Whenever an employee is required to submit to a physical examination.

   b. Whenever an employee suffers a work-related injury that requires medical treatment. Testing will also be required of any employee involved in a reportable work-related accident regardless of whether that employee sustained injury.

   c. Whenever there are reasonable grounds to believe that an employee's ability to perform his or her job is impaired due to the use of drugs/alcohol.

3. Any employee whose drugs/alcohol test is confirmed positive will be subject to the following action:

   a. The employee will receive written instructions from the company stating that the employee will not be permitted to return to work unless the employee provides a confirmed negative drugs/alcohol test to the company within 45 days of the date of instructions.

b. If the employee fails to provide a negative test result within the 45-day period, he or she will be subject to dismissal for failure to obey written instructions and for violation of the company's drugs/alcohol policy.

c. If the employee provides a confirmed negative test result within the 45-day period, the employee will be permitted to return to work, provided there is work available. The employee will be instructed in writing that the use of drugs/alcohol is contrary to company policy and that the employee must remain free of such drugs/alcohol. The employee may also be required periodically by the Personnel Department to submit to drugs/alcohol testing for a three-year period from the date of the employee's return to work. If any test during this period is confirmed positive, the employee will be subject to dismissal for failure to obey instructions and for violation of the company's drugs/alcohol policy.

4. Any drugs/alcohol testing conducted under company policy shall be performed at a medical facility/laboratory designated by the company. For purposes of administering this policy, the company will not accept test results from any facility other than the one designated by the company.

5. Any employee's refusal to either (a) submit to a drugs/alcohol test, or (b) submit to such testing at a company-designated facility shall subject the employee to disciplinary action up to and including discharge.

6. Employees undergoing medical treatment who are required to use prescription drugs on the job must provide the Personnel Department with a copy of the prescription and a letter from a treating physician which describes any potential side effects associated with the prescribed drug and which certifies that the drug will not impair the employee's job performance.

7. Under no circumstances will intoxicating beverages or illegal drugs be consumed on plant property. Employees having possession of such beverages or drugs will be subject to discharge.

Sample Policies: AIDS _____

Commentary on employee handbook policy statements dealing with AIDS: Unlike many past and current employee handbooks, employers drafting new or revised employee handbooks are considering the need to prepare, publish, and distribute a policy statement on the latest tragic and emotional critical issue regarding Acquired Immune Deficiency Syndrome (AIDS). The major concern of employees, management, as well as those outside the working population, is that of communicability of the virus in normal areas of the workplace.

It has been well communicated from medical authorities that AIDS is not transmitted by casual employee contacts. Therefore, it is recommended that employers developing a new or revised policy on AIDS do so with the spirit of educating employees and their families about this fearful illness. Moreover, the policy statement should communicate to employees how your company plans to face up to this issue. This section provides sample policies on AIDS to include the following guidelines:

a. Effectual statement that AIDS is not communicated or transmitted by casual contacts of employees in the workplace.

b. Company benefit and communication programs that are available to employees and/or their dependents that have the AIDS virus.

c. An understanding of any company-provided accommodations or benefits for employees who may become a victim of AIDS.

d. A positive statement to lessen numerous employee fears and phobias about AIDS.

e. The company position that it will make every effort to comply in good faith with federal, state, and local disability, health and safety, or handicap regulations when dealing with the AIDS issues in the workplace.

It is to be remembered that federal law, the Rehabilitation Act, prohibits discrimination against persons with AIDS under Section 503. The law applies to covered government contractors and subcontractors from discriminating against qualified handicap applicants and employees, including the requirement that the covered contractors take affirmative action to employ such persons. The Supreme Court has already held that an employee with a contagious illness is "handicapped" within the meaning of the Rehabilitation Act.

Over 40 states currently prohibit discrimination against handicapped or disabled employees. Many have already addressed the issue of HIV infections, AIDS, and most have held that employees with these infections are protected from discrimination. Therefore, it is highly important that the employer's employment lawyer or legal counsel be consulted in reviewing proposed drafts of new or revised AIDS policy statements in employee handbooks.

Sample Policy 1

Our company recognizes that employees with a life-threatening illness such as AIDS may wish to continue their employment and, in fact, that continued employment may be therapeutically important to their recovery process. The company also recognizes that it must satisfy its legal obligation to provide a safe work environment for all employees, customers, and other visitors to our premises. As long as employees who have AIDS are able to maintain acceptable performance standards in accordance with established company policies and procedures, and the weight of medical evidence continues to indicate that AIDS cannot be transmitted by casual workplace contact, employees with AIDS will be permitted to continue to work.

In determining such an employee's ability to continue in employment, the company will consider making reasonable accommodations to the employee's condition, consistent with applicable federal, state, and local laws.

As part of its overall AIDS program, we conduct ongoing training sessions with employees to provide information about the nature of this disease and to help allay the fear often expressed by employees owing to a lack of understanding of AIDS and especially of how it can be transmitted. Also stressed during such sessions will be the services we offer to individuals with AIDS, including our employee assistance program (EAP), which offers counseling and referral to appropriate community organizations, and the medical and other benefits, offered by our company to employees with AIDS and their dependents.

If you have AIDS or any other life-threatening illness, please contact the Human Resources Department or Medical Department. The Human Resources Department, in conjunction with the Medical Department, will provide you with information about the illness and about programs that are available to assist you and your family. Further, we will take all reasonable precautions, to the maximum extent possible, to ensure that information about your condition remains confidential.

Our Medical Department will also determine what information should be obtained from your physician, so that the company can explore the types of possible reasonable accommodations that may be recommended for you, consistent with the business needs of your department, established company policy, and applicable federal, state, and local laws.

Sample Policy 2

After consultation with medical experts, and in view of the gravity of this issue, as well as its potential impact on our staff, the company asks for your serious attention and cooperation regarding this issue.

Our policy is to be both compassionate and in line with current medical and legal counsel. Simply stated, AIDS and pre-AIDS employees are fully entitled to the ethical considerations and legal rights awarded anyone with any other illness. This includes protection of their privacy, confidentiality, and civil liberties. This disease should be considered as any medical problem with attendant absence and disability.

Medical evidence available indicates that AIDS is not communicated by normal activity within an office or manufacturing environment. There is no evidence that other employees are exposed to an increased risk because of the presence of AIDS or pre-AIDS employees.

Sample Policy 3

The company is committed to maintaining a safe and healthy work environment for all employees. Consistent with this commitment, the company will treat AIDS the same as other life-threatening illnesses, in terms of all our employee policies and benefits. Employees who are affected by AIDS or any other life-threatening illness will be treated with compassion and understanding and will be given support to the fullest extent possible in dealing with their personal crisis.

Based on the overwhelming preponderance of available medical and scientific opinion, there is no evidence that the AIDS virus is casually transmitted in ordinary social or occupational settings or conditions. Therefore, subject to changes in available medical information, it is the policy of the company to allow employees with AIDS or any of its related conditions to continue to work as long as they are medically able to perform and do not pose a danger to their own health and safety or the health and safety of others. Concomitantly, co-workers have no basis upon which to refuse to work or withhold their services for fear of contracting AIDS by working with an AIDS-affected person. Employees who engage in such refusals or withholding of services or who harass or otherwise discriminate against an AIDS-affected employee will be subject to discipline.

Employees who are affected by AIDS or any of its related conditions or who are concerned about AIDS are encouraged to contact their Human Resources Representative to discuss their concerns and to obtain additional information.

The company will treat all medical information obtained from employees with AIDS or any of its related conditions confidentially as required by law.

Sample Policies: Employee Assistance Program _____

Sample Policy 1

Our company recognizes that a wide range of problems—such as marital or family distress, alcoholism, and drug abuse—not directly associated with an individual's job function can nonetheless be detrimental to an employee's performance on the job. Consequently, we believe it is in the interest of employees and the company to provide an effective program to assist employees and their families in resolving problems such as these as the need arises. To this end, EAP provides consultation services for referrals to local community treatment sources. All employees are free to use this program and are encouraged to do so. Employee visits to the EAP are held in confidence to the maximum possible extent.

Participation in our EAP does not excuse employees from complying with normal company policies or from meeting normal job requirements during or after receiving EAP assistance. Nor will participation in our EAP prevent us from taking disciplinary action against any employee for performance problems that occur before or after the employee's seeking assistance through the EAP.

Employees interested in learning more about our EAP or in discussing a personal or job-related problem should contact the company's EAP counselor in the Human Resources Department.

Sample Policy 2

The EAP is designed to help employees and their family members attain a healthy and productive life through a variety of personalized and professional services. Our EAP, which will be handled by Corporate and Employee Assistance Program, Inc., will provide confidential assessment, counseling, and referral assistance to all salaried employees and family members in areas such as stress, marital and other family conflicts, alcohol and drug abuse, and financial/legal difficulties.

Our company wants to assist employees to resolve personal difficulties at early stages before they become costly in terms of either personal distress or work productivity. This service is being offered because the company is concerned about our employees' personal well-being and because it makes good sense.

The introduction of the EAP is an important benefit to the company and its employees. We encourage you and your family to make full use of this resource designed to help maintain high employee productivity, health, and well-being in all aspects of life.

Sample Policies: Health and Safety ————————————

Sample Policy 1

It is the intention of our company to furnish all employees with a safe and healthy place to work. Yet, no matter how safe working conditions may be, carelessness or horseplay on your part can make you or your co-worker a casualty. You should know and follow all commonsense and posted safety and fire regulations and utilize safety equipment properly to protect you and your fellow employees from inconvenience or serious injury. Use of safety glasses, where applicable, is mandatory.

Employees are responsible for following all safety rules for using safety equipment furnished by the company. It is your duty to report any unsafe conditions and defective working tools or equipment to your supervisor. Any and all accidents, no matter how small, should be immediately reported to your supervisor.

Failure to adhere to established safety practices will result in disciplinary action, up to and including dismissal.

Sample Policy 2

It is our policy to provide a safe workplace for all our employees. Having accepted this responsibility, we feel that you, in turn, must accept the responsibility to work safely because of your life and the life of your co-workers. This means working intelligently with common sense and with foresight. Every employee is expected to follow safety standards which apply to our operations and adhere to all OSHA regulations.

Injury to an employee causes physical suffering and loss of income, as well as loss of productivity and damage to the morale of the work group. Your own judgment and common sense will help you to avoid an on-the-job accident.

Good housekeeping practices must be followed at all times. Papers and other waste must be placed in the containers provided. A neat, clean work area not only reduces the chance of an injury but makes for a more pleasant and attractive place to work.

If you notice a condition or practice which seems unsafe, you should immediately call it to the attention of your supervisor or readily correct it personally if safely possible to do so.

Rules alone will not prevent accidents; it takes the cooperation of all of us to see that accidents are eliminated. Report any unsafe conditions to your supervisor and always try to THINK SAFETY.

Sample Policy 3

Our company is vitally interested in your safety and health, both on and off the job. The basic company Safety Policy is

No operating condition or urgency of service can ever justify endangering the life of anyone.

The Safety Program includes the following objectives:

1. To completely integrate safety with production and operation.

2. To provide safe working conditions.

3. To train employees in practices for the safe conduct of their work.

4. To enforce safety measures.

You have definite responsibilities which the company expects you to fulfill with respect to (1) safety to yourself, (2) safety to your fellow employees, (3) protection to the public, and (4) protection to the company equipment and property. The acceptance and fulfillment of the above responsibilities is a condition of employment.

Accidents are preventable, and your company takes every possible precaution to make your working conditions safe. Safety guards, personal protective devices, equipment, and special tools are provided to eliminate specific job hazards. But, in the final analysis, the real safety job is up to you—you need to *think, act, and work safely at all times.*

The company has a safety manual which you will be expected to study and follow in the performance of your duties.

Before starting work under conditions which you believe are unsafe, you must call these conditions to the attention of the person in charge. You are expected to report to your immediate supervisor any unsafe conditions you may observe.

Your suggestions and ideas toward improving methods and making conditions safer are earnestly sought. If you have any ideas or suggestions regarding safety or the safety programs, report them to your supervisor immediately; do not wait for a safety meeting.

All accidents, whether resulting in a personal injury or not, must be reported to your supervisor, regardless of how minor they may be. The accident is to be reported to the supervisor on the shift during which the accident occurred. Even minor accidents may indicate an unsafe condition which should be corrected.

Teamwork and cooperation are expected from each employee in safety matters, the same as they are in all other activities making up our company's operations.

Sample Policy 4

It is only by reporting every injury that the proper treatment of injuries can be given and plans for prevention of similar injuries developed.

If you should become injured on the job in any manner, the injury must be reported to your supervisor immediately.

The supervisor will see that first aid is given and further medical attention is provided if necessary.

Occupational injuries that require medical treatment other than first aid or that result in lost time, are required by state and federal laws to be reported by the company. In either of these instances, the facts are to be reported to your supervisor as soon as possible after the occurrence.

Sample Policy 5

The company provides all the necessary safety equipment, such as safeguards on all machinery, goggles, ventilators, and protective clothing and safety boots. It is mandatory that these devices be used at all times when needed. Any employee discovered not using the appropriate safety equipment will be subject to corrective action.

The following safety rules must be obeyed:

1. Always wear safety boots of a type furnished or authorized by the company.

2. Do not run in the plant or on plant property.

3. Wear your safety glasses at all times in the plant area.

4. Do not smoke in a No-Smoking area.

5. Make sure all safety devices are properly adjusted.

6. Practice good housekeeping on the job.

7. Do not wear loose clothing around moving machinery.

8. Report all injuries immediately to your supervisor.

9. Have respect for electricity.

10. Have respect for *hot metal*—aluminum is the same color at 1000 degrees as it is at room temperature. *Be careful!*

11. *Think safety! Think safety!*

12. Personal hearing protection must be worn in required plant areas.

Clothing: The company will supply protective clothing as warranted. When working in casting, run-off tables, or other areas where there is hot metal, all personnel will wear heavy, long-sleeved shirts with the sleeves down. At no time will any employee be permitted to work without a shirt or to work wearing tank tops, "muscle shirts," rolled-up trousers, or shorts. Immediate corrective action will be taken with anyone violating this rule.

Safety Boots: The company provides safety boots for all employees following the orientation period. (Footguards are to be provided during the orientation period.) Anyone needing new safety shoes should contact your supervisor that the proper size and style may be ordered.

Safety Glasses: It is mandatory that all employees and visitors wear safety glasses while in the plant. Glasses will be furnished by the company and loaned to each employee. Visitors will be furnished glasses by either the plant manager or the personnel manager.

In the event an employee loses his or her glasses or fails to return them upon termination of employment, a direct charge will be made to the individual concerned.

The following policy will cover prescription safety lenses/glasses:

1. A new employee will be issued "clip-on" safety lenses or some suitable protective device for the first six months of employment or until he or she has an eye examination after the first ninety days of employment.

2. Any employee requiring prescription glasses will pick up a prescription form from the personnel office and:

   a. Choose the type of frames desired from those available.

   b. Take the prescription form to the optometrist or an MD eye specialist of his or her choice for the examination. (The eye examination will be at the expense of the employee.)

   c. Return the completed form to the personnel office. (The company will pay for the prescription glasses.)

   d. The employee will be notified by the doctor or personnel office when the glasses are ready to be fitted. NOTE: No prescription that is two years old or older will be honored for safety glasses.

3. Any prescription safety glasses or regular safety glasses that are broken in a plant accident will be replaced or repaired by the company. The company will not replace safety lenses because of pitting or scratching. Employees are expected to wear protective devices over their personal prescription glasses because the company will not be financially responsible for any damage. The company reserves the right to replace prescription safety lenses damaged as the result of pitting or scratching.

Sample Policies: Fire Plan

Sample Policy 1

Fires in plants do happen and caution must be used to guard against them. Because many people are on duty at all times during the 24 hours, good fire prevention habits go a long way toward preventing fires. Safety for the employees is everybody's responsibility. Of primary importance is *prevention*.

The City of (name of city) is responsible for furnishing fire protection for this company.

A fire containment program is posted on the bulletin board.

In case of fire, evacuate the building in accordance with the established fire drill plan. Individuals, previously designated by the supervisor, will be responsible to see that all windows are closed, fire doors closed, and fire-fighting equipment is manned.

In case of fire at the *presses:*

1. Sound the fire alarm—long blast!
2. Operator cuts off all pumps and motors.
3. Leadperson cuts off billet oven.
4. Holeperson, stretcher, cutoff, and runoff get fire extinguishers. No. 1 and No. 2 saw helpers close all windows and doors.
5. All supervisors in the plant go to the fire area.
6. All maintenance persons go to the fire area.
7. Supervisors decide if the fire department is needed.
8. All other employees stay away from the fire area, unless instructed by supervisors or leadperson.

In case of *cast house* fire:

1. Sound fire alarm—long blast!
2. Holeperson to plug off molten metal and help caster shut down casting.
3. Leadperson cuts off all equipment as soon as possible.
4. Charger and tow motor helper get fire extinguishers.
5. Sawperson, helper, and saw helper close all doors and windows and then help with fire extinguishers.
6. All supervisors in the plant go to the fire area.
7. All maintenance persons go to the fire area.
8. Supervisors decide if the fire department is needed.

9. All other employees stay away from the fire area, unless instructed otherwise by supervisors or leadperson.

In case of fire in *shipping department:*

1. Sound fire alarm—long blast!

2. Leadperson cuts off age ovens.

3. Scale person and two senior packers get fire hoses and extinguishers.

4. Two packers close all windows and doors.

5. All supervisors in the plant go to the fire area.

6. All maintenance persons go to the fire area.

7. Supervisors decide if the fire department is needed.

8. All other employees stay away from the fire area unless instructed otherwise by supervisors and leadperson.

All employees not involved in fighting the fire are to assemble in the rear parking lot.

Sample Policies: Hearing Conservation _____

Sample Policy 1

A mandatory hearing conservation program has been adopted by our company. Prescribed personal hearing protectors must be worn by all employees working or visiting high-noise areas at all times. The company will furnish and maintain OSHA-approved personal hearing protectors. Personal hearing protectors will be furnished at company expense. All employees who work in designated areas of noise concentration will be given a hearing test.

Your complete cooperation in this program is required. If you have problems or questions concerning your protectors, see your supervisor.

<u>Purpose:</u>

1. To protect and conserve the hearing of every employee of our company who is exposed to 85 decibels or more of noise (defined as a high-noise area) as required by federal law under the Occupational Safety and Health Act.

2. To use feasible engineering methods to effectively reduce noise levels below 85 decibels whenever possible but, when this is impractical or impossible, to implement controls as a means of personal protection for the employees.

3. Training classes will be instituted to explain why hearing protection is necessary and to instruct in the proper use of personal hearing protectors. Visual aids such as films or posters will be used in these classes.

4. Noise surveys and analysis:

   All areas of the plant are to have annual noise surveys of OSHA-approved sound level meters and/or audiodosimeters. These noise level readings will be analyzed and recommendations made by competent audiometrically and/or medically trained personnel.

5. Audiometric testing:

   A certified audiometric technician using OSHA-approved audiometric testing equipment will annually test all employees exposed to 85 decibels or above. This testing is to be done at company expense. These tests are also to become a part of the regular pre-employment examinations.

6. Medical surveillance:

   A licensed otolaryngologist will interpret all audiograms and indicate those individuals in need of further attention. Medical referral services to appropriate clinics or other medical and/or audiological consultants will be provided.

7. Recordkeeping:

   Arrangements for an efficient recordkeeping system for audiograms, noise surveys, and audiometric calibrations will be provided and maintained for the duration of employment, plus five years.

8. Ear protection:

The company will provide and maintain OSHA-approved personal hearing protection equipment appropriate for all employees.

9. Warning notices:

Clearly printed hearing protection warning notices will be posted at entrances to or on the periphery of areas with noise exposure.

All of the previously mentioned policies will be conducted in accordance with all state and federal regulations regarding hearing conservation programs.

Sample Policies: Smoking —————————————

Sample Policy 1

Smoking is permitted, except in areas which are restricted. Do not throw a burning cigarette away—be sure it is out before it is disposed of. Please use ashtrays and do not throw butts on the floor.

Ashtrays have been provided in all areas where smoking is permitted. Employees using wastebaskets or other unsafe receptacles as ashtrays will be subject to disciplinary action.

Fire extinguishers have been placed in strategic locations throughout the building.

In case of fire (1) call the fire department first, (2) then alert all occupants in the building, (3) then use fire extinguisher, unless fire has gained headway. In no case endanger your means of escape. Your company carries fire insurance—so save yourself FIRST.

Sample Policy 2

Because we are expected to maintain the highest possible safety conditions, *you must not smoke in restricted areas.* Smoking is permitted in authorized areas during break and lunch only. Smoking in unauthorized areas will result in disciplinary action up to and including dismissal.

Sample Policy 3

Because we are expected to maintain the highest possible safety conditions and because we are concerned for our employees' health, you are encouraged not to smoke and are expected not to do so in restricted areas. Safe smoking habits must be observed at all times.

All employees will refrain from smoking in the presence of our customers. When you are waiting on a customer, you are involved in serious business, and the relaxation or privilege of smoking should not be going on at the same time.

When you smoke in authorized areas, please be sure to extinguish your cigarettes in the proper receptacles.

Sample Policy 4

As a health care company, ABC Company fully supports the desire for a smoke-free workplace. In light of this support, the company has developed the following guidelines:

- Certain buildings are designated as "smoke-free," either with or without designated smoking areas. Notices are posted in the lobby and at various other locations throughout each of these buildings.

- The company encourages smokers to quit smoking. This encouragement involves sponsoring the "Great American Smoke Out" program, eliminating cigarette machines from company facilities, and sponsoring periodic smoking cessation programs.

Sample Policy 5

Due to the nature of our products and because of the health hazards, most of us are not allowed to smoke at our work stations. You may smoke, of course, in designated areas of the canteen and cafeteria during break periods and lunchtime. When you do smoke, please place your ashes in the ashtrays or stands provided; this reduces the hazard of a fire which could put us all out of a job. It also makes your break area more attractive.

4.13 Employee Handbook Development Checklist

Customer Service and Quality Standards

The following checklist can be used to help determine the various subjects to include in your handbook. Sample handbook statements covering many of the items in this checklist appear in this section. They can be used to help draft your personalized employee handbook statements.

Our Employee Handbook Should Include:

1. Does a formal policy presently exist on customer service? Yes ___ No ___ Maybe ___

2. Are employees aware of our company's policy on customer service? Yes ___ No ___ Maybe ___

3. Should we include a customer service policy in the new or revised employee handbook? Yes ___ No ___ Maybe ___

4. Should our policy statement describe our company's position in the industry? Yes ___ No ___ Maybe ___

5. Should our policy statement set forth our company's unique position in the area of customer service apart from our competitors? Yes ___ No ___ Maybe ___

6. Should our policy statement describe how we can meet our customers' needs and expectations more completely and efficiently? Yes ___ No ___ Maybe ___

7. Should our policy statement refer to customer services promoted in company's advertising and product literature? Yes ___ No ___ Maybe ___

8. Should our policy statement describe the kind of customer service we would like to be able to provide? Yes ___ No ___ Maybe ___

9. Should the policy statement explain what services our customers expect from us? Yes ___ No ___ Maybe ___

10. Should our policy statement describe which customer services give us a competitive edge? Yes ___ No ___ Maybe ___

11. Should our policy statement explain the high priority our company gives to customer service? Yes ___ No ___ Maybe ___

12. Should our policy statement explain who is responsible for customer service within our organization? Yes ___ No ___ Maybe ___

13. Should our policy statement explain realistic
    customer service goals?   Yes ___ No ___ Maybe ___

14. Should our policy explain quality standards of our
    products and/or services?   Yes ___ No ___ Maybe ___

Sample Policies: Customer Service and Quality Standards

Sample Policy 1

Our company's continued success is directly dependent upon having satisfied customers. For this reason, it is important that all employees of the company understand the necessity of maintaining good relationships with our customers.

The existence of good customer relations makes friends, prevents misunderstandings, builds morale, improves our performance, and makes our daily jobs more pleasant. Also, since all of us come into contact with our customers and the public, we should do everything we can to keep our relationships with them on as high a level as possible.

Here are a few ways we as employees can help maintain good customer and public relations:

- Be polite at all times, to all persons. The importance of this cannot be too highly emphasized.

- Put forth your best "personal image," such as neatness of dress, a pleasant smile, an interest in your work, and a willing and cooperative attitude toward your associates and our customers.

- Be aware that your telephone manners are very important. Treat customers and the public with respect and dignity when talking on the telephone just as you would in meeting people face to face.

- Take an interest in civic affairs.

- Remember that in order to gain and hold the respect of others, you must earn such respect by your own actions. Good reputations are built by the total of many acts but can be quickly lost by one inconsiderate or thoughtless act.

Sample Policy 2

We must be honest and straightforward with our customers and be sure that they not only are told the facts but also understand the facts. To the best of our ability, we want to be sure that the products we sell serve the needs of the customer, even when he is too naive to understand these needs exactly. When we sell a product to a customer, we want to be sure the corporation fulfills the obligations we took on with the sale. We sell our corporation, not a single individual, to our customers, and we must be sure all our commitments are met.

Sample Policy 3

Our company is committed to these consumer rights:

Dependable high-quality services at reasonable prices. Our company strives to provide quality telecommunications services and products for all consumers at fair and reasonable prices.

Courteous, helpful assistance. Consumers deserve courteous, helpful assistance in all their transactions with our employees.

Full information about all products and services. Consumers have a right to the information necessary to make sound buying decisions. It is our policy to provide consumers with the information they need about our product and service options, including the lowest price service available, and pricing and payment options.

Choice of products and services. We believe consumers should have free and open choices of telecommunications products and services. When dealing with us, the consumer should have the opportunity to select from all available service options and products.

Safe products and services. We strive to provide and maintain safe, nonhazardous telecommunications products and services to our customers and to the communities we serve.

Telecommunications privacy. We fully safeguard every individual's right to privacy as an essential aspect of our service. We carefully strive to protect communications services from unlawful wiretapping or other illegal interception. Customer service records, credit information, and related confidential personal account information are fully protected.

An accurate, easily understood bill and reasonable billing procedure. We believe consumers should receive an accurate, easily understood bill, and one that makes clear when payment is due. Consumers are entitled to reasonable billing procedures and clear explanations about deposits, late payment of bills, collections, suspension, or disconnection of services for nonpayment. In case of bona fide emergencies, we try to avoid disconnection of service for nonpayment.

Fair resolution of complaints. It is our policy that consumers, wherever located, have access to a readily available process to provide them with fair resolution of their complaints and grievances concerning services, billing, and other practices and procedures. Accordingly, we provide consumers with helpful information about where and how to express their concerns and complaints to the company and to regulatory agencies.

The opportunity to be heard. We believe in listening to consumers and taking their advice, counsel, and criticism into careful consideration in our policy and decision making. We also believe consumers should have the opportunity to be heard on issues affecting our business.

Sample Policy 4
Our business has been built on the fundamental concept of achieving superiority versus competition in identifying the wants and needs of customers, both end consumers and trade; providing high-quality products and/or services to meet those needs in unique or advantageous ways; marketing those products/services to reinforce their appeal and achieve superior acceptance.

Sample Policy 5

We want consumers to have an enjoyable experience—so that they "feel good"—shopping at our store. We want to instill confidence in consumers that in all of our actions we are competent, fair, and of the highest integrity.

We want consumers to regard their shopping experience as enjoyable because of the sense of organization, intimacy of the surroundings, and character of service provided.

We will be sensitive to meeting our target consumers' expectations for shopping assistance and support services, such as credit, product services, and catalog desks. All of our associates will conduct themselves in a friendly, knowledgeable way, and present an appearance that supports the character of the store and merchandise.

Everything we do gives a signal to consumers as to who we are, what we believe in, and what we want to be.

Sample Policy 6

Our consumer relations policy is to respond to all consumer inquiries within 72 hours.

Consumer problems or complaints are handled through direct correspondence and/or direct telephone calls from the home office, with assistance, when necessary, from the national field sales organization. The Consumer Affairs department has the authority to determine whatever course of action should be taken regarding a consumer problem.

Each product comes packaged with an owner's manual which stresses that consumers should contact the Consumer Affairs department if problems with the product arise.

Sample Policy 7

The purpose of the consumer affairs unit is to enhance the loyalty of existing customers, attract new customers, and provide useful information to our personnel about customer ideas, needs, and problems.

The strategy for accomplishing these goals is to provide our consumers with personal service that is friendly, courteous, efficient, and helpful. We should provide the best service in our industry and offer service for consumers that is on a par with other consumer product companies of comparable reputation.

Our presumption in dealing with consumers is that they have contacted us with a legitimate need or problem. We want them to feel satisfied as a result of their contact with the company, and we want them to tell others about how pleased they are about the way they were treated.

Our experience to date suggests that we can be generous about replacing garments when there is consumer dissatisfaction without incurring unwarranted costs.

Sample Policy 8

Our customer service policy for years has been simply: "Satisfaction Guaranteed or Your Money Back." This promise has worked effectively over the years. Very few people take advantage of the offer. If you consider that a customer might spend $20,000 over a lifetime, it would seem foolish to risk that business because of a return worth just a fraction of that amount.

Our company considers customer service and satisfaction to be a responsibility of all employees. Each salesperson is trained to listen to customer complaints, apologize for the inconvenience, ask what the customer wants us to do, and then finally do it.

Sample Policy 9

Principles of Doing Business

Principle 1. We do everything we can to make our products better. We improve material and add back features and construction details that others have taken out over the years. We never reduce the quality of a product to make it cheaper.

Principle 2. We price our products fairly and honestly. We do not, have not, and will not participate in the common retailing practice of inflating mark-ups to set up a future phony "sale."

Principle 3. We accept any return, for any reason, at any time. Our products are guaranteed. No fine print. No arguments. We mean exactly what we say: GUARANTEED. PERIOD.

Principle 4. We ship faster than anyone else we know of. We ship items in stock the day after we receive the order. At the height of the last Christmas season, the longest time an order was in the house was 36 hours, with the exception of monograms, which took another 12 hours.

Principle 5. We believe that what is best for our customer is best for all of us. Everyone here understands that concept. Our sales and service people are trained to know our products and to be friendly and helpful. They are urged to take all the time necessary to take care of you. We even pay for your call, for whatever reason you call.

Principle 6. We are able to sell at lower prices because we have eliminated middlemen, because we don't buy branded merchandise with high protected mark-ups, and because we have placed our contracts with manufacturers who have proved that they are cost conscious and efficient.

Principle 7. We are able to sell at lower prices because we operate efficiently. Our people are hardworking, intelligent, and share in the success of the company.

Principle 8. We are able to sell at lower prices because we support no fancy emporiums with their high overhead.

4.14 Employee Responsibilities and Business Ethics

SESCO Observations and Recommendations
Developing Policies on Employee Responsibilities and Business Ethics

A review of most employee handbooks that have been drafted, published, and distributed in the past shows few formalized business ethics policy statements. However, there is definitely a trend toward drafting a formalized policy statement on business ethics in contemporary employee handbooks by major companies. It is recommended that your employee handbook contain a policy statement dealing with your company's business ethics.

Unless American management places an equal priority on ethical behavior in business as it does on technology and on-the-job knowledge and training, a company can jeopardize its bottom line. Most employers and employees have witnessed the devastating effects of unethical behavior in the insider trading scandals, Watergate, and Golden Parachutes.

Since the overwhelming majority of American businessmen and women firmly believe that "there is no right way to do a wrong thing," all employees in every organization should be given clearly stated business ethics statements as well as training in the ethical standards, performance, and expectations of the company. Equal emphasis should be placed on the "quality" of business standards and ethics as is placed on "quality control" in manufacturing and customer service.

A company does not have to be as large as IBM to have the need to clearly state its employee expectations for ethical performance and behavior in serving clients and customers and in complying with internal established company policies and procedures. "Good ethics is good business!"

Management credibility (trust, confidence, and respect) is largely earned by the quality and examples set forth by top management in all business organizations. Behavior modeling is still the best, most persuasive way to teach middle management, front-line supervisors, and all nonsupervisory employees the value of ethical standards. Employees model themselves on their superiors in American management.

It is American management's responsibility to create a workplace environment for performance standards that are truly ethical in all respects. Most of the Fortune 500 companies have policy statements that clearly provide goals and objectives pertaining to business ethics, credibility, integrity, and quality standards. A number of employers today establish "ethics committees" to establish standards of ethics and ethical business practices governing a broad range of operational concerns and customer relations.

The typical policy statement on business ethics and employee responsibilities provides detailed policy and procedures involving the use of company property, company assets, outside employment, financial interest in other businesses, compliance with federal and state laws, confidentiality, expense accounts, and other important interests and concerns involving employee relations.

The policy statement on business ethics and standards of performance should form the basic foundation for future employee conduct and standards of performance in the workplace. A properly worded policy statement on business ethics and the employees' responsibilities in complying with such policy should clearly communicate "what management expects of employees and what employees can expect from management," adhering to the company's policy of ethical conduct and business ethics.

The following are practical steps in the initial development and drafting of a business ethics policy for management and employees in all classifications:

1. Identify company values
   a. Historic
   b. Current

2. Draft an ethics policy

3. Gain approval of the policy
   a. Board of Directors
   b. Top management

4. Communicate the policy

5. Provide training in the policy

6. Develop monitoring devices

The purpose of any policy statement on business ethics and employee responsibilities, including on-the-job conduct and performance, is to provide "standards of conduct" for employees of the management team in order to guide them in their day-to-day business decision making and on-the-job employee behavior. Every employee and manager would be expected to think and act in compliance with the company's "code of conduct."

Those seeking additional resource help in establishing and maintaining a realistic business ethics program including those responsible for management development and training, may wish to contact one of the following two organizations:

Ethics Resource Center
1025 Connecticut Avenue, NW
Washington, DC 20036

The Center for Business Ethics
Bentley College
Beaver & Forest Streets
Waltham, MA 02254

4.14 Employee Handbook Development Checklist

Employee Responsibilities and Business Ethics

The following checklist can be used to help determine the various subjects to include in your handbook. Sample handbook statements covering many of the items in this checklist appear in this section. They can be used to help draft your personalized employee handbook statements.

Our Employee Handbook Should Include:

EMPLOYEE RESPONSIBILITIES

1. Employee's responsibility to the company   Yes ___ No ___ Maybe ___

2. Appearance and grooming   Yes ___ No ___ Maybe ___

3. No solicitation—no distribution rules   Yes ___ No ___ Maybe ___

4. Housekeeping and cleanliness   Yes ___ No ___ Maybe ___

5. Outside employment   Yes ___ No ___ Maybe ___

6. Personnel records   Yes ___ No ___ Maybe ___

7. Requests for employee information   Yes ___ No ___ Maybe ___

     A. Written requests   Yes ___ No ___ Maybe ___
     B. Telephone requests   Yes ___ No ___ Maybe ___
     C. Requests from government agencies—federal, state, county, unemployment, etc.   Yes ___ No ___ Maybe ___
     D. Requests from tax units   Yes ___ No ___ Maybe ___
     E. Requests from courts and law enforcement agencies   Yes ___ No ___ Maybe ___
     F. Subpoena   Yes ___ No ___ Maybe ___
     G. Employee release   Yes ___ No ___ Maybe ___

8. Company confidential information   Yes ___ No ___ Maybe ___

9. Care and maintenance of equipment   Yes ___ No ___ Maybe ___

10. Credit standing and garnishments   Yes ___ No ___ Maybe ___

11. Company bulletin boards and contents   Yes ___ No ___ Maybe ___

12. Telephone usage and courtesy   Yes ___ No ___ Maybe ___

13. Involvement in community affairs   Yes ___ No ___ Maybe ___

BUSINESS ETHICS

1. Compliance with laws and regulations   Yes ___ No ___ Maybe ___

2. Dealing with customers, suppliers, etc.   Yes ___ No ___ Maybe ___

    A. Contract negotiations   Yes ___ No ___ Maybe ___
    B. Product quality   Yes ___ No ___ Maybe ___
    C. Information from competitors   Yes ___ No ___ Maybe ___
    D. Costs/timecards and reporting   Yes ___ No ___ Maybe ___
    E. Hiring restrictions   Yes ___ No ___ Maybe ___

3. Company resources   Yes ___ No ___ Maybe ___

    A. Political contributions   Yes ___ No ___ Maybe ___
    B. Business gifts   Yes ___ No ___ Maybe ___
    C. U.S. government regulations   Yes ___ No ___ Maybe ___
    D. Relations with foreign officials   Yes ___ No ___ Maybe ___
    E. Financial responsibility   Yes ___ No ___ Maybe ___

4. Conflict of interest   Yes ___ No ___ Maybe ___

5. Insider trading   Yes ___ No ___ Maybe ___

6. Acceptance of business gifts, etc.   Yes ___ No ___ Maybe ___

7. Restricted company information   Yes ___ No ___ Maybe ___

8. Classified information   Yes ___ No ___ Maybe ___

9. Reporting violations   Yes ___ No ___ Maybe ___

10. Discipline procedures   Yes ___ No ___ Maybe ___

PERSONAL COMPUTERS AND SOFTWARE

1. Access to PCs and authorization to use   Yes ___ No ___ Maybe ___

2. Control of data (programs, files, etc.)   Yes ___ No ___ Maybe ___

3. Record of PC use   Yes ___ No ___ Maybe ___

4. Security of files (backup, etc.)   Yes ___ No ___ Maybe ___

5. oan of PCs to employees   Yes ___ No ___ Maybe ___

6. Safeguarding equipment/software   Yes ___ No ___ Maybe ___

7. Access to company files/records   Yes ___ No ___ Maybe ___

Sample Policies: Employee Responsibilities ——————

Sample Policy 1

Both employee and employer have expectations of each other in the workplace.

The company expects employees to

- Follow company rules and procedures;

- Follow the supervisor's instructions;

- Be prompt and regular in attendance;

- Be efficient and productive;

- Be safe and careful;

- Produce quality products and professional work;

- Provide a fair day's work for a fair day's pay; and

- Speak for themselves and maintain an open, honest communication with the supervisor and other management.

The employee can expect to

- Be treated with respect and fairness;

- Receive training and instruction for the assigned job;

- Receive recognition for good work and be corrected for unsatisfactory work;

- Have reasonable working hours;

- Receive open, honest communication throughout the company; and

- Have a safe and healthful workplace.

Sample Policy 2

Along with the advantages and opportunities offered by our bank go certain responsibilities—obligations that you will want to meet. Your primary and most important responsibility, of course, is to do a good job on the work assigned to you by your supervisor. He or she is responsible for what you do, so it is a good idea to respect his or her experience, listen to instructions carefully, and carry them out promptly and cheerfully. Completing each assignment to your supervisor's satisfaction is the surest way to make progress. In addition to following instructions, doing a good job requires you to think for yourself—to ask questions and make constructive suggestions. You will find that your supervisor is interested in your ideas and will appreciate your efforts to do an outstanding job.

Doing a good job also implies certain other obligations on your part, such as maintaining good health and mental alertness, using good judgment, being prompt and regular in attendance, cooperating with your fellow workers, and being loyal to our bank—its people, its customers, and its services. You will want to keep well informed about your bank so that you will be able to talk intelligently about it to your friends and neighbors. To them you represent the bank, and what you say can do much to shape their final opinion of it. This can also help to shape your own future.

Sample Policies: Appearance and Grooming _____

Sample Policy 1

An employee is expected to dress in good taste. Those employees having regular contact with customers are expected to dress in businesslike attire that is similar to the normal business dress modes of our customers. Specific divisions may find it necessary to establish, and are authorized to require, a more stringent dress code.

Sample Policy 2

In our business we are selling not only our skills but also ourselves. Therefore, it is extremely important that our employees present a good impression in appearance and grooming. (Name of company) requires all its employees to maintain a professional, businesslike appearance and attire consistent with the normal business dress modes of our customers. As a condition of employment this standard of dress and appearance is required.

Sample Policy 3

Because of the nature of our people-oriented business, our employees are expected to present the professional image we wish to portray to the public. Employees contribute personally to this desired image by their dress and grooming.

Each individual is expected to be groomed in a manner that is consistent with the job performed and with community standards, and in a manner that will not be offensive. Since dress is a matter of individual taste, we do not wish to set forth strict guidelines. However, all personnel will maintain a clean and neat appearance.

Certain employees are required to wear uniforms which are provided by the company. Wearing a clean uniform is important, and you are required to ensure your uniforms are properly maintained.

Sample Policy 4

In reality, we all work for the public, and the public often judges us by our outward appearance. It is important that attire be appropriate for the job and that we portray a neat and clean image.

All employees are expected to be groomed in a manner consistent with community standards and their position in the company. Casual attire, including jeans, tennis shoes, tee shirts, etc., will be considered inappropriate. Any employee appearing for work whose dress is identified by management as inappropriate, for any reason, will be asked to leave and to return acceptably attired. Should you have any questions regarding acceptable attire, please see your supervisor.

Sample Policy 5

Each individual is to be neat and well groomed. Attire should be appropriate to your particular job. Since dress is a matter of individual taste, we do not wish to set forth strict guidelines. You are expected to be groomed consistent with community standards and in a manner not to offend our visitors, customers, and fellow employees. Male employees must be clean shaven or wear a well-groomed beard and/or moustache. Hair must not be below the collar. Shirts must be properly buttoned and tucked in. Belts must be worn. Female employees are required to wear appropriate foundation garments. No tennis shoes or sandals will be permitted.

Sample Policy 6

The way our employees dress affects both their ability to do their work safely and the impressions of visitors to the office and manufacturing areas. For these reasons, office employees are requested to dress in neat, conservative business attire. Information on appropriate dress for employees working in the manufacturing areas of the company is available from the areas' supervisors.

Sample Policies: No Solicitation and Distribution Rules

Sample Policy 1

In order to prevent disruptions in the operations of the company, and in order to protect employees from harassment and interference with their work, the following rules regarding solicitation and distribution of literature on company property must be observed. Violation of these rules will be cause for appropriate discipline.

Employees

a. During working time, no employee shall solicit or distribute literature to another employee for any purpose. "Working time" refers to that portion of any working day in which the employee is supposed to be performing actual job duties; it does not include such times as lunch, break time, or time before or after a shift. Thus no employee who is on "working time" shall solicit or distribute literature to another employee. No employee who is on "nonworking time" shall solicit or distribute literature to an employee who is on "working time."

b. No employee shall distribute literature to another employee for any purpose in working areas of the company.

c. No employee shall solicit or distribute literature to any visitors at any time for any purpose.

Nonemployees

Persons who are not employed by the company shall not distribute literature or solicit employees or visitors at any time for any purpose on company grounds or inside the company's plant or offices.

Sample Policy 2

Employees are prohibited from soliciting during working time. Distribution of literature and other material is also prohibited in work areas at all times and in nonwork areas during working time.

Solicitation and distribution may not be engaged in during either the working time of the employee subjected to the solicitation and distribution or the working time of the employee engaging in such conduct. Working time is defined as all time when an employee is supposed to be engaged in performing work tasks, but it does not include meal times, breaks, or other specified periods during the workday when the employee is properly not engaged in performing his or her work tasks. No littering with solicitation literature is permitted at any time.

Sample Policy 3

Out of respect for the private lives of company employees and in the interest of keeping a clean, orderly, and professional workplace, the company will enforce the following policy with regard to solicitations and the distribution of literature:

- Employees may not solicit funds, or otherwise solicit among employees, for any purpose during actual working time when full attention to work is required. Working time does not include lunch hours, coffee breaks, or other rest or break periods when full attention to work is not required. The only exception to this rule is the annual company-sponsored United Way campaign.

- Any solicitation must be conducted in an unintrusive, courteous, and professional manner; must not disrupt or interfere with the soliciting employee's work or the work of any employee; and must not harass any employee.

- any disruption, harassment, or neglect of work that accompanies any solicitation will result in appropriate disciplinary action. Employees who have been harassed or whose work has been disrupted or interfered with by a soliciting employee should bring it promptly to the attention of their supervisor for corrective action.

- Employees may not distribute or circulate any printed or written material in any work area at any time, concerning matters other than those directly related to company business.

- Gambling, lotteries, pools, raffles, and commercial sales or enterprises are strictly forbidden on company property at any time.

- Employees may not post signs, advertisements, or notices that are not related solely to company business or to company-sponsored events or announcements.

- Individuals who are not employed by our company may not solicit employees or distribute or circulate printed or written material on company property at any time.

Sample Policy 4

In the interest of maintaining a proper business environment and preventing interference with work and inconvenience to others, employees may not distribute literature or printed materials of any kind, sell merchandise, solicit financial contributions, or solicit for any other cause during working time. Employees who are not on working time (e.g., those on lunch hour or breaks) may not solicit employees who are on working time for any cause or distribute literature of any kind to them. Furthermore, employees may not distribute literature or printed material of any kind in working areas at any time.

Nonemployees are likewise prohibited from distributing material or soliciting employees on our premises at any time.

Sample Policy 5

To avoid disruption of operations, the following rules apply to solicitation and distribution of material (i.e., selling of products, handbills, advertisements, literature, etc.) on company owned or leased property.

Persons not employed may not solicit or distribute literature to employees on company owned or leased property at any time for any purpose. Employees are expected to report any violations to the security department.

Employees may not distribute any noncompany literature or engage in any solicitation during work time or in designated work areas. Work areas include all areas except the cafeteria, restrooms, lobbies, and parking areas. Work time includes the work time of both the employee doing the soliciting or distributing and the employee to whom the solicitation is directed. Non-work time is prior to start time, designated break time, lunchtime, and after work.

Sample Policies: Housekeeping and Cleanliness _____

Sample Policy 1

By keeping our plant clean, we get better quality work and make everyone a little happier. Everyone has to do his or her part. We expect employees to spend any time they have available from production work in policing their machines and the areas around them. In certain departments and on some machines, daily cleanup is required, and in others a weekly cleanup is sufficient. Ask your supervisor for help regarding a cleanup schedule.

Good housekeeping promotes good workmanship and safety. Keep your equipment in good order and practice good housekeeping.

Sample Policy 2

Good housekeeping is a safety measure; a clean plant is a safe plant. See that your workplace is clean and orderly. Keep aisles clear and do not block exits. Stack materials in an orderly and safe manner.

Employees will be judged by the way their work area is maintained and their good housekeeping practices of cleaning up after each job.

Housekeeping (whether good or bad) creates a lasting impression on company visitors. Our daily visitors include customers, prospective customers, suppliers, and representatives of other business concerns.

The courteous reception they receive from employees and the neat appearance of the office or plant greatly influence the impressions and opinions they form.

Sample Policy 3

We ask that all employees take pride in good housekeeping and to make a special effort to keep our company as clean as possible at all times.

Customers and visitors immediately notice the cleanliness of our work areas, including buildings, grounds, and other facilities, and obtain a positive impression of the company and its employees when attention to neatness and cleanliness is observed.

Sample Policy 4

One sure indication of an efficient worker is the condition and appearance of his or her work area. Orderliness in your work area reduces accidents, improves health conditions, reduces fire hazards, adds to the efficiency of your work, and improves the quality of our service. You are expected to help by placing trash and refuse in the containers provided and by applying a few simple rules of tidiness. It is your responsibility to help keep company premises clean and sanitary.

Sample Policy 5

A clean plant is a more pleasant and safe place to work. The company stresses cleanliness and orderliness in the plant and offices. All washrooms shall be kept in a clean and sanitary condition in accordance with sanitation standards set by OSHA.

To ensure that our plant is being maintained in the best possible condition, periodic inspections will be conducted in all departments by management personnel. At the conclusion of the inspections, specific criticisms and suggested improvements regarding fire hazards and good housekeeping will be made to the individuals concerned.

Each employee is urged to cooperate to the fullest extent in these matters. Corrective action will be taken for violation of housekeeping and sanitation rules.

Sample Policies: Outside Employment _____

Sample Policy 1

It is expected that full-time employees' primary employment obligation is with (name of company). Therefore, any outside employment should not conflict with your job or the scheduling of work shifts.

While some part-time and temporary employees have other employment obligations, it is important that the employee and the supervisor establish work schedules that are mutually advantageous to both the employee and (name of company).

Sample Policy 2

In accepting a job with (name of company), we must insist that you maintain a certain loyalty—loyalty to the company and to your fellow employees. You are expected to arrange your living habits so that you will be alert, efficient, and enthusiastic on your job at all times.

Any employee who engages in additional employment outside the company in any phase of the graphic arts industry, either with another employer or through self-employment, may be dismissed. The company cannot accept your divided loyalty, and it will not compete with you after regular working hours.

If you must accept outside employment in a business unrelated to the graphic arts, in order to supplement your income, this work must not interfere with overtime demands of your regular job or diminish your capacity to fulfill your regular duties or carry out your moral obligation to the company.

Sample Policy 3

We do not attempt to control your personal affairs nor to regulate the use of your leisure time. However, since working for more than one employer may interfere with your efficiency, create conflicts if working for a competitor, and possibly complicate your eligibility for workers' compensation in the event you become disabled while employed elsewhere, we expect you to give full attention to your job here.

Sample Policy 4

Outside employment could give rise to a conflict of interest with respect to your employment at (name of company). Your duties in outside employment may detract from the business opportunities or reputation of (name of company) or they may adversely affect your job performance. Because a conflict of interest could exist without your being aware of it, it is mandatory that you notify your supervisor to determine if there is a conflict before accepting any supplemental job. You must also notify your supervisor if your duties in outside employment change significantly.

Sample Policy 5

We appreciate the ability, energies, and loyalty you bring to your job. In fairness to fellow workers and to us, employees are not permitted to hold employment with another organization or have an interest in any business which may in any way result in a conflict of interest or which would adversely affect their employment here. However, should employees wish to involve themselves with work which cannot be described by the above stipulation, they are free to do so, provided it is not done on company time and will not interfere with their performance as an employee. All employment that is in addition to employment with the company must be approved by the president.

Sample Policy 6

We offer you an opportunity for earning a livelihood for your family. In all fairness to each of your fellow workers and to us, you are not permitted to hold employment at another company or business which is in any way competitive with our business or which would adversely affect your employment here. Involvement in other unrelated jobs or interests on company time will not be tolerated.

Sample Policies: Personnel Records ————————————

Sample Policy 1

The company maintains a personnel file for each employee. The file contains the individual's employment application, offer letter, "conditions of employment" document, the two most current performance appraisals, and any formal disciplinary documentation. In general, a personnel file will not contain any material that has not been reviewed with the employee. The Benefits Department also maintains employee files to administer benefits coverage. The contents of employee files are strictly confidential, and access will be limited to authorized individuals.

The employee can ask to see his/her personnel files by contacting the Personnel representative. The employee may review his/her file in the Personnel Department in the presence of the Personnel representative and may make copies of any of its contents.

In addition to personnel and benefits files, authorized medical staff will maintain employee files for health-related information. Only the employee and the medical staff have access to medical information.

Sample Policy 2

An employee is to notify the corporation at once whenever there is a change in address, name, telephone number, marital status, person to notify in case of accident or illness, number of dependents, or insurance beneficiary.

Sample Policy 3

Employees are expected to keep (name of company) informed of any change regarding their records. Changes in any of the following categories should be reported to the Personnel Office as soon as they occur:

1. Change of address
2. Change of telephone number
3. Change of person to be notified in case of emergency
4. Legal change of name
5. Change in marital status

Sample Policy 4

The accuracy of personnel records is essential for the proper handling of many items of great personal importance to you, including proper handling of emergency notification of your family, income tax deductions, insurance coverage, beneficiaries for insurance, etc. The accuracy of your personnel record is your responsibility. Please report promptly to the office any change in your address, telephone number, marital status, or number of dependents.

Sample Policy 5

When you applied for employment with us, it was necessary to complete an application form. This information was transferred to a permanent and confidential file, which is the company's employment record of you as an individual. Keeping this record correct and up to date is important to you because it enables us to reach you in an emergency, forward your mail, properly maintain your insurance and other benefits, compute your payroll deductions, etc.

Your supervisor should be notified promptly of changes in the following:

1. Address and telephone number

2. Marital status

3. Name

4. Beneficiary of dependents listed in your insurance policy

5. Number of dependents for withholding tax purposes

6. Person to notify in case of accident

7. Any change or restriction in your driver's license

Sample Policies: Requests for Employee Information ———

Sample Policy 1

The company is committed to protecting the privacy of its current and former employees. To assist employees who want the company to provide confidential information on their behalf, the personnel department will coordinate the response to requests for information about current and former employees. Only authorized personnel representatives will respond to requests for salary, work history, and other confidential information.

Sample Policy 2

Employees who receive calls or written requests to release information about current or former employees should refer these requests to the Personnel Department. Any employee who releases information about a current or former employee without specific authorization by the employee will be subject to disciplinary action up to and including termination of employment.

Sample Policy 3

Current employees who need verification of their employment and salary to obtain a mortgage or credit card or for other personal reasons should submit a written request to the Personnel Department. Current employees may authorize their supervisor or other company representatives to provide a personal reference that includes an assessment of the employee's job performance and accomplishments. A supervisor or any other employee who is asked by an active employee to provide a personal reference must consult with Personnel for advice on providing a balanced, objective view of the employee's work record.

Sample Policy 4

Before employees leave the company, they will have an exit interview with a personnel representative. At the exit interview, employees will be asked to complete a "Personnel Reference Authorization" form to indicate what information, if any, the company may release if a prospective employer requests information about the former employee's work record. At the employee's request, the supervisor and personnel representative will provide a letter that summarizes the employee's work history and comments on the employee's performance and accomplishments. A copy of this letter will remain in the former employee's personnel file and will serve as the basis for future references that are authorized by the former employee.

Sample Policy 5

The company will release information about current and former employees if the request is accompanied by a subpoena or if releasing the information is required by law. The Personnel Department will handle these requests for information. Sample Policies: Company Confidential Information

Sample Policies: Company Confidential Information _____

Sample Policy 1

Many of our company employees have been placed in a position of trust because of the work they perform and are, therefore, exposed to or have access to company funds, employee payroll data, personnel record information, employee billing records, customer records, credit management, vendor contracts, computerized information, financial information, and other types of sensitive information that are considered confidential in nature.

You are reminded that revealing any type of confidential information to unauthorized persons or tampering with or altering company records and/or property is a violation of that trust which can result in disciplinary action up to and including discharge.

Should you have doubts about what is considered confidential information or a violation of trust, you should seek advice from your supervisor.

Sample Policy 2

In the course of your work, you may have access to confidential information regarding the company or those we serve. It is one of your prime responsibilities to be sure that you in no way reveal or divulge any such information and that you use it only in the performance of your duties. Divulging confidential information will result in immediate suspension, leading to dismissal.

Sample Policy 3

Employees are asked not to divulge, during any term of employment or after employment is terminated, any information acquired during employment with the company concerning any of the activities or affairs of the company's clients or concerning any company transactions with its clients or any other individuals or bodies, nor divulge any affairs of the company.

Sample Policy 4

In the course of your work, you will undoubtedly have access to confidential information regarding our company or respected clients. It's one of your most serious responsibilities that you in no way reveal or divulge any such information and that you use it only in the performance of your duties. All of us pledge ourselves to respect this information and keep it confidential.

Sample Policy 5

It is the policy of our company to ensure that the operations, activities, and business affairs of the company and our customers are kept confidential to the greatest possible extent. If, during the course of their employment, employees acquire confidential or proprietary information about our company and its customers, such information is to be handled in strict confidence and not to be discussed with outsiders. Employees are also responsible for the internal security of such information.

In addition, employees are prohibited from engaging in securities transactions on the basis of information not available to the general public and which, if known to outsiders, might affect their investment decisions. The dissemination of such information to others who might make use of that knowledge to trade in securities is also prohibited.

Employees will be asked to sign a statement of confidentiality at the time of hire and periodically throughout their terms of employment to acknowledge their awareness of, and reaffirm their commitment to, this policy.

Employees found to be violating this policy are subject to disciplinary action, up to and including termination, and may also be subject to civil and/or criminal penalties for violations of, among other things, applicable securities laws.

Sample Policy 6

Because of our philosophy regarding the protection of confidential information, a great deal of proprietary and other confidential data are disseminated that must be restricted to employees only and not become known to competitors or others outside the company.

Proprietary and confidential data can take many shapes, including, but not limited to, documents, cassette tapes, word processing or computer diskettes and related equipment, and carbon typewriter ribbons. Employees who handle this type of material are personally responsible for its safekeeping. Employees are not to discuss any of the following items outside of the company without the express authority from a senior executive of the company:

- Research work, including formulae, compounds and related material, and their biological evaluation

- Research proposals, pending patent applications, and their disposition

- Processes, including all aspects of laboratory and full-scale production, plus prototypes, designs, and blueprints thereof

- All phases of new and existing product development, including clinical trials, marketing plans, possible uses, etc.

- Operating and strategic plans

- Regulatory information and communications

- Acquisition and divestiture data, including licensing agreements and negotiations, as well as possible future acquisitions or divestitures of assets, technology, or securities

- Financial data such as sales volumes, profit margins, costs of goods sold, etc.

- Any data affecting business or profit

Sample Policies: Care and Maintenance of Equipment _____

Sample Policy 1

Your cooperation in the care and use of company equipment is necessary to maintain it in good operating condition. You should use it only for the purpose intended and as instructed by your supervisor. If any of our equipment is defective or not in a safe working order, please notify your supervisor so that a repair or replacement can be made.

Company vehicles are for business use only and are to be driven only by authorized employees. Employee drivers must have with them, at all times, a valid (state) driver's license and are expected to practice safe and courteous driving habits. Any accident must be reported to your supervisor immediately.

Failure to use company property and vehicles properly can result in disciplinary action, up to and including dismissal.

Sample Policy 2

The business in which this company competes requires specialized machinery and equipment. This machinery and equipment requires constant attention, skillful use, and regular maintenance. As an employee, it is your responsibility to provide all machinery and equipment you use with the required levels of attention, skill, and maintenance.

You must not attempt to use any machinery or equipment with which you are not familiar without first getting instructions from your supervisor. If any of our tools or equipment are defective, broken, or are not the best for the job, notify your supervisor immediately so that repairs can be made or replacements considered.

No company tools, machinery, or equipment will be loaned to employees for their personal use under any circumstances.

Sample Policy 3

Our company has invested thousands of dollars in the equipment which is necessary to perform your job. Your cooperation in the care and use of this equipment is necessary to maintain it in operating condition. Your maintenance roster should be used in connection with the care and upkeep of equipment. If any of our equipment is defective or not in a safe working order, please notify us so that a replacement or repair can be made. Equipment is to be kept as clean as possible at all times.

Care should be exercised at all times because gross employee negligence, causing damage to company property, equipment, or customer vehicles, may result in the employee being held financially liable for the damage.

Sample Policies: Credit Standing and Garnishments ———

Sample Policy 1
Anyone may get into personal financial difficulties once in a while, but your company, like all reputable business firms, does not like wage assignments or garnishments. A garnishment is a court order to a company to pay your debts through the court before giving you your paycheck. Since executing garnishments is an inconvenience to the company, we hope you will conduct your financial affairs in a manner that will make them unnecessary. You are encouraged to discuss such problems with management before legal action is taken against you. All such discussions are held in the strictest confidence and every effort will be made to help you.

Sample Policy 2
A garnishment is a court order to a company to pay an employee's debts through the court before issuing his or her pay check. Since executing garnishments is a costly inconvenience to the company, (name of company) hopes you will conduct your financial affairs in a manner that will make them unnecessary.

Sample Policy 3
The assignment of wages, or an order for garnishment of wages for credit for any employee, is regarded as a serious matter. If a creditor obtains a garnishment on your earnings, the company is required by law to deduct the necessary payment. If you cannot clear the indebtedness, we will be required, by law, to deduct the garnishment from your wages. The first garnishment occurrence against an employee will result in a written correction notice; any occurrence thereafter may result in dismissal.

Sample Policy 4
We are expected to conduct our personal lives in a manner which will reflect credit upon our company. One of the most important things is to show our ability to properly manage our own personal finances and to meet our financial obligations promptly.

Anything done by employees in their personal affairs which might involve the company in legal proceedings started by their creditors is looked upon as a serious matter. If unusual or emergency situations develop that create a financial burden upon you, it is imperative that provisions for these be made so that neither actions for collection nor garnishment of wages will occur. If a creditor obtains a garnishment on your earnings, we are required by law to deduct the necessary payment.

Sample Policies: Company Bulletin Boards and Contents

Sample Policy 1

Bulletin boards have been placed in convenient locations throughout the company to provide information to employees. You are urged to observe the bulletin boards closest to your work area daily for improvement announcements and other information.

All postings are to be cleared through your supervisor and the Human Resources Department prior to posting. There are separate bulletin boards for company postings and for employee postings (i.e., "For sale," "Ride wanted," etc.).

Sample Policy 2

Our company maintains bulletin boards throughout its facilities to furnish you with up-to-date information on events and matters of interest which are important to its employees. You should check the bulletin boards regularly so that you will be well informed on company matters. All materials and information must be approved by the president before posting.

Sample Policy 3

Information of general interest is regularly posted on our bulletin boards. Please form the habit of checking the bulletin boards daily, so that you will be familiar with the information posted there.

Only notices of an official nature will be placed on these boards.

Sample Policy 4

In order to communicate current important topics with our employees, we maintain bulletin boards. Bulletin boards are located throughout our facilities, in areas that employees frequently visit, in order to ensure that employees have constant access to posted information. The company's bulletin boards are uniform in size, glass-enclosed, and locked for security and cleanliness.

Our bulletin boards are used to communicate official government information on EEO, wage and hour, health and safety, and other issues. They are also used to communicate information regarding company policy and company business and announcements, including but not limited to job postings, safety rules, health items, benefit programs, and notices announcing special events, such as our annual blood donor drive.

Employees may not post, tape, tack, or affix in any way any form of literature, printed or written materials, photographs, or notices of any kind on the company's bulletin boards or their glass coverings, on the walls, in time clock areas, or anywhere else on company property. Violation of this policy shall be grounds for disciplinary action, up to and including discharge.

Bulletin boards may not be used by employees or outside parties for the posting of commercial notes and advertisements, announcements and witticisms, sales of personal property, or any other matters, work related or not. Employees and outside parties are also prohibited from distributing literature and soliciting other employees except as stated in the company's solicitation and distribution of literature policy.

Our human resources department maintains keys for all bulletin boards. All postings are performed by members of the human resources department, who are responsible for keeping the company's bulletin boards up to date.

Sample Policies: Telephone Usage and Courtesy _____

Sample Policy 1

The telephone is maintained for business purposes only. You must not make personal calls unless specifically authorized to do so. Incoming calls to you will not be allowed unless an emergency requires that you be called. If no emergency exists, the caller's name and number will be given to you.

Sample Policy 2

Our telephone facilities are reserved for business purposes. All personal incoming and outgoing calls should be limited to matters of emergencies, such as illness, accident, unanticipated overtime work, and calls of a similar nature. Incoming messages during the normal work day, unless emergencies, will be taken by the receptionist and a message relayed to the employee. All calls outside the normal work day will be taken by the shift supervisor.

All nonbusiness outgoing calls are to be made on the pay telephones which have been installed for the convenience of the employees.

Sample Policy 3

All telephones in the company have been installed for the purpose of carrying on and conducting our business; thus, personal calls must be limited and should be restricted to emergency situations during production time and to a three-minute maximum during your lunch period. Should you have an emergency call to place, go to your supervisor and get his or her approval to use the company phone. Incoming calls of an emergency nature will be accepted, and you will be immediately notified of any such calls. Other calls of a personal nature cannot be accepted.

Sample Policy 4

Our telephone courtesy is most important. People judge us and our bank by our telephone manners. Please remember these things: answer pleasantly, give your name and department, take the message or offer to call back if you cannot answer the question, get the message straight, write it down and read it back, don't depend on your memory. Telephones should be answered promptly. If a party ordinarily handling calls for a department must leave the vicinity of the telephone, he or she should delegate someone to handle such calls until his or her return. If a person answering the telephone discovers, after talking to the party calling, that the call was meant for another department or that it involves several departments, he or she should take the message and offer to call the party back. By no means should the call be transferred to two or more people with a party having to relay the message again.

Sample Policy 5

Company telephones and voice mail are provided for the conduct of company business. However, it is recognized that some nonbusiness calls are necessary. For this reason, the company does not desire to prohibit the use of telephones or voice mail for personal use. Such calls should be limited in number and duration and you should not abuse this privilege. When nonbusiness or personal long-distance telephone calls are placed from any company facility, charges should be "reversed" or charged to the employee's home telephone number.

Telephones should be answered promptly at all times during working hours. You should make arrangements for someone to take your calls or to have calls forwarded when you are absent from your work area.

Sample Policy 6

The telephone is a very important business tool. Customers call in orders, our suppliers call us, prospects make inquiries, and customer needs are satisfied through the use of company telephones.

You may make important local personal calls before or after work, but do not tie up the lines with private calls from 8 a.m. to 5 p.m., except for real emergencies. Ask any persistent friend calling to do the same. *Use of company phones for personal long-distance calls is not allowed.* In cases of emergency, we will assist you in any telephoning that is necessary. Pay phones are strategically located in the cafeteria areas to provide outside access during employee work breaks.

Sample Policies: Involvement in Community Activities ____

Sample Policy 1

In general, the company encourages you to be active, involved members of your community. The opportunities that outside activities present for personal growth and fulfillment, as well as for professional growth, are many.

The primary responsibility of all employees is to carry out the work assigned to them by the company, and they should not participate in any outside activity which conflicts with such responsibility or with the interest of the company.

There are various outside activities which might interfere, directly or indirectly, with your obligation to the company. When there is a possibility of interference or conflict, the best interests of both the employee and the company require that the particular activity have company approval. Therefore, as a general rule, you should inform your supervisor of all such proposed activities and obtain approval.

Sample Policy 2

You are encouraged to take an active part in community and civic activities. Whether it be civic or service organizations or "drives," such as the United Way Fund, it is hoped that each of you will do your part to make our community a more desirable place in which to live. Employees who assume civic responsibilities within their community develop the qualities of leadership which will contribute to their progress in the bank.

Sample Policy 3

We recognize that our company is an important factor in the life of each community in which it operates and that it has a responsibility to cooperate with local government and with organizations interested in the welfare of these communities. It is our hope that all our employees accept this responsibility and that they take part in discussions and activities designed to solve community problems in the best interest of our community, our personnel, and our company.

Our record of good citizenship is important to us. Public relations can be good, bad, or indifferent. We appreciate your efforts to build good friendships for our company.

Sample Policies: Business Ethics ————————

Sample Policy 1

The Code of Business Practices and Ethics should guide and direct employees' company-related actions and activities.

The company considers respect for the highest ethical standards to be more important than any short-term or temporary gain the company or the employee may receive. The company policy strongly suggests that all employees act as leaders and set an example among their business, personal, and professional acquaintances by their conduct.

Management responsibilities. Executives, managers, and supervisors must be sure that their employees understand and comply with the Code of Ethics. They should also actively encourage employees to become so familiar with the code that acting properly is second nature.

At least once a year, each supervisor must certify to his division head that he and his subordinates have complied with the code during the preceding year.

Financial Officers' Responsibilities. Financial officers must make sure all transactions and financial activities are conducted according to the strictest legal and ethical standards. They must report to the controller any actual, apparent, or potential transaction that violates the Code of Ethics.

Ethics Committee. The president will name a nine-member Ethics Committee to promote active compliance with the Code of Ethics. The Ethics Committee should also promote improved standards of ethical behavior within the industry and the community by supporting appropriate programs, procedures, and legislation.

Permanent members of the committee should be the president and the legal counsel. Other members should include management, supervision, collective bargaining representatives, and employees. They should serve staggered terms of one to three years.

The Ethics Committee will advise all employees in specific situations. It will decide on the proper course of action when questionable practices are brought to its attention. The committee will also serve as the judge of all serious violations or apparent violations of the code. It may delegate to management the power to determine the appropriate course of action for less serious code violations.

Obligation to Report. Each employee has the direct obligation and responsibility to report his or her own and any other real or apparent violations of the Code of Ethics.

Employees should first report questionable practices to their department head, but they may go directly to the office of the legal counsel or the Ethics Committee.

Depending on the seriousness of the situation, the manager or the committee should quickly respond to the report and take all necessary action to make sure that the violation is corrected or the situation clarified.

If an employee is not satisfied with the initial response, he or she should appeal directly to the president. No reprisals or other harm may come to any employee for reporting a real or apparent violation.

However, if an employee is aware of, but fails to report, a situation, he or she will be held responsible for this failure. It could lead to disciplinary action.

Enforcement and Sanctions. The company considers any violation of the code to be an important matter. The Ethics Committee or its delegated representative may take easy appropriate disciplinary action, including demotion, suspension, reprimand, and discharge, in response to violations. They will consider the circumstances of the situation, the employee's actions or decision, and the employee's response to the allegation; but lack of knowledge of the Code of Ethics will never be considered a legitimate excuse.

The company prefers not to maintain such strict disciplinary procedures. It would prefer that employees act according to the dictates of their consciences. But in an imperfect world, the company must make it clear that each employee is expected to apply the Code of Ethics to all business activities.

Compliance with the Law. Company policy is to obey the law and regulations of every state and country in which the company does business. The company recognizes that with the law, many interpretations often exist. And employees who are untrained in the law may find it difficult to distinguish proper from improper conduct.

In such cases, each employee should seek the advice of respected managers, legal staff, or the Ethics Committee before he or she acts. However, when the needed advice cannot be obtained quickly enough, the employee should act as his or her best judgment and conscience dictate. No employee should act, or be required to act, in a manner that he or she would be embarrassed or ashamed to read about in the newspapers.

Another rule is that employees should avoid the appearance or suspicion of improper or illegal conduct in any business affair. If they are in doubt, they should refrain from taking the questionable action.

Company Loyalty. Each employee should always act in the best interests of the law and in accordance with the highest ethical standards. In doing so, he or she will always be acting in the company's best interests. No employee should be influenced by outside interests or relationships which jeopardize the company's or the employee's reputation and integrity.

Discounts, Rebates, Credits, and Preferential Treatment. Employees should avoid improper or questionable credits, rebates, discounts, or allowances on any company product or service.

The Ethics Committee will determine accepted practices in this area.

Each employee involved in such transactions must maintain exact records as required by law and the company when granting such preferences.

Naturally, the company will engage in legal and accepted competitive practices. That is the essence of a free enterprise system.

Employees should be thoroughly familiar with applicable laws, particularly the price discrimination provisions of the Robinson Patman Act. They should refer any questions to the legal staff.

Personal Use of Company Property. Employees may not use, divert, or appropriate company property, equipment, services, or assets for personal use or benefit. The improper and unauthorized use of any of these will be treated as theft.

Even such seemingly minor activities as using the copying machines for personal needs erode company profits and create unhealthy precedents.

Employees may use certain equipment and office supplies, provided they obtain their supervisors' permission and immediately reimburse the company for the value of the items or service. No exceptions are allowed.

Expense Accounts. Company expense accounts require special treatment. "Padding" of expense accounts is prohibited. Other unacceptable practices include swapping airplane tickets and pocketing the difference, exaggerating business entertainment costs, double-billing, registering in a hotel and not making use of the room while staying for free elsewhere, and so forth.

If an employee is caught, he or she is liable for federal tax penalties, including jail. However, the company's reputation and integrity will also be harmed, and the company becomes liable for federal penalties on unpaid withholding taxes.

These factors make accurate expense account management an essential job responsibility for each employee concerned .

Confidential Company Information. Confidential company information is considered company property and may be used or disclosed only with proper authorization and only in the exercise of an employee's duties.

The company, through its disclosure policy, will keep the amount of information it considers confidential to a minimum. However, it has the right to protect certain types of information, especially that which might jeopardize the company's existence, give competitors overwhelming advantages, and harm company investors and employees.

Categories of Information. The Ethics Committee will decide which categories of information are to be considered confidential. When determining standards, the guiding principle should be a clear "business need" to protect the information.

Confidential categories of information include proposed or advance plans for new products, facilities' construction, earnings, dividends, managerial or organizational changes, and unpublished or proprietary information about product design, development, research, manufacture, and distribution.

Employees' Responsibility. Each employee must protect confidential information to which he or she has authorized access, or to which he or she gains inadvertent access. Access in itself never confers the privilege to disclose the information.

Release of Information. Confidential information may only be released by official company announcement from the office of the president or with the president's written permission. Release of such information must be approved by the Executive Committee.

Improper Use. The company considers the following actions to be improper and unlawful use of confidential information:

- Using the information for personal benefit.

- Using "inside" information to buy or give advice about buying company securities. y Discussing confidential information with family, relatives, friends, or business and professional associates.

Such improper and illegal disclosure will be treated in the strictest legal manner, and the company may exercise its right to file civil and criminal actions.

Sample Policy 2

The company's reputation and the trust and confidence of those with whom we deal are among our most vital corporate resources. Our company is committed to conducting its affairs in a uniformly ethical manner and pursuant to a standard of fundamental honesty and fair dealing. This standard requires adherence to all laws, regulations, and normal ethical practices that apply to the company's business activities.

Areas for Potential Conflict—Employees have a responsibility to work in the best interests of the company and to avoid situations and actions that may be, or create the appearance of being, in conflict with the company's objectives and principles. While it is not possible to list every circumstance that may lead to a conflict of interest, the following are examples of activities that must be avoided:

- Holding a substantial financial interest in any enterprise with which the company has business dealings (e.g., competitors, suppliers, and customers). (Interest of less than $10,000 or which, regardless of value, amount to less than 1 percent, of an enterprise are not considered to be substantial.)

- Accepting, directly or indirectly, from any vendor or supplier of services, by an employee or any member of an employee's immediate family, any vacations, cash payment (other than reimbursement of reasonable out-of-pocket expenses), service, loan (except from banks or other financial institutions), or discount (except those offered to employees of the company).

- Accepting gifts from any vendor or supplier of materials or services.

In addition to the above prohibitions, there are borderline situations that give rise to possible conflicts of interest. The following serves as a guide to the types of activities that should be fully reported to the company:

- Acting as a director, officer, employee, or otherwise for any business or other institution with which the company has a competitive or significant business relationship.

The employee should report to his or her supervisor any situation in which members of the employee's immediate household hold positions that are likely to cause the employee to have a conflict between the interests of the company and another institution.

- Competing with the company in the purchase or sale of any kind of property (tangible or intangible) or diverting a business opportunity from the company for the employee's personal interest.

- Using company assets (e.g., funds, facilities, know-how, or personnel) for the benefit of other business or personal Interests.

- Engaging in outside activities that reduce the employee's impartiality, judgment, or that may interfere with or adversely affect the employee's ability to perform company work.

Honoraria—From time to time, employees may be asked to represent the company before an outside group or trade association. In such instances, employees may accept expense reimbursement but should decline any fees offered. If an honorarium cannot be declined, the employee should request that the granting organization contribute the honorarium to a charity or some other nonprofit agency. If the granting organization will not comply with this request, the employee must donate the money to a charity or some other nonprofit agency.

Approvals and Advice—Employees are encouraged to discuss issues and concerns pertaining to the company's commitment to ethical business practices with their supervisors. All managers shall be responsible for the enforcement of compliance with this policy.

Employees must obtain approval from their supervisor, the appropriate area or functional Vice-President, and an authorized representative from the Law Department before undertaking any of the activities identified as possible conflicts of interest in this Business Ethics Policy.

4.15 Disclaimers and Handbook Acknowledgment/Receipt Statements

SESCO Observations and Recommendations
Drafting Disclaimer Statements and Acknowledgment/Receipt Pages

Over the past several years, many state laws have been amended or changed as a result of challenges to the employers' and the states' "employment-at-will" doctrine. One exception is referred to as the "implied contract" doctrine. Contents of employee handbooks and other written company personnel policies and benefit programs have been used in state lawsuits by employees in an attempt to establish an employment agreement or "employee contract" between the employer and employee. Most often these cases have arisen when employees have been discharged or terminated from employment, soon followed by a "wrongful discharge" lawsuit against the employer.

In numerous cases, improperly or poorly worded policy statements in employee handbooks have become the basis of legally enforceable "employee contracts" between an employee and a former employer if the handbook language is interpreted by the court as binding on the employer.

Numerous employers and their legal counsel have reacted to some of these state employment-at-will cases by avoiding the development and publication of employee handbooks for their employees. Others have revised their employee handbooks to avoid inconsistent personnel policies and procedures or "trigger" words that undercut the employer's "employment-at-will" rights if in compliance with current state law. Some employers believe that by not establishing written personnel policies and procedures and publishing them in employee handbooks and by avoiding distribution of written personnel policies and procedures, that they can protect themselves from future employment-at-will lawsuits or financial liabilities if challenged by former employees in the state courts.

Unfortunately, a number of employers have learned that simply not putting their personnel policies in a distributed employee handbook is no guarantee against costly employee lawsuits. Numerous state courts have already held that *verbal statements and verbal communications by supervisors and managers in pre-employment interviews, employee performance appraisals, and other day-to-day supervisor-employee communications are often held to be legally enforceable promises.* This simply means that verbal promises and verbal statements made by management, when documented by former employees who are initiating lawsuits, can be legally binding. They can force the employer to live up to verbal promises concerning employee benefit eligibility, long-term employment, or an employee's protection from being terminated "at any time for any reason."

In short, employers today cannot avoid employment-at-will or wrongful discharge lawsuits in state courts simply by not publishing and distributing their personnel policies, standards of performance, conduct work rules, and other company policies. Operating in a "communications vacuum" on the basis of unwritten, unpublished company personnel policies and procedures can even be more costly and dangerous to employers if supervisors and managers are permitted to interpret verbally their understanding and intent of an employer's existing "unwritten," unpublished personnel policies, benefit programs, and standards of performance.

Recommendations for Avoiding "Verbal" Contract Statements with Employees and Job Applicants

In addition to establishing and publishing properly worded disclaimer statements in the body of your new or revised employee handbook, it is recommended that employers remind everyone involved in the human resources, personnel departments, particularly those responsible for pre-employment interviewing and hiring, as well as all supervisory personnel, of certain important guidelines and "employment-at-will" vulnerability areas. This will help maintain employment-at-will rights and avoid potential lawsuits alleging "wrongful discharge" by former employees.

It is further recommended that the disclaimer statement in the introductory portion of most employee handbooks contain a statement by those individuals in top management who have the authority and responsibility to modify or establish any specific period of employment or to make any promises or commitments that guarantee continued employment. (See sample introductory disclaimer statements in this section.)

Employee handbooks that are properly worded and kept current and updated on employment and benefit personnel policies and procedures can be an employer's most valued documentation in preventing and defeating employment-at-will or wrongful discharge lawsuits and costly litigation and unfavorable media publicity. Properly worded disclaimers in the introductory section of your employee handbook, as well as in the acknowledgment/receipt page, can properly reaffirm your states' "employment-at-will" doctrine.

It is highly recommended that disclaimer statements be worded in a positive, tactful way to avoid offending employees and their families. Your goal is to have employees understand that your employee handbook is a management-employee communications guide and *not* a legally enforceable employee contract.

Although used by most employers in drafting and publishing new or revised employee handbooks, disclaimer statements do not provide a 100 percent guarantee that the employer will not have to defend a lawsuit by a former employee claiming certain "contractual" benefits in the future.

Disclaimers published in employee handbooks are an effective defense against employee claims which are alleged to come from policy statement language in the employee handbook. However, disclaimer statements in employee handbooks will not protect an employer if they are not properly worded and communicated to employees.

Employers should consider customizing their disclaimer statements so that there may be one type of disclaimer for hourly or salaried employees that work in a union-free environment and a second, perhaps more strongly worded, disclaimer for exempt salaried managerial, professional, and executive employees. In publishing and distributing employee handbooks for a union-free environment, informing employees in writing that they may be terminated with or without good cause, depending upon the circumstances of their employment or performance, may make the company more vulnerable to union organizers. It gives a persuasive union organizer "written proof" that employees in that union-free company have no real job security unless they sign a union authorization card and ask the union to represent them and protect them against discipline or discharge "without just cause," as provided in most labor agreements.

Future state court decisions may become more "pro-employee" and refuse to recognize the legal effect of disclaimers in employee handbooks. Because of the obvious "disparity in bargaining strength" between employers and employees in a non-union environment, disclaimers may be considered to be one-sided by future state court judges and given little or no legal weight by the court. Thus, a disclaimer may not completely guarantee protection.

An employer should consider the possible advantages of clearly providing in the employee handbook a disciplinary section detailing work rules and progressive discipline procedures which state that employees will be subject to discipline or terminated only "for cause." In view of the numerous federal employment laws that prohibit discrimination because of race, religion, sex, age, national origin, etc., employers are already required to bear the burden of proof in disciplinary or discharge cases in defending discrimination charges investigated by the NLRB, the EEOC, the OFCC, the Federal Wage-Hour Division, and other federal agencies. A strong case can be made that for positive, pro-employee—employer relations in maintaining valued employees and promoting job security in a union-free environment, the employer must be willing to commit to fair, firm, and consistent disciplinary treatment, including discipline or discharge only for just or proper cause, rather than "at the will" of the employer for good cause or no cause at all.

After reviewing and reading the sample disclaimer statements that follow, one can certainly understand why disclaimers do have a negative impact on the employer-employee relationship and employee morale. The only effective way to prevent such negative, unfavorable reactions is for employers to clearly explain to employees why there is a published disclaimer on their employment application forms or in their employee handbooks. Such reasons should include the need for the management of the company to be able to have the flexibility to change personnel policies and procedures as required to stay ahead of the competition within the industry and to operate profitably and efficiently.

Employee handbook disclaimers should be drafted so that employees know that the new or revised handbook is a "guide" and not a legally enforceable employee contract. Disclaimer statements should be clearly worded, in a positive tone. Employees should be reminded in disclaimer statements that they, too, have the right to terminate their employment at any time for any reason during their employment.

A disclaimer statement should be clearly and conspicuously placed in the employee handbook without any intent to play it down, keep it subtle, or "hide it" from employees. It does not necessarily have to be printed in bold letters on the inside cover of the employee handbook. A disclaimer statement is often woven into the introductory letter printed in the first part of the employee handbook and signed by the CEO or general manager. It is also usually found in most handbooks on the receipt/acknowledgment page that employees sign to indicate that they have received the employee handbook.

In the opinion of many employment attorneys who represent management, written, published disclaimers that specify employment may be terminated at the will of either the employer or the employee remain an effective means of defending employers against wrongful discharge suits. However, a number of employer attorneys predict that state courts will begin evaluating the presence and wording of disclaimer statements in personnel policy manuals and employee handbooks and on employment applications to determine whether or not employees received adequate notice about the disclaimer statement and whether or not they understood the language in the disclaimer statement.

State courts will be asked by employee plaintiffs in the future to evaluate the wording of disclaimer statements to determine if they are clearly worded, understood by the employee, and presented in a form that employees cannot ignore or be unaware of their existence.

Management/Supervisor Do's and Don'ts

1. Do not make verbal statements to job applicants during pre-employment interviews of any "guaranteed" period or length of employment. Avoid verbal statements that employees can have "good job security" as long as they meet certain quality or quantity of work standards or production quotas.

2. Do not make verbal statements concerning the length of a "probationary period." Avoid using the term *probationary* if possible. Instead, use the term *tryout* or *period of adjustment*. If such a tryout period is for 30 workdays, 60 workdays or 90 workdays, avoid verbal statements that imply the new employee will have the right to work the full length of the the period. The employment application or pre-employment "agreement" should clarify that a new employee has the right to terminate employment at any time and that the employer retains the same right. (See sample policy statements in this section for appropriate wording.)

3. Do not make any verbal statement that new employees will be eligible for promotion or upgrading to a higher-paying position or job classification as a result of length of service, time on the job, or achievement of a series of job accomplishments.

4. Do not verbally promise new employees that the employee performance evaluation and review at the end of their tryout period implies a guaranteed term of employment.

5. Do not make a verbal statement that termination of employment will occur only "as a last resort" after the supervisor and employee have gone the last mile.

6. Do not make a verbal statement that an employee may be disciplined or terminated only for "just cause," "proper cause," or "for cause."

7. Do not make a verbal statement that will condition future employment on the employees' receiving a "satisfactory performance" or "acceptable performance" rating in their performance review.

8. Do not make verbal statements during employment interviews with job applicants about "job security" and "steady work" or assurances of continued employment.

The don'ts suggested above, as well as other relevant guidelines that are based upon your respective state employment law decisions, should be prepared in writing, updated, and provided to all human resources personnel and company supervisors during scheduled company management meetings and briefing sessions.

4.15 Employee Handbook Development Checklist

Disclaimers and Handbook Acknowledgment/Receipt Statements

The following checklist can be used to help determine the various subjects to include in your handbook. Sample handbook statements covering many of the items in this checklist appear in this section. They can be used to help draft your personalized employee handbook statements.

Our Employee Handbook Should Include:

DISCLAIMER STATEMENTS

1. Defining absenteeism: Yes ___ No ___ Maybe ___

1. Does our corporate personnel policy and procedures
    manual contain a sample or model disclaimer
    statement?   Yes ___ No ___ Maybe ___

2. Does our present employee handbook contain a
    disclaimer statement in the introductory section?   Yes ___ No ___ Maybe ___

3. Does our present employee handbook contain a
    disclaimer statement in the "Summary" or
    "Acknowledgment/Receipt" page?   Yes ___ No ___ Maybe ___

4. Has the disclaimer statement been reviewed by an
    employment attorney for compliance?   Yes ___ No ___ Maybe ___

5. Should the disclaimer statement clearly indicate that
    the new, revised employee handbook is not a
    contract?   Yes ___ No ___ Maybe ___

6. Should the disclaimer statement confirm that
    employment may be terminated at any time for any
    reason?   Yes ___ No ___ Maybe ___

7. Should the disclaimer statement include the
    company's "employment-at-will" rights?   Yes ___ No ___ Maybe ___

8. Will the disclaimer statement indicate that
    employees also have the right to terminate their
    employment at any time for any reason?   Yes ___ No ___ Maybe ___

9. Should the employee "discipline and conduct"
    section of the handbook avoid progressive discipline
    or a statement that employees will be disciplined or
    terminated only for "just cause"?   Yes ___ No ___ Maybe ___

10. Should a "tryout period" statement provide that at any time during that period an employee may resign or be terminated without prior notice or obligation?   Yes ___ No ___ Maybe ___

11. Should the introductory disclaimer statement provide that the handbook is neither a contract nor an agreement of employment for a definite period of time but a summary of company policies, work rules, and benefits?   Yes ___ No ___ Maybe ___

12. Should the introductory disclaimer statement provide the right for management to change, amend, or delete some of the personnel policies and benefits contained in the handbook, with notification by management when new or revised policies are implemented?   Yes ___ No ___ Maybe ___

ACKNOWLEDGMENT/RECEIPT PAGE

1. Should the acknowledgment/receipt page contain "employment-at-will" disclaimer statement?   Yes ___ No ___ Maybe ___

2. Has the presently worded, existing acknowledgment/receipt page been reviewed by an employment attorney for compliance with federal and/or state "employment-at-will" statutes?   Yes ___ No ___ Maybe ___

3. Should the acknowledgment/receipt page clearly provide that the new, revised employee handbook is not an employment contract?   Yes ___ No ___ Maybe ___

4. Should the acknowledgment/receipt page confirm that employment may be terminated at any time for any reason?   Yes ___ No ___ Maybe ___

5. Should the acknowledgment/receipt page include the company's "employment-at-will" rights?   Yes ___ No ___ Maybe ___

6. Will the acknowledgment/receipt page provide that employees also have the right to terminate their employment at any time for any reason?   Yes ___ No ___ Maybe ___

7. Should the acknowledgment/receipt page provide that the handbook is neither a contract nor an agreement of employment for a definite period of time but is a summary of company policies, work rules, and benefits for employees?   Yes ___ No ___ Maybe ___

8. Should the acknowledgment/receipt page provide the right for management to change, amend, or delete some of the personnel policies and benefits contained in the handbook, with notification by management when new or revised policies are implemented?　　　　　　　　　　　　　　　Yes ___ No ___ Maybe ___

9. Should the acknowledgment/receipt page avoid the requirement that employees "obey," "comply with," or "abide" by the policies and procedures outlined in the employee handbook?　　　　　　　　　　Yes ___ No ___ Maybe ___

10. If the handbook contains a "union-free" policy statement, will the acknowledgment/receipt page avoid any wording requiring employees to acknowledge" in consideration of my employment, I agree to comply with all personnel policies and requirements of the company"?　　　　　　　Yes ___ No ___ Maybe ___

11. Should the acknowledgment/receipt page include this statement: "The handbook policies described herein are not conditions of employment and the language is not intended to create a contract between the company and its employees"?　　Yes ___ No ___ Maybe ___

Sample Policies: Disclaimer Statements _____

Sample Policy 1

[Introductory Page Handbook Disclaimer Statement]

This handbook has been prepared to help you become familiar with your new employer and to make your transition smooth and effective. It is neither a contract nor an agreement of employment for a definite period of time; rather, it is a summary of company policies, work rules, and benefits you enjoy as an employee. From time to time, conditions or circumstances may require management to change, amend, or delete some of the policies and benefits contained in this handbook. When such changes are made, management, of course, will notify you of the new or revised policy.

The contents of this handbook are presented as a matter of information only. None of the benefits or policies in this handbook are intended by reason of their publication to confer any rights or privileges upon you, or to entitle you to be or remain employed by the employer. While we hope that your employment with the employer will be long-lasting, employees are, of course, free to resign at any time, just as the company is free to terminate your employment at any time.

Sample Policy 2

[Pre-Employment Letter Containing Disclaimer Statement]

In consideration of my employment, I agree to conform to the rules and regulations of the employer, and my employment and compensation can be terminated, with or without cause, and with or without notice, at any time, at the option of either the employer or myself. I understand that no manager or representative of the employer, other than [designate specific representative], has any authority to enter into any agreement for employment for any specified period of time, or to make any agreement contrary to the foregoing.

Sample Policy 3

[Another employer had his attorney prepare a draft of a letter the employer would use as a pre-hire agreement at the time employee applicants applied for a position with the new company. The purpose and intent of the following pre-employment agreement is to protect the employer from potential future liability when investigating the job applicant's prior employment record, as well as to disclaim any verbal or oral promises made to job applicants by managers or persons involved in the pre-employment interview process.]

[Pre-Employment Interview Agreement with Job Applicants]

I hereby give [name of employer] the right to make a thorough investigation of my past employment, education, and activities; and I release from all liability all persons, companies, and corporations supplying such information. I agree to indemnify [name of employer] and its officers and employees against any liability which might result from making such investigation. I understand that any false answer or statements or implication made by me in this application or other document shall be considered sufficient cause for denial of employment or discharge.

Additionally, I understand that nothing contained in this employment application or in the granting of an interview is intended to create an employment contract between [name of employer] and myself for either employment or for the providing of any benefit. No promises regarding employment have been made to me, and I understand that no such promise or guarantee is binding upon [name of employer] unless made in writing. If an employment relationship is established, I understand that I have the right to terminate my employment at any time and that [name of employer] retains the same right.

I understand that if employment is offered in response to this application, my employment may be terminated by me or by the [name of employer] at any time at the convenience of the terminating party, with or without cause, and with or without notice. I understand that no representative of the [name of employer] other than [specify the person or job title], has authority to enter into an agreement for any specified period of time, or contrary to the foregoing. I agree that my employment may be terminated by the [name of employer] at any time without liability for wages or salary except such as may have been earned at the time of such termination.

Sample Policy 4
[The following is a typical disclaimer statement that appears on an employer's acknowledgment/receipt page of the employee handbook.]

[Disclaimer Statement Found on Employee Handbook Acknowledgment/Receipt Page]

We have prepared this handbook as a guide for policies, benefits, and general information which should assist you during your employment. However, neither this handbook nor any other company communication or practice creates an employment contract. The company reserves the right to make changes in content or application of its policies as it deems appropriate, and these changes may be implemented even if they have not been communicated, reprinted, or substituted in this handbook. It is also understood that nothing in this handbook or any other policy or communication changes the fact that employment is at-will for an indefinite period, unless terminated at any time by you or the company.

I understand that no employee or representative of the company, other than the President, has any authority to enter into an employment contract or to change the at-will employment relationship or to make any agreement contrary to the foregoing. I acknowledge receipt of the employee handbook and understand that my continued employment constitutes acceptance of any changes that may be made in content or application of the handbook.

Sample Policies: Employment-at-Will Disclaimers _____

Sample Policy 1

This is not a contract of employment. Any individual may voluntarily leave employment upon proper notice or may be terminated by the employer at any time and for any reason. Any oral or written statements or promises to the contrary are hereby expressly disavowed and should not be relied upon by any prospective or existing employee. The contents of this handbook are subject to change at any time at the discretion of the employer.

_____   _____
(Date)   (Employee Signature)

Sample Policy 2

"Employment-at-will" simply refers to the traditional relationship between employer and employee, specifying that the employment relationship may be terminated by either party unilaterally. Thus, this handbook is not an expressed or implied contract of employment, but rather an overview of working rules and benefits at our company.

_____   _____
(Date)   (Employee Signature)

Sample Policy 3

The contents of this handbook are presented as a matter of information only. The personnel policies and procedures and employee benefits described are not conditions of employment. Our company reserves the right to modify, revoke, suspend, change, or terminate any or all such personnel policies and benefit plans, in whole or in part, at any time, with or without notice. The policy statements that appear in this handbook are not intended to create or to be construed to constitute a contract between our company and any one or all of our employees.

Sample Policies: Acknowledgment/Receipt Pages ⸻

Sample Policy 1

I have received my copy of (name of company) Employee Handbook. I understand that this handbook is intended as a guide for personnel policies, benefits, and general information and that these guidelines should not be construed as an employment contract.

I understand management reserves the right to make changes in the guidelines or their application as it deems appropriate, and these changes may be made with or without notice. I also understand that employment is terminable at the will of either myself or the company at any time, and that no representative of the company other than the President has any authority to make any contrary agreement.

Sample Policy 2

This notice acknowledges that you have received your employee handbook from our company. Please fill in your name, sign and date this form, and return it to the Human Resources Department within five workdays after you have received your employee handbook. This will confirm to us that you have received your revised, new employee handbook.

Printed Name of Employee: _____

Signature of Employee: _____

Date: _____

Sample Policy 3

We have prepared this handbook as a guide for policies, benefits, and general information which should assist you during your employment. However, these guidelines should not be construed as a contract. The company reserves the right to make changes in content or application as it deems appropriate, and these changes may be implemented even if they have not been communicated, reprinted, or substituted in this handbook. It should also be understood that nothing in this handbook changes the fact that employment is at-will for an indefinite period unless terminated at any time by you or the company.

I acknowledge receipt of the Employee Handbook, and I agree to read and abide by the policies set forth in the handbook.

Sample Policy 4

This certifies that I have received the Employee Handbook outlining the company's policies, rules, and general information. I understand that this handbook is not an expressed or implied contract of employment, but is an overview of working rules and benefits, which can be changed at management's discretion.

Furthermore, I acknowledge that my employment is not guaranteed for any particular length of time and that either party remains free to terminate the employment relationship at any time.

_____   _____
(Date)   (Employee Signature)

Sample Policy 5

On this date I have received a copy of the Employee Handbook. This handbook contains a brief description of the employee benefits, company policies, and other important job-related information.

This handbook is also designed to answer many of the questions which may arise in connection with my employment with (name of company). Neither the handbook nor any of its individual terms constitutes or represents contracted commitments between the company and its employees or modifies the prevailing employment-at-will relationship.

_____   _____
(Date)   (Employee Signature)

Sample Policy 6

[Acknowledging Receipt and Reading of Employee Handbook]

I understand that the [name of employer]'s employment application and any other [name of employer] documents, including the [name of employer]'s employee handbook which I have received and read, are guidelines only and are not to be interpreted as a contract between myself and the [name of employer], and that I may voluntarily leave employment upon proper notice and may be terminated by the [name of employer] at any time and for any reason. I understand that any oral or written statements to the contrary are hereby expressly disavowed and should not be relied upon by myself. I further understand that the [name of employer] reserves the right to change, modify, or delete any of its rules and provisions of its handbook at any time.

Relevant Federal and State Regulations and Court Decisions

CONTENTS

Relevant Federal and State Regulations and Court Decisions

**SESCO Observations and Recommendations
Maintaining Employee Handbooks in a Workplace Regulated by Federal/State Court Decisions and Regulations**

Section 1 of this manual contains a list of important objectives, advantages, and benefits to an employer for having an up-to-date published employee handbook. The section also included a list of advantages of publishing a new handbook and revising a current handbook.

One of the important employer advantages listed was as follows:

> An employee handbook can be a valuable legal defense for an employer if and when faced with an employee lawsuit alleging that a former employee was "wrongfully discharged."

In reviewing relevant state court decisions involving "employment-at-will" cases where certain states have recognized "implied contracts" as cause for wrongful discharge from the verbal or "oral representations of job security" by supervisors and managers, or implications of an implied contract from printed statements in employee handbooks and personnel policy manuals, it becomes persuasive that if those employers had had a properly worded, clear disclaimer statement in a current, updated employee handbook distributed to all employees, including those former employees who were suing their former employer for "wrongful discharge," the employer would have had an invaluable defense documentation.

With a properly worded published disclaimer statement prominently placed in the employee handbook and understood by all employees, the employer would have been less vulnerable to a lawsuit based upon "oral" or "verbal" promises made to former employees during their employment that related to job security, permanency of employment, job tenure, etc., during the hiring process or during performance appraisal reviews by supervision.

5.01 Employment-at-Will—Yesterday and Today

In those states where traditional "employment-at-will" law exists, an employer still has a right to terminate or discharge an employee for just cause or for no proper cause. Today, it is estimated that close to 70 percent of working men and women in the United States, almost 76 million men and women, are employed by employers on an "at-will" basis. In short, these working employees have not been hired on the basis of an employer-employee contract agreement, nor have they been employed or are they working under any provisions of a bona fide collective bargaining agreement negotiated between the employer and a union representative. Most of these labor agreements require that employees be disciplined and/or discharged for "just cause" or "proper cause." Thus, in the past, employees protected from "employment-at-will" managerial prerogatives have included the following:

- Union members represented by labor unions with collective bargaining agreements

- Civil service employees

- Other employees covered by expressed or implied employment contracts

Therefore, the *employment-at-will issue* historically has been one of an individual's job rights compared to an employer's right to employ whomever he wishes and terminate whomever he wishes.

The old English "common law" permitted employers the right to exercise almost total control of the employer-employee relationship. This enabled such employers to employ or terminate anyone at their own will and discretion. This grew out of the historical "master-servant" relationship in which the master had the absolute right to discharge the servant for any reason or for no reason at all. The current lingo known as "employment-at-will" was developed during the industrial revolution in the late 1800s. This "freedom of contract" idea or "employment-at-will" also gave employees the right to quit their jobs whenever they wanted to and also gave the employers the right to hire or fire for any reason at any time.

5.02 The Beginning of Federal Regulations and Restrictions on "Employment-at-Will"

Beginning in the early 1900s, a number of federal employment laws were passed by Congress that restricted the right of the employer to terminate employees for any reason or for no reason at all. One of the most significant federal labor laws passed was in 1935, a bill sponsored by Senator Wagner of New York—The Wagner Act, also better known as the National Labor Relations Act. Not only did it give employees the right to form and join a labor union for purposes of collective bargaining over their wages, benefits and working conditions, it also established protection of that right by prohibiting employers from disciplining or discharging employees for engaging in union activity for purposes of collective bargaining or concerted activity for their mutual aid or protection (Section 7).

Since then, more than 25 other federal employment laws have been passed by Congress that restrict the employer's right to hire and fire "at the will of the employer." Most of these federal employment laws are well known to most human resource professionals and personnel managers. They are highlighted in the appendix to this section in the chart, "Who Is Challenging Your Right to Hire and Fire?"

In addition, almost two-thirds of our states have amended a number of old, established common-law employment-at-will doctrines resulting in substantially fewer employer rights to terminate employees at the will of either party where there is no specified term of employment in an employment agreement or where there is no existence of a labor agreement. Under traditional common-law "employment-at-will" state statutes, an employer could hire an employee for any period of time, and employee could be terminated by the employer at any time during the term of employment, with or without notice, with or without just cause when there existed no employment contract or state law limiting the right to terminate or employ at will.

5.03 Wrongful Discharge Lawsuits v. Employee Handbooks

In recent years, a number of state courts have ruled on a significant number of "employment-at-will" cases in which former employees have filed lawsuits against their former employer alleging that they were terminated improperly or "wrongfully." Their attorneys have attempted to support such lawsuits with policy statements or language in employee handbooks that were distributed to employees during the employment process or by *verbal or oral statements made to them* during pre-employment interviews, performance evaluation reviews, or disciplinary interviews by supervision. (See chart in the appendix to this section "State Laws that Recognize Implied Contracts as Cause for Wrongful Discharge.")

One of the most important "employment-at-will" cases involved the *Blue Cross/Blue Shield Company v. Toussaint,* heard before Michigan Supreme Court in 1980. When interviewed and hired, a new employee asked the employer questions about future "job security." During the trial, the former employee testified that management told him he could be employed "as long as I did my job." Furthermore, the employer presented him with an employee handbook in which existed a disciplinary policy stating that employees would be terminated only for "just cause." Following his termination of employment, the employee sued his former employer for "breach of contract."

Blue Cross/Blue Shield was found to have breached an employment agreement with the former employee because of poor wording in the employee handbook, as well as the promise to the new employee that he would have job security and steady work "as long as he did his job."

The Michigan court concluded that such wording, *verbal or written, may become "part of the employment contract, either by express agreement, oral or written, or as a result of an employee's legitimate expectations grounded in an employer's policy statements."*

It is in the termination of employment that most employers are haunted by poorly worded employee handbooks or by uninformed, ill-thought-out statements made to employees in the pre-employment interviewing or hiring process or doing their disciplinary or performance evaluation reviews. It is obviously more difficult for an employer to monitor statements, promises, and opinions voiced to employees by management in these cases than it is to monitor and clean up properly worded policy statements involving discipline or discharge or guarantees of employment status in employee handbooks.

5.04 Court Rulings Involving Employee Handbooks

One of the most effective employer defenses in wrongful discharge cases is a properly worded, currently issued employee handbook. How and what the employee handbook language states as well as its intent is one of the most important management documents used in employment law litigation today. Following are several significant employment law cases dealing with discipline and discharge which reinforce important guidelines on having properly worded employee handbooks. These cases also confirm the importance of having the final draft of any revised or new employee handbook thoroughly read by a professional consultant who is competent in the drafting and editing of employee or personnel policy handbook language or by the employer's legal department or outside employment law counsel.

A U.S. District Court issued a decision in 1985 concerning an employee handbook in *Thompson v. American Motor Inns*, 623 F. Supp. 409 (W.D.Va 1985). Thompson was a full-time desk clerk and night auditor for American Motor Inns. The employee handbook provided that after serving a probationary period, an employee became a "permanent" employee. The handbook also provided for a discipline system which employed written and verbal warnings, and stated that three such warnings could result in dismissal.

One evening in 1982, a counselor of a children's shelter brought five children to the Holiday Inn where Thompson was on duty. The counselor filled out the registration and attempted to pay for the lodging by personal check. Thompson refused the check because the counselor had no personal identification. The counselor left the Holiday Inn without any mention of who he was or why he needed the room. Shortly thereafter, Thompson was discharged on account of the incident.

He filed an action against his employer alleging that he had been discriminated against because of his age and that his employer had breached its "contract" with him. Although the court acknowledged that the employment-at-will doctrine is recognized in Virginia, the court referred to this doctrine as "anachronistic" and "antiquated." The court ultimately concluded that the employment-at-will doctrine was not a substantive rule of law, but merely a rebuttable presumption.

With reference to the handbook, the court found that the employer had "made specific promises" to its employees *not to dismiss them without utilization of the warning system,* and that Thompson was an excellent employee who had not been given notice of failure to comply with company policy. *It was clear to the court that Thompson had been discharged wrongfully.*

Another Virginia employer was sued in the Circuit Court of Scott County, Virginia, by a former employee who alleged a cause of action arising from a *breach of employment contract.* The employee admitted that his employee handbook was the employment contract referred to in the complaint. At the time of his employment, the employee read and agreed to a section called "Conditions of Employment" which stated that he could be "terminated... at any time without liability" and "that no employment contract is being offered." More significantly, the employee agreed that his "employment . . . will not imply that any employment contract is being offered."

Regardless of the employee's assumption that he could not be discharged without what he felt was "good reason," it was clear that the plaintiff had no contract with the defendant which required "good cause" or "just cause" for his termination. Because the employee could not prove a contractual relationship with his employer, the employee could not prove a breach of contract, and the Court entered summary judgment for the employer. See *Hillman v. Louisiana-Pacific Corporation,* Chancery No. 2832 (1989).

In *Sullivan v. Snap-On Tools Corporation,* Sullivan contended that his employment contract contained a "just cause" provision which removed him from *at-will* status. There was no written "just cause" agreement, but the employee argued for such a requirement because of the suggested disciplinary procedures set forth in the handbook. According to the court, however, the "strongest indicator of the nature of the employment relation" was found in the express at-will language contained in the handbook, wherein it was provided that "an employee may be dismissed at the discretion of the employer." Quoting *Miller v. SEVAMP, Supra,* the court concluded that a "clearer expression of intent to create at-will employment can hardly be imagined." *Sullivan v. Snap-On Tools Corporation,* Civil Action No. 88-0443-R (E.D. Va 1989).

In *Castiglione v. The Johns Hopkins Hospital,* 69 Md.App. 325,517 Atl.2d 786, 105 Lab.Cas. ¶55,629 (1986), a dischargee had no cause of action against her former employer for breach of contract. The employee handbook conspicuously stated that it was not an employment contract and that the employer retained the right to direct and discipline the workforce. *The employee could not be said to have a legitimate expectation of interest in her job where the handbook disclaimed the employer's intention to create such expectations.* Her argument that the disclaimer should not be enforced because it was inequitable also was rejected, because she had not alleged fraud, mistake, or oppression.

An important U.S. Court of Appeals (Cincinnati) decision relevant to those preparing new or revised employee handbook ruled that the at-will language in an employee handbook created an at-will employment relationship even though the handbook also outlined specific causes that could lead to dismissal.

The case arose when a worker was fired for refusing to apologize to a manager after accusing him of making obscene phone calls to his wife. The employee sued the firm for wrongful discharge, claiming that the employee handbook, which listed specific dischargeable offenses, meant that dismissals could only be for just cause.

Finding that the last page of the handbook specifically stated that employment was terminable at will, the court ruled that the handbook's listing did not indicate that the acts it specified were the only ones that might lead to dismissal. Moreover, the court points out, the list did not detract from the handbook's explicit at-will language. *Pratt v. Brown Machine Co.,* CA6, 1988, 3 IER Cases 1121.

5.05 "Implied Contracts" v. Employee Handbook Policy Statements

A number of state courts have recognized exceptions to state employment-at-will statutes based on one or more of the following theories:

- Implied contracts (such as employee handbooks, personnel policy manuals, oral representation, and promissory estoppel)

- A covenant of "good faith" and fair dealings

- Public policy

In most wrongful discharge claims filed in state courts, it is usually the nature of the claim that determines the financial remedy for an employee who prevails in a wrongful discharge lawsuit. For example, if the employee's attorney sues on an alleged "contractual" cause of action, an employee may collect back pay, front pay, and other compensatory damages.

Properly worded employee handbooks that are free from confusing, inconsistent, or restrictive policy statements pertaining to progressive discipline and language restricting the right of the employer to terminate at will, such as "for proper or just cause" can assist in an employer's defense against a wrongful discharge lawsuit by disproving that the employee handbook policy statement is an "implied contract" that prohibits the employer from terminating an employee at will. The chart in the appendix to this section provides an analysis of states which recognize "implied contracts" as a cause for wrongful discharge. Such "implied contracts" include *oral representations of job security, a covenant of good faith and fair dealing, an employer's written discipline or discharge policy and procedure, and promissory estoppel.* One example of "promissory estoppel" occurs when a prospective applicant quits his or her job to accept an offer of employment but fails to receive the promised job opportunity or, if hired, is terminated shortly thereafter.

Oral Representations—A number of states have upheld wrongful discharge lawsuits filed by employees who claim an employer or management representative made a verbal or oral statement that allegedly created an "implied contract," thus restricting the employer's right to terminate the employee at will. Oral promises to employees that they will be terminated only "for just cause" is an example of an oral representation of job security that could haunt an employer who does not wish to follow a progressive discipline system prior to terminating employees. (See appendix.)

Covenant of Good Faith and Fair Dealing—Some state courts enforce the belief that there is an implied contract in the employer-employee relationship that applies to employees hired or terminated at will. The essence of this belief is that an employee "contract" or "covenant" is implied in every employer-employee relationship in order to prevent an employee from being discharged in bad faith.

Because of the trend of state courts holding that employers are often bound by employee handbook policy statements, most revised or new employee handbooks contain "disclaimer" statements in the introduction or in the introductory section of the handbook, and/or on the acknowledgment/receipt page. Disclaimer statements usually provide that neither the employee handbook nor any policy statements published are for the purpose of creating any type of an employment agreement or contract between the employer and employee. The primary purpose of a disclaimer statement is to give an employer a "good faith defense" to any future claim by a former employee that the employee handbook is a bona fide contract. (See Section 4.15 for a handbook checklist on disclaimer statements and sample disclaimer statements.)

5.06 Employer Guidelines for Preventing Wrongful Discharge Lawsuits

1. All pre-employment personnel forms, including job applications, should clearly state in a special statement, to be signed by the job applicant, that employment is at will. (See Section 4.15 for recommended pre-employment statement.)

2. Employee handbooks, personnel policy manuals, new employee orientation manuals, and any other printed company materials given to new employees should be carefully reviewed and revised as necessary to remove any implications that employment is other than at the will of the employer.

    Carefully review all bulletin board postings of "company policy and procedures" to minimize the risk that they create an "implied contract" on behalf of employees. Consider inserting your "employment-at-will" policy statement in stock option plans, bonus plans, and employee promotion documents.

3. New employees should be given realistic job interviews which include a review of criteria, based job descriptions, outlining performance expectations for an employee to achieve upgraded job opportunities within the organization.

4. Human resource personnel and supervisors involved in the pre-employment interview process should be aware, and alert to any legal implications of verbal promises made to job applicants that could involve an "implied contract" by oral statements.

5. Employee performance appraisals and reviews conducted by supervision must be conducted honestly, objectively, and accurately to truly reflect the employee's negative performance as well as positive appraisals. Using *criteria-based job descriptions*, employees' performance evaluations should be carefully documented and signed off by *at least two members of management*. If an employee is discharged in the future, any performance evaluations that show only positive results can haunt the employer in alleged wrongful discharge lawsuits. Proper documentation of the employer's dissatisfaction with the employee's performance should be properly recorded and communicated to the employee during a performance

review. Be certain the employee understands the areas of poor performance and dissatisfaction and provide the employee reasonable time to improve the on-the-job performance before terminating him or her for poor performance (as opposed to clear misconduct).

6. Employers should establish a well-communicated, published complaint resolution procedure that permits employees to discuss on-the-job complaints and grievances with management. A peer review procedure or conflict resolution procedure providing for a fair hearing at higher levels of management will help the employer defend a wrongful discharge case if such complaint procedure steps have been complied with.

7. It is recommended that all terminations be the end result of progressive, corrective discipline wherever possible. It makes sense to apply the "golden rule" before summarily discharging any employee. If an employee feels he has been abused or unfairly discharged, he is more likely to bring a wrongful discharge lawsuit against his former employer.

8. In order to create a more positive feeling following termination for any reason, it is recommended that companies provide exit interviews that allow employees to express their feelings about the work environment prior to their termination. In addition, employers should provide outplacement counseling services to terminated employees, including assistance in preparing resumes and offering suggestions on how they may search for job opportunities. Counseling should help alleviate employees' feelings of hostility or bitterness against their former employer and lessen the possibility of a wrongful discharge lawsuit or the filing of discrimination charges against the employer.

9. Always listen carefully and get the employee's side of the story before finalizing any termination decision. It is recommended that all decisions to terminate employees be reviewed by an impartial "third party" within the company, such as the Director of Human Resources, who should also seek outside professional or legal advice where necessary or appropriate.

10. Avoid inaccurate statements of the reasons for discharge of employees. Carefully protect bona fide reasons for discharge with few people within or outside the company.

11. Consider using a formal "severance agreement" with appropriately worded releases drafted by company counsel.

5.07 Federal Regulations Affecting Personnel Policies and Procedures

This section is a guide to help you understand some of the more important federal regulations that affect the employer-employee relationship. It is not intended to be an exhaustive summary but a *handy reference source for you.* In addition, remember that in many jurisdictions there are also state and local laws that address the same issues as federal labor laws.

Private Employers

Age Discrimination in Employment Act of 1967
29 USC Sections 621–634

Coverage: Employers with 20 or more employees who are engaged in an industry affecting commerce are prohibited from discriminating against individuals on the basis of age in hiring or discharge decisions or with respect to compensation, terms, conditions, or privileges of employment. The act protects employees who are at least 40 years of age. Employees of federal, state, and local governments are also protected.

Americans with Disabilities Act of 1990
42 USC 12101

Prohibits employment discrimination against a qualified individual with a disability in application, hiring, advancing, training, compensation, and other terms and conditions of employment. Also prohibits discrimination on the basis of disability in the enjoyment of goods, services, facilities, transportation, privileges, advantages and accommodations provided by a place of business intended for non-residential use and that affects commerce.

Bankruptcy Act
(As amended by the Bankruptcy Act Amendments of 1984)
11 USC Section 525

Coverage: Any private employer or the federal government may not terminate the employment of, or discriminate in terms and conditions of employment against, an individual who is or has been a debtor under the Bankruptcy Act.

Civil Rights Act of 1964
Title VI—Nondiscrimination in Federally Assisted Programs
2 USC Section 2000d

Coverage: Programs and activities that receive federal financial assistance are prohibited from excluding persons on the basis of race, color, or national origin.

Civil Rights Act of 1964
Title VII Equal Employment Opportunity
42 USC Section 2000e et seq.

Coverage: Employers with 15 or more employees are prohibited from discriminating against any individual with respect to compensation, terms, conditions, or privileges of employment because of that individual's race, color, religion, sex, or national origin.

Consolidated Omnibus Budget Reconciliation Act of 1986 (COBRA)
IRC Section 162(k)

All employers in the U.S., excluding church groups and federal employers, with 20 or more employees must offer employees and their dependents the right to continue group health (and dental) plan coverage up to 36 months beyond the date it would otherwise end.

Consumer Credit Protection Act
15 USC Section 1673

Coverage: All employees are protected by this act. This act sets a national maximum of the amount of an employee's wages that can be withheld to satisfy a wage garnishment.

The amount withheld cannot exceed either (1) 25 percent of the employee's weekly disposable earnings or (2) the amount by which the employee's weekly disposable earnings exceed 30 times the current minimum wage set by the Department of Labor. Each state has its own statutes on garnishments; the federal standard is designed only to set the maximum that can be withheld under state law. The federal act does not limit court-ordered wage deductions for the support of any person or wage deductions for state and federal tax debts. The act also prohibits an employer from discharging an employee whose wages are garnished for one indebtedness.

Employee Polygraph Protection Act of 1988

Prohibits most private employers from using lie detector tests for applicants and employees.

Employee Retirement Income Security Act of 1974
29 USC Sections 1001–1461

Coverage: The Employee Retirement Income Security Act (ERISA) sets standards and requirements for the substantive provisions and administration of employee benefit plans and employee welfare benefit plans, including, for example, pension and profit-sharing plans. ERISA does not apply to plans maintained solely to comply with workers' compensation, unemployment compensation, or disability insurance laws; plans maintained outside the United States for nonresident aliens; and excess benefit plans.

Equal Pay Act of 1963
29 USC Section 206(d)

Coverage: The Equal Pay Act is an amendment to the Fair Labor Standards Act (FLSA), and covers the same employers. The requirements of the Equal Pay Act, however, are extended to apply to executive, administrative, or professional employees, and outside salesmen, even though other FLSA requirements do not. The act prohibits an employer from discriminating on the basis of sex by paying persons of one sex less than the wage paid to persons of the opposite sex in the same establishment "for equal work on jobs the performance of which requires equal skill, effort, and responsibility and which are performed under similar working conditions." Excepted are wage differentials based on seniority, merit pay, and piecework, and a "differential based on any other factor other than sex."

Fair Labor Standards Act of 1938
29 USC Sections 201–219

Coverage: The Fair Labor Standards Act (FLSA) covers most employers in the public and private sectors. The act requires, first, that employees be paid at least at the minimum wage; second, in general, that they be paid time and one-half for hours worked in excess of 40 in any given week; third, that persons employed in hazardous occupations be over 18 years of age; and fourth, that minors employed in other occupations be above 14 or 16 years of age, depending on the type of work and employer. The act was amended in 1985 to permit public employers to give compensatory time off in lieu of overtime pay.

Federal Election Campaign Act of 1971
2 USC Sections 431–455

Coverage: The act limits the means that a corporate employer may use to solicit contributions from employees for the employer's political fund. The act also makes it unlawful for any corporation to make a contribution or expenditure in connection with any election at which citizens vote for presidential and vice-presidential electors or a senator or representative in Congress. Contributions and expenditures are prohibited in connection with any primary election or political convention or caucus held to select candidates for any such office. Note that, while this act applies to elections for federal office, many states have similar statutes limiting the contributions of corporations in state and local elections. Corporations are permitted by the federal act to establish a separate segregated fund that may be utilized for political purposes.

Immigration Reform and Control Act
8 USC Section 1324(a) & (b) (1986)

Coverage: All employers, including state and local government employers, must verify that employees hired on or after November 7, 1986, are either U.S. citizens or authorized to work in the United States. There is no exception for employers with a small number of employees. Verification requires that new hires produce specific documents proving their identity and employment eligibility and, further, that both employee and employer complete a government form, INS Form I-9, indicating that the new hire is eligible for employment. Form I-9 must be retained for three years from the date of hire or until one year after termination, whichever is later. Any employer who knowingly hires or continues to employ an unauthorized alien is subject to civil, and in some cases criminal, penalties.

In addition, the act makes it unlawful for employers having four or more employees to discriminate by hiring, recruiting, referring, or discharging employees on the basis of national origin, citizenship, or intention to obtain citizenship, to the extent that such discrimination is not covered by Title VII of the Civil Rights Act of 1964. It also grants amnesty to aliens who were previously illegal, but who have resided continuously in the U.S. since January 1, 1982, have been physically present in the U.S. since the act was passed, and are otherwise admissible as immigrants. (See Section 4.03 for policy on Immigration Reform Act.)

Internal Revenue Code
26 USC Sections 1–9602

Coverage: Covering all employers, the code defines the tax treatment of the full range of business expenditures and, therefore, has important implications for the benefits to be granted to employees.

Jurors' Protection Act
28 USC Sections 1363, 1875

Coverage: These statutes prohibit all employers from disciplining any regular employee for the employee's participation in jury service.

Labor-Management Reporting and Disclosure Act, 1957
29 USC Section 153

Coverage: The purpose of this act was aimed at eliminating the practices of wrongdoing on the part of certain unions and their officers. A code of conduct was established for unions, union officers, employers, and consultants which guarantees certain inalienable rights to union members within their union and imposes certain obligations on unions, union officers, employers, and consultants.

National Labor Relations Act of 1935
29 USC Sections 151–169

Coverage: The National Labor Relations Act (NLRA) applies to employees in all industries affecting commerce and to all employees except agricultural laborers, individuals employed in the domestic service of a family or person, individuals employed by their parent or spouse, independent contractors, and supervisors. The NLRA gives employees the right to form, join, and assist labor organizations or to refrain from such activities and to bargain collectively with employers.

Norris-LaGuardia Act, 1932
29 USC Sections 101–110

The Norris-LaGuardia Act accords full freedom to employees to organize and to negotiate the terms and conditions of their employment through representatives of their own choosing and limits the jurisdiction and authority of the courts of the U.S. to issue restraining orders and injunctions.

Occupational Safety and Health Act of 1970
29 USC Sections 651–678

Coverage: Because the act applies to employers in business affecting commerce, most private employers are covered by the act. Those which are excluded are, generally, subject to safety and health requirements established by other agencies. Employers are required to maintain a workplace that is free from recognized hazards likely to cause death or serious injury and to comply with the workplace safety and health standards promulgated by the Occupational Safety and Health Administration (OSHA). Employers are prohibited from discharging or in any other way discriminating against employees who exercise their rights under the act. This precludes an employer from discharging an employee who, acting under a reasonable apprehension, refuses in good faith to expose himself to a hazardous workplace condition.

Older Workers Benefit Protection Act of 1990
29 USC 630 et seq.

The act prohibits employers from reducing benefits because of an employee's age and specifies rules for obtaining ADEA waivers.

Portal to Portal Pay Act of 1947
29 USC Sections 251–262

Coverage: This act applies to all employees subject to the Fair Labor Standards Act (FLSA), and the intent of the legislation was to abrogate certain judicial interpretation of the act. The Supreme Court had held that the time employees spent in walking from the plant gates to their workbenches and in tasks that were preparatory to their day's work must be counted as hours worked in computing pay and overtime. To alter this holding, the act bans suits by employees to recover back pay for time spent on site before and after the completion of the employees' "principal activities" unless that time was considered compensable under a contract, custom, or practice in the plant.

Pregnancy Discrimination Act of 1978
42 USC Section 2000

The Pregnancy Discrimination Act prohibits disparate treatment of pregnant women for all employment-related purposes. This act prohibits termination or refusal to hire or promote a woman solely because she is pregnant; bars mandatory leaves for pregnant women arbitrarily set at a certain time in their pregnancy and not based on their individual inability to work; protects reinstatement rights of women on leave for pregnancy-related reasons including rights in regard to credit for previous service, accrued retirement benefits, and accumulated seniority; and requires employers to treat pregnancy and childbirth the same way they treat other causes of disability under fringe benefit plans.

Veterans Reemployment Rights Act of 1974
38 USC Sections 2021 et seq.

Coverage: The act protects all employees who are inducted into the Armed Services and requires the employer to restore the veteran to a position of like seniority, status, and pay if he or she applies to return to work within 90 days of satisfactory completion of military service. For veterans who remain active with the military reserve components, the act requires the employer to grant a leave of absence for up to 90 days each year to permit the employee to participate in annual training duty.

Worker Adjustment and Retraining Notification Act (Plant Closing Law)
20 CFR-TT 639

Coverage: The plant closing law requires employers of 100 or more employees to give 60 days' notice before closing a facility or starting a layoff of 50 people or more. Part-time employees, who are described as working fewer than twenty (20) hours per week or who have been employed for fewer than six (6) of the twelve (12) months preceding the date on which the notices are required, are not counted when adding the number of employees under the law.

Federal Contractors

Executive Order No. 11246 of September 26, 1965
30 Fed. Reg. 12319

Coverage: By this order, every employer who holds a federal contract of $10,000 or more is prohibited from discriminating against employees or job applicants on the basis of race, color, religion, sex, or national origin. For contractors employing 50 or more employees and holding contracts exceeding $50,000, the order requires written affirmative action plans regarding the utilization of minority persons and females.

Service Contract Act
41 USC Sections 351–358

Coverage: Employees engaged in contracts executed by the United States or the District of Columbia are entitled to minimum wages by reasons of the Service Contract Act of 1965 if the principal purpose of the contract is to furnish services in the United States through the use of service employees. Both prime contractors and subcontractors are subject to the provisions of the statute.

Regardless of the contract amount, no employee performing work under such contract or subcontract may be paid less than the highest of the minimum wage schedules specified in the Fair Labor Standards Act.

Vietnam-Era Veterans' Readjustment Assistance Act of 1974
38 USC Sections 2011–2012

Coverage: Employers who have federal contracts of $10,000 or more are prohibited from discriminating against and are required to take affirmative action to employ and advance employment-qualified disabled veterans and Vietnam-era veterans. A written affirmative action plan is required of employers who hold contracts of $50,000 or more and who have 50 or more employees.

The Vocational Rehabilitation Act of 1973
29 USC Sections 701–796i, 793–794

Coverage: The mandate of the act is divided in two parts. The first part, commonly referred to as Section 503, covers private employers who are government contractors. The second part, Section 504, applies to programs and activities that receive federal financial assistance. For employers holding government contracts and subcontracts in excess of $2,500, Section 503 of the act prohibits discrimination against handicapped individuals. If the employer's contract is $50,000 or greater and the employer has 50 or more employees, the employer is required to develop a written affirmative action program for the employment of the handicapped. Section 504, on the other hand, only prohibits discrimination against the handicapped and does not require an affirmative action plan.

Walsh-Healey Act
41 USC Section 35

The Walsh-Healey Act establishes minimum wage, overtime, and child labor standards for employees of companies with a $10,000 or larger contract to sell goods to the federal government.

Who is Challenging Your Right to Hire and Fire?
(Understanding the Rules of Your Governmental Partners of Federal Contractors)

Government Act and Agency	Basis of Coverage	Type of Employee Protection	Applies to Us?	Posters Required?	Penalty for Noncompliance	Statute of Limitations
Government Supply Contracts (DOL)	Supplies exceeding $10,000	• Minium wages • Overtime pay • Child labor • Homework • Safety and health		Yes	• Liquidated damages • Contract cancellation • Blacklisting	2 years 3 years (willful)
Government Service Contracts (DOL)	All employees	• Minimum wages • Safety and health • Equal pay (regardless of sex) • Overtime pay		Yes	• Backpay • Withholding contract payments • Contract cancellation • Blacklisting	N/A
Public Works Contracts (DOL)	Government contracts $2,000	• Minimum wages • Fringe benefits • Anti kickback • Overtime pay		Yes	• Withholding contract payments • Blacklisting	N/A
Executive Order 11246 (OFCCP)	Government contracts $10,000 Government contracts $50,000 and 50 employees	Prohibits discrimination of race, color, sex, religion, or national origin. Requires written Affirmative Action Program (AAP)		Yes	• Back pay • Contract cancellation • Judicial enforcement	N/A
Drug-Free Workplace Act (DOL)	Government contracts $25,000	• Drug-Free Awareness Program • Report drug convictions • Good-faith drug-free effort		Yes	• Debarment up to 5 years	N/A
Vocational Rehabilitation Act (DOL)	Government contracts $2,500 Small Business Administration Loans Government contracts $50,000 and 50 employees	Requires affirmative action to employ and promote handicapped persons. Rquires written AAP		Yes	• Withholding contract payments • Contract cancellation and debarment • Judicial enforcement	N/A
Vietnam Era Veterans' Readjustment Assistance Act (DOL)	Government contracts $10,000 Government contracts $50,000/50 employees	Requires affirmative action to employ and advance disabled and Vietnam-era veterans. Requires written AAP		Yes	• Withholding contract payments • Contract cancellation and debarment	N/A
Executive Order 11141 (EEOC)	Government contracts $10,000	Prohibits discrimination based on age		Yes (EEOC)	• Withholding contract payments • Contract cancellation and debarment	N/A

Who is Challenging Your Right to Hire and Fire?
(Understanding the Rules of Your Governmental Partners)

Government Act and Agency	Basis of Coverage	Type of Employee Protection	Applies to Us?	Posters Required?	Penalty for Noncompliance	Statute of Limitations
Fair Labor Standards Act (DOL)	At least two employees whose work affects goods for commerce. All employees of any business with $500,000 annual gross sales.	• Minimum wage • Overtime pay • Recording of hours • Garnishment protection • Child labor (Recordkeeping requirements)		Yes	• Injunctions • Back Pay • Liquidated Damages • Fines (up to $10,000) • Legal Costs	2 years 3 years—willful violations 5 years—criminal violations
Equal Pay Act (EEOC)	All employees of a single location	No wage differential based on sex. Differences OK if based on merit, performance, seniority.		Yes (EEOC)	• Back pay, including wages theoretically lost	180 days* (300 days in deferral states)
Immigration Reform and Control Act (DOJ)	Four or more employees	Employers must verify U.S. citizenship or legal alien status		No	• Fines (up to $10,000) • Jail	N/A
Federal and State Laws Unemployment Compensation (State Employment Agencies)	All employers	Compensation for temporary involuntary unemployment		Yes	• Increased state tax based on claims	N/A
State Laws Workers' Compensation (State Agencies)	All employees	Compensation for injured workers and occupational diseases. Some states don't allow termination.		Yes	• Reinstatement/backpay, medical costs, disability and death payments, rehabilitation costs, legal fees and costs	6 months
Employee Polygraph Protection Act (DOL)	Most private employers	Prohibits use of lie detector tests for applicants and employees		Yes	• Fines (up to $10,000) • Court actions	N/A
Occupational Safety and Health Act (OSHA) (State and Federal Agencies)	Any person engaged in a business affecting commerce	Prohibits workplace of unsafe and unhealthy conditions (Recordkeeping requirements)		Yes	• Fines • Close facilities • Imprisonment	N/A
National Labor Relations Act (NLRB)	Two employees Interstate commerce $50,000/year	Protected to engage in: • Union activity • Concerted activity		No, except in violations	• Reinstatement • Back pay • Post Notice • Recognize union	180 days

*46 of 50 states have state EEO laws; statute of limitations extends from 180 to 300 days in these states; plus state statute may be as long as one year.

Government Act and Agency	Basis of Coverage	Type of Employee Protection	Applies to Us?	Posters Required?	Penalty for Noncompliance	Statute of Limitations
Civil Rights Act-Title VII (EEOC) (State and Federal Agencies)	15 or more employees working 10 or more calendar weeks	Prohibits discrimination of race, color, religion, sex, and national origin, handicap, veterans status (Recordkeeping requirements)		Yes	• Reinstatement • Back pay, including wages theoretically lost • Can be class action	180 days* (300 days in deferral states)
Pregnancy Discrimination Act (EEOC)	15 or more employees working 20 or more calendar weeks	Required to consider pregnancy as disability		Yes (EEOC)	• Reinstatement • Back pay • Can be class action	180 days* (300 days in deferral states)
Americans with Disabilities Act (ADA) (EEOC, DOJ)	Title I 25 employees (7/92) 15 employees (7/94)	Prohibits discrimination against a qualified individual with a disability in application, hiring, advancing, training, compensating, discharging, and other terms and conditions.		Yes	• Injunctions • Reinstatement • Hiring • Back pay • Attorney fees and costs	180 days* (300 days in deferral states)
(DOJ)	Title III Any place of public accommodation and services (1/92)	Forbids discrimination on basis of disability in enjoyment of goods, services, facilities, privileges, advantages, and accommodations.		No	• Judicial enforcement • Fines up to $100,000 • Attorney fees and costs	N/A
Age Discrimination in Employment Act (EEOC)	Employer with 20 or more employees	Prohibits discrimination on basis of age over 40		Yes (EEOC)	• Reinstatement • Back pay	180 days* (300 days in deferral states)
Consolidated Omnibus Budget Reconciliation Act (COBRA) (IRS)	20 or more employees with a qualifying event of resignation, termination, divorce, layoff, death, or disability	Allows for contribution of health care protection up to 36 months		Notice to employee/spouse	• $100 per day fine • Attorney's fees and costs	No limitation if employee is never notified.
Employee Retirement Income Security Act (ERISA) (DOL)	Any employer engaged in business or in any industry or activity affecting commerce	• Eligibility • Funding • Standards for managing • Information disclosure		No	• Injunctions • Equitable, remedial relief, including removal from office • Up to $10,000 fine, jail	N/A
Workers' Adjustment and Retraining Notification Act (DOL)	100 or more employees	• Layoffs and closings		Written notice	• Back pay and benefits • Civil penalty up to $30,000 • Attorney's fees	N/A
Fair Employment Practices Laws (FEPs) (State Agencies)	Often extend to smaller employers	Often more comprehensive and more restrictive		Yes	• Individual state statutes	Individual state statutes
State Courts	Violation of the employment-at-will doctrine	• Violation of public policy • Bad-faith dealings • Duration of agreement, either expressed or implied		No	• Unlimited financial recovery	Individual state statutes

*46 of 50 states have state EEO laws; statute of limitations extends from 180 to 300 days in these states; plus state statute may be as long as one year.

State Laws That Recognize "Implied Contracts" as Cause for Wrongful Discharge

KEY: **N/C** No court case has been issued so far.
   N/R No ruling. The highest court of the state has not clearly expressed its position on this issue and the lower courts are divided, or the federal courts, interpreting state law, are the only courts to have issued a decision.

State Jurisdiction	Handbooks/ Manuals	Covenant of Good Faith and Fair Dealing	Oral Representations of Job Security	Promissory Estoppel[1]
Alabama	Yes	Yes	Yes	Yes
Alaska	Yes	Yes	Yes	N/R
Arizona	Yes	Yes	Yes	N/C
Arkansas	Yes	No	Yes	N/C
California	Yes	Yes	Yes	Yes
Colorado	Yes	Yes	Yes	Yes
Connecticut	Yes	Yes	Yes	Yes
Delaware	No	No	N/C	N/C
District of Columbia	Yes	N/C	Yes	Yes
Florida	Yes	N/C	No	Yes
Georgia	Yes	No	No	No
Hawaii	Yes	N/C	Yes	N/C
Idaho	Yes	N/C	Yes	Yes
Illinois	Yes	No	Yes	Yes
Indiana	No	No	Yes	Yes
Iowa	N/R	Yes	Yes	Yes
Kansas	Yes	No	Yes	Yes
Kentucky	N/C	N/C	Yes	No
Louisiana	N/C	N/C	No	No
Maine	Yes	No	Yes	N/C
Maryland	Yes	No	No	No
Massachusetts	Yes	Yes	No	No
Michigan	Yes	N/C	Yes	Yes
Minnesota	Yes	No	Yes	Yes
Mississippi	N/C	N/C	N/C	N/C
Missouri	Yes	N/C	No	Yes
Montana	The statute preempts all causes of action arising from terminating at-will			
Nebraska	N/C	N/C	No	Yes
Nevada	N/C	Yes	N/C	N/C
New Hampshire	N/C	Yes	Yes	Yes
New Jersey	Yes	No	Yes	Yes
New Mexico	Yes	No	Yes	Yes
New York	Yes	No	Yes	N/R
North Carolina	No	N/C	No	Yes
North Dakota	Yes	No	N/C	N/C
Ohio	Yes	N/C	Yes	Yes
Oklahoma	Yes	Yes	N/C	N/C
Oregon	Yes	N/C	Yes	N/R
Pennsylvania	No	No	Yes	Yes
Rhode Island	N/C	N/C	N/R	N/C
South Carolina	Yes	N/C	No	N/R
South Dakota	Yes	No	No	No
Tennessee	No	N/C	N/R	N/R
Texas	N/R	N/C	Yes	Yes
Utah	N/C	N/C	N/C	N/C
Vermont	Yes	N/C	N/C	N/C
Virginia	Yes	N/R	N/C	Yes
Washington	Yes	No	N/C	N/C
West Virginia	Yes	N/C	N/C	N/C
Wisconsin	No	No	Yes	No
Wyoming	No	No	Yes	Yes

[1]Promise by employer that causes an employee or prospective employee to substantially alter his or her life circumstances.

INDEX OF SAMPLE POLICIES

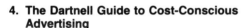
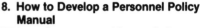

9. Greatest Direct Mail Sales Letters of All Time

What makes some sales letters work — again and again? Direct mail expert Richard S. Hodgson has selected and analyzed over 100 of the most successful direct mail sales letters ever written. He provides the complete text of each letter, then examines and explains in detail what makes each one work. You also get special sections on how to create successful letters.

8 1/2" x 11" Padded 3-Ring Binder $91.50

10. Questions That Make the Sale

Propel your sales to ever-higher levels by asking the right questions. Ten information-packed chapters show you how to:
• Rivet attention on your presentations
• Identify/clarify customers and needs
• Motivate, qualify, prospect, probe and close with greater success.
The final chapter contains 365 questions — "a question a day"— to achieve greater sales success.

Paperback $19.95

11. Idea-A-Day Guide to Super Selling and Customer Service

<u>Fifteen minutes a day</u> is all you'll need to ensure sales success all year long. The *Idea-a-Day Guide* is loaded with sales success ideas — 250 of them — one for each working day of the year. Not just another how-to book, *Idea-a-Day*'s unique organization gives you a new money-making idea on every page to give you a one-of-a-kind, hands-on reference you'll use every day of the year.

Paperback $19.95

12. How to Develop an Employee Handbook

Writing an employee handbook can be a difficult, time-consuming task. That's where *How to Develop an Employee Handbook* can help you. It's loaded with checklists and guidelines, more than 400 sample policy statements in use today by actual companies just like yours, and guidelines to help you adapt samples to your special needs. Also includes three supplemental books.

8 1/2" x 11" 3-Ring Binder $91.50

13. Customers: How to Get Them, How to Serve Them, How to Keep Them

Move ahead of the competition for good by energizing everyone in your company to give the kind of customer service that will win customers and bring them back again and again. Get practical advice on how to boost customer awareness, deal effectively with problems, win long-term customer commitment, and measure customer satisfaction. Forms, checklists, and cases give life to difficult problems and practical solutions.

8 1/2" x 11" 3-Ring Binder $91.5

14. Successful Telemarketing

Increase the impact of your current marketing and sales programs with this step-by-step guide to today's most cost-effective sales techniques. A comprehensive package including master planner, checklists, sample scripts, meeting formats, decision sheets, and case studies shows you how to apply basic techniques, target profitable accounts, pick market strategy, train staff, and measure results.

8 1/2" x 11" 3-Ring Binder $91.5

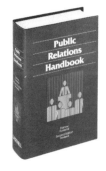

15. Copywriting Secrets and Tactics

Words can make a difference — especially when those words are meant to sell your product. Whether you're writing copy for direct mail, catalogs or other print media, *Copywriting Secrets and Tactics* by Herschell Gordon Lewis will enable you to turn your prose into sales copy that will cut through the clutter and invoke action.

8 1/2" x 11" 3-Ring Binder $91.5

16. Public Relations Handbook

Whatever your public relations needs, you'll turn to this comprehensive volume first for authoritative guidance. You'll get practical insights from two of the leading practitioners in the field, plus more than 40 case histories and articles. Practical information on asking the right questions, where to look for the answers, how to get the job done — it's all in one handy volume.

Hardcover, 6" x 9" $49.9